Back from the Deep

How Gene and Sandy Ralston
Serve the Living by Finding the Dead

Doug Horner

STEERFORTH PRESS
LEBANON, NEW HAMPSHIRE

For information about permission to reproduce
selections from this book, write to:
Steerforth Press L.L.C., 31 Hanover Street, Suite 1
Lebanon, New Hampshire 03766

Cataloging-in-Publication Data is available from the Library of Congress

ISBN 978-1-58642-384-1
Printed in the United States of America

CONTENTS

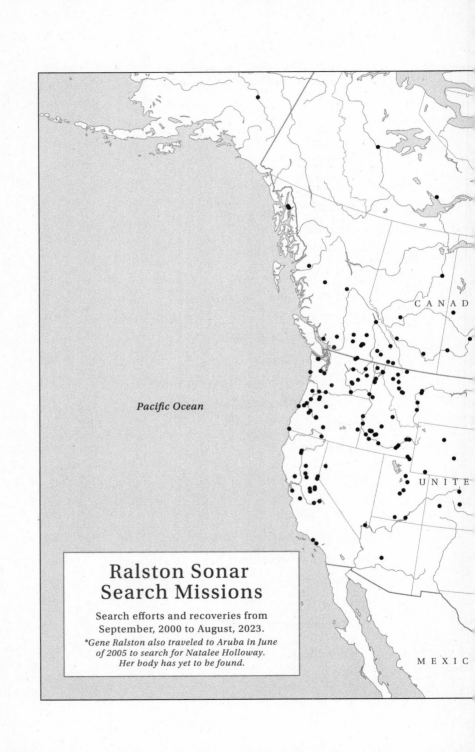

Pacific Ocean

CANAD

UNITE

MEXIC

Ralston Sonar
Search Missions

Search efforts and recoveries from
September, 2000 to August, 2023.

*Gene Ralston also traveled to Aruba in June
of 2005 to search for Natalee Holloway.
Her body has yet to be found.*

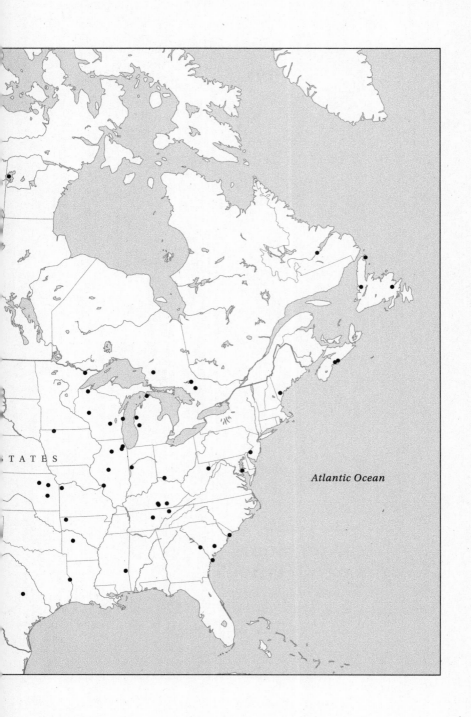

Atlantic Ocean

CHAPTER ONE

The *Kathy G*

On a rainy afternoon in early April 2021, the *Kathy G* was parked on a concrete pad between a vegetable garden and the house of Corporal Peter Westra, an officer with the Royal Canadian Mounted Police (RCMP). Beads of water clung to the hull and small pilothouse of the twenty-three-foot aluminum boat. It had a short mast and boom that looked like a miniature crane. A six-foot-long steel torpedo was fastened to the bow.

The boat, and the motor home parked nearby, belonged to Gene and Sandy Ralston, a married couple in their midseventies from a rural area outside of Boise, Idaho. They used a particular type of sonar to search lakes and rivers throughout Canada and the United States for the bodies of people who had drowned. They were self-taught, but they were among the best underwater search-and-recovery specialists in the world. As of two and a half weeks before, they'd found 124 corpses. Most of those people would still be missing if not for the Ralstons, who were the option of last resort. They would get the call to help only after the local and official resources were exhausted. And they offered their boat and expertise on a volunteer basis, charging only expenses — basically gas money and whatever it cost to park their motor home. The going commercial rate for this type of equipment and expertise varied, but $4,000 a day was considered reasonable.

I drove six hundred miles, up and over two mountain ranges, to join Gene and Sandy in Maple Ridge, British Columbia, a small city not far east of Vancouver and Canada's Pacific coastline. The local police, known as the Ridge Meadows RCMP, had asked them to help on two searches. (The RCMP is a federal policing agency in Canada that also provides regional and municipal services on a contract basis. The Ridge Meadows detachment had 112 officers and about 50 civilian staff at the time.) One search was for a thirty-seven-year-old man who had drowned in Alouette Lake the past October. The other was for a small plane, and its two pilots, that had crashed into a river about a year before. The Ralstons had also committed to a third search, this one in a lake about a three-hour drive east of Maple Ridge, for a young man from Wyoming.

And then, if they had time, Corporal Westra, the missing persons coordinator with the local RCMP, had told them about four other cold cases involving people presumed to have drowned in Alouette Lake that he would like to get solved once and for all. One of those incidents happened in the summer of 1974. Two friends were out fishing when a wave rolled over the back of the boat and it sank. The men swam for shore. One was rescued by a passing boat. The other drowned. Police, family, and volunteers searched the shorelines. The family hired scuba divers, but Alouette was more than five hundred feet deep in places — way beyond the capability of all but the most advanced divers. Searchers had tried to recover the body of the young man by dragging metal hooks across the lake bottom.

~

For most of human history, deep lakes have not relinquished their dead. In warm, shallow water, decomposition goes fast and creates gases that can surface a corpse within two to three days. Cold temperatures dramatically slow the natural process of decay. People who drown in water that is a hundred or more feet deep may never surface. The weight of the water traps the body on the bottom.

The oldest corpse that the Ralstons have found was missing for twenty-nine years. The man had been wearing heavy, durable clothing when he drowned, which helped to keep his body intact. The sonar image shows the body lying on its back on an otherwise smooth lake bottom at a depth of 570 feet. It's one of the sharpest outlines of a body that Gene and Sandy ever recorded.

The Ralstons' search gear, known as side-scan sonar, uses sound instead of light to create a picture of the bottom of a lake, river, or ocean. The transducer, the device that generates the sound pulses and records their echoes, is housed in a torpedo-shaped casing called a towfish, which is pulled behind the boat and close to the bottom. The Ralstons' towfish was custom made so they could plumb the deepest lakes on the continent. It weighs 150 pounds. They have enough cable on board to search down to a thousand feet. Reading a sonar image involves deciphering the shadows that different objects cast on the bottom. The sound generated by the sonar reflects off the contours of solid objects — rocks, logs, bodies, sunken treasure — and makes them appear bright and distinct on the computer screen on the boat. The resolution is high enough that Gene and Sandy can pick out beer cans and fishing rods.

This type of sonar was invented in the 1950s but was kept secret by the American military for decades. The technology became more widely available in the 1980s, but it took a long time for people to grasp the potential. Side-scan sonar has revolutionized underwater exploration. The invention was akin to someone flicking a switch and turning on the lights in the dark corners of the deepest waters. Everyone from treasure hunters to archaeologists and engineers suddenly had the power to see through the abyss in real time.

The Ralstons bought their system in the fall of the year 2000 and unwittingly became pioneers in using the technology to find corpses. Their original plan was to use the sonar primarily for their business. At the time, Gene and Sandy ran their own environmental consulting firm doing a variety of work on the water, like investigating the effects of a proposed hydroelectric dam or measuring changes in sediment levels in reservoirs used for drinking water. They thought the sonar would be handy for mapping river bottoms to help engineers decide on the best places to build bridges. But within weeks of getting it up and running, Gene and Sandy imaged the body of twenty-three-year-old Brandon Larsen on the bottom of Bear Lake, Utah. Word spread about a couple from Idaho with a mysterious technology that could reveal the secrets of the deep. Over the next few years, more and more of the Ralstons' business projects gave way to search missions. Same with vacations, hobbies, friends, and family — all those things that make up what most people consider a normal life.

The Ralstons never set out to become experts at finding drowning victims. They stumbled upon a major gap in the services available to the families of people who go missing in water. Police and volunteer search-and-rescue organizations are limited in terms of resources and expertise when it comes to deep water. If the initial search fails, families are often left to figure out and fund any additional efforts. They can hire a commercial outfit, which costs thousands of dollars a day. Or they can call Gene and Sandy.

I first met the Ralstons in early 2017 at a public library in a strip mall south of Boise. I had heard of them about a month earlier from a friend of my parents who had a summer cottage on Shuswap Lake in British Columbia. The family friend told me about how the Ralstons had recovered the body of a twenty-five-year-old man from Calgary, my hometown.

Kevin Boutilier jumped off a houseboat during the summer of 2013 to retrieve his baseball hat, which was blown off his head by a gust of wind. His family and the local authorities tried everything to find his body — sonar, underwater submersible, scuba divers — over a period of eleven months. The Ralstons arrived and located Kevin their second day on the water. I learned that not only do Gene and Sandy do unusual work, but they're also unusually good at that unusual work.

I emailed Gene to discuss writing a magazine story about them, and we set up a time to meet in person. We talked for a few hours each afternoon over three days in a private room at the Lake Hazel Library. Gene was mannerly and chatty. He wore a collared flannel shirt tucked into jeans. His brown hair was graying and parted neatly to the side. Age had begun to soften the sharp edges of his body and face, but he looked strong and capable. Sandy had expansive blue eyes. Their striking color contrasted with the whiteness of her shoulder-length hair, which was pinned to the side and off her face with a small plastic clip. She wore roomy sweatshirts and cardigans that emphasized her small stature and frame. Sandy was more guarded than Gene. She had a no-nonsense demeanor and would sometimes flick the fingers of one hand to hurry her husband to the point of his story.

As I talked to the Ralstons, it became hard to keep all the different parts of all their different searches and recoveries straight. There was the time they helped the FBI find the bodies of four murder victims on the bottom of a reservoir in California. That was what Gene called a "six-pack-of-beer story," his unit of storytelling that comes after a "really long story." On their next search they imaged a 1927 Chevrolet sedan on the bottom of a lake in Washington State. This discovery solved the mystery of what had happened to Blanche and Russell Warren, a married couple who had vanished on a summer afternoon in 1929, leaving behind two young sons. And then there was the time they had an astronaut from NASA aboard to help search for the wreckage of the space shuttle *Columbia* in a reservoir in Texas. I flew home from Idaho with a full notebook.

I met Barb Boutilier a couple of weeks later in Calgary. A retired teacher, she'd raised Kevin and his older sister on her own. She was proud of her son, of his vitality and big circle of close friends. She had been a hockey mom, driving Kevin to an endless stream of practices and games. She described one of her favorite memories of her son: It was a brief moment, a snapshot she had caught of him and his friends through the living room window on a summer afternoon. He had recently gotten his driver's license and was in the family car, a white four-door sedan. His friends in the back seat were holding on to hockey nets, their arms out the windows on both sides of the car. They were headed down the street to a park. "They played hockey even in the summertime, those guys. It was kind of their life," she said.

Barb showed me the sonar image that the Ralstons had made of her son's body on the bottom of Shuswap Lake. She kept a copy on her cellphone. "So that's kind of what it looks like, that's actually him, off Gene and Sandy's computer," she said. The Ralstons had shown me similar images back in Idaho. A human body was easy to recognize in some sonar images, a bright-yellow figure on an otherwise flat and barren surface. It was what you couldn't see, what your mind instantly inferred — the three hundred or so feet of water in Kevin's case — that gave the images such a haunting quality.

"You need to bring him home. Everybody says it's closure — I don't know if it brings closure." Barb told me that she still had Kevin's ashes in her house. She had another more permanent place for his remains arranged, but she wasn't yet ready to take that step. "It's much better for him to be here than at the bottom of that lake. Every parent, anyone, would prefer to have their loved ones someplace they know. I guess they're not safe, but close by."

Barb struggled to find the words to explain the service, the gift, that Gene and Sandy had provided. Bringing a body back from the deep never means bringing a person back from the dead, but it was crucial for Barb and her family to have Kevin's body home and to have somewhere she could visit and remember and feel close to her son. I wanted to write about the Ralstons because I wanted to write about the people they have helped in this very specific and yet hard-to-put-your-finger-on kind of way.

But it was all so sad. Even when the Ralstons succeeded, it was sad. I felt guilty for dredging up those memories for Barb. It was clear, however, that she wanted to talk about her son and about the Ralstons — less because she wanted to be part of an article and more because she wanted to pay Gene and Sandy back somehow. "They are the only ones who can do this," she said.

I joined the Ralstons on a search that spring in 2017 for a man in his early sixties who was presumed to have drowned in Slocan Lake, BC. Gene and Sandy spent two weeks scanning several square miles of the bottom, but never found him. Next I followed them for part of another search that summer, then a three-day training session in the fall on how to use sonar to find drowning victims, which they hosted for military and law enforcement officials in California. I was with the Ralstons in the spring of 2019 when they found the body of a twenty-year-old man who had drowned after his canoe capsized. That day happened to be Gene's seventy-fourth birthday.

I eventually wrote the article about the Ralstons but kept in touch, meeting them on the occasional search when they were close to Calgary. I was curious about why they stayed so busy even after this type of sonar had become more widely available. Gene and Sandy often found someone after other search teams using the same technology had come up empty handed. They have an uncanny knack for finding bodies in water.

The Ralstons talked to Barb during the summer of 2014 about retiring. They had set themselves a goal of finding a hundred corpses. Kevin's body was the ninety-fifth. Almost a decade and dozens more recoveries later, however, and Gene and Sandy continue to respond to requests for help. Someday, maybe soon, they will be forced to stop because they can no longer manage the physical demands of searching. The practical mechanics of finding and recovering corpses are no doubt disturbing. But it's that proximity to death and decay that highlights the humanity required to see the job through. And so I decided in the spring of 2021 to drive to Maple Ridge and join the Ralstons one last time to learn as much as I could about this married couple from rural Idaho who serve the living by finding the dead.

CHAPTER TWO

Point of Last Seen

"Oh, gosh. Well, I guess you could call it three searches," Gene said to me after I sat down on the couch in the motor home for a debrief about the upcoming searches. He was sitting at a table with his back to the front passenger seat. He wore his usual uniform of a plaid flannel shirt and jeans. Gene always dressed neatly, but in clothes made of a durable enough material that he wouldn't hesitate to slide under the motor home on the side of the highway to fix something.

Sandy was to my right, standing in the kitchen. She was using a paper towel to dry off an orange rain hat. It had earflaps and a brim and was made from a heavy-duty waterproof material. The Ralstons had arrived a few hours ago and gone with Corporal Westra (they called him Pete) to evaluate the boat launch they would use to access the Fraser River. Past the kitchen was a bathroom and then a bedroom at the end of a short, narrow hallway. The motor home was clean and cozy. Sandy wore fuzzy slippers. Rain drummed softly on the metal roof.

"There are five people in Alouette alone," Gene said. "So if you say three searches, Alouette's one for five people. Fraser River is an airplane plus two people, and Nicola is one, the cowboy, but he may or may not be in the lake."

Gene's arms were crossed, and he was leaning back in his chair. He seemed both anxious and energized by the task at hand. His favorite movies were old westerns, the kind where a mysterious stranger rides into town, saves the day, and then rides off into the sunset. The ringtone on his cellphone was the theme music from *The Good, the Bad and the Ugly*, the classic spaghetti western in which a young Clint Eastwood played a stoic cowboy searching for buried treasure amid the chaos of the American Civil War. Unlike Eastwood's character, Gene was gregarious. He loved cheesy jokes that involved puns. He would repeat them a second time if no one laughed the first go-round.

"How many years ago did he disappear?" Sandy asked about the man they were planning to search for in Nicola Lake. She had finished drying the hat but was still standing in the kitchen. Sandy's expressive eyes were often quick to register impatience. She was the master of a thousand scowls, most of them exaggerated for humorous effect and directed at her husband of forty-nine years.

"Two years," Gene replied.

"I thought it was more than two years," she said.

"Two years in January," he said.

Ben Tyner was thirty-one years old when he landed his dream job. He moved from Laramie, Wyoming, to the Nicola Valley, an arid and mountainous region of BC, in the fall of 2018 to take over management of a sprawling cattle ranch. Three months later, early on a Monday morning, someone found Ben's horse, outfitted with his personal saddle and reins, wandering alone on the side of a logging road some distance from the ranch. What began as a search-and-rescue mission had quickly turned into a homicide investigation. Gene had received a call from Ben's dad, Richard Tyner, earlier that year to see if they would be up for searching Nicola Lake, a long and narrow body of water not far from the ranch headquarters and the house where

Ben had lived. Richard was in regular contact with the RCMP and the FBI about the ongoing investigation of his son's murder. He told Gene that he was not aware of any evidence to indicate that someone had disposed of Ben's body in the lake, but there wasn't any information to the contrary. And they had already conducted several comprehensive searches on land. Nicola Lake, it seemed, was one of the last places left to look for Ben. Gene told Richard they were willing to try.

"None of this is going to be easy. None of it. Not a single thing is going to be easy," Gene said about the upcoming searches. Which was to say that sometimes, at least for the Ralstons, it was easy. They once spent several days traveling to Juneau, Alaska, to search for a man who had fallen off a dock and into Auke Bay. They found him in twelve minutes. The same sort of thing happened on a search in a lake in Newfoundland, Canada, in 2007. Nineteen-year-old Stephan Hopkins had been missing for more than two months when the Ralstons arrived in their motor home. They found him within half an hour of launching the *Kathy G*. The local community was so impressed they raised more than $300,000 (CAD), bought their own boat, and then outfitted it with the same type of sonar gear.

And once, in a lake in northern Idaho, Gene lowered the towfish right on top of a corpse. Turns out it was somebody who had drowned two years earlier and not the young man the Ralstons had originally been called to help find. Seven minutes into a new search that same afternoon, the Ralstons found that guy, too. Gene compared finding a person on your first pass with the sonar in a big lake to pulling your chosen card from the deck at random. And it happened twice that day. "Is that divine guidance?" Gene or Sandy sometimes asked after telling one of these sorts of stories. They didn't attend church, and they were not religious in any official way, but the Ralstons did wonder about the influence of a larger, unseen power on the work that they did and the path that their lives had taken.

Each of these searches on Alouette Lake, Nicola Lake, and the Fraser River presented significant challenges, Gene explained. Sandy nodded. Neither of them anticipated a straightforward or quick resolution for this trip to Canada.

First off, the search for Ben Tyner didn't include any clues about the point of last seen. The rule of thumb was that a body would be found on the bottom of a lake within a radius equal to the depth of the water. So if you knew where someone went under, the point of last seen, then you knew where to start looking. Without that crucial information, even with a powerful technology like sonar, the search was reduced to the proverbial needle in a haystack, except you didn't even know the whereabouts of the haystack.

Gene and Sandy had worked several homicide cases before. They knew what to look for in terms of the kinds of places on shore that someone could use to dispose of a body. But Nicola Lake was fourteen miles long and had highways that ran along both the south and north shores. The Tyner family — Richard; his wife, Jen; and Ben's younger brother, Jack — were planning to join the Ralstons for the search. The border between Canada and the United States, however, was closed because of the pandemic. The Tyners were unsure if they would be able to cross. The Ralstons had been allowed into Canada that morning because they were considered essential workers and had letters from two different RCMP detachments outlining why they were the only people who could do this particular job. Gene said that the search for Ben would take priority if the Tyners made it across the border. He expected them to try sometime in the next few days.

The Ralstons generally operated on a first come, first served basis. They tried to plan trips based on who asked for help first, but there were a multitude of factors they had to consider when deciding what searches to take on and when. They used to be less discerning. Gene and Sandy would drive cross-country or cross-continent after getting a request. They spent upward of two hundred days a year on searches. It has been more like seventy to eighty days the past few years. They were taking more time nowadays to weigh the likelihood of whether they could help, whether their sonar would be effective for the specific conditions of the lake or river in question. And they were sticking closer to home, agreeing to the searches they could get to within a day or two. Plus, Gene had a growing network of other search specialists he could consult with and mobilize if it was too far for them to make the trip.

Even though the Ralstons have slowed down, the requests for their help have not. It was depressing, Gene told me once, that the need was so great. People reached out over email for the most part. A few short paragraphs that outlined another worst-case scenario: a boat that capsized, a truck that veered off the road, a brother who jumped off a bridge. Sometimes it was a phone call. And sometimes that phone call came in the middle of the night, like the one two months before regarding the search for a twelve-year-old boy caught by a rogue wave off the coast of California. The Ralstons turned down several inquiries related to that incident because the surf was too rough for the sonar to work. You needed relatively calm water to get a clear image of the bottom. Their home phone number and email were listed on their webpage, which appeared with most internet searches related to missing drowning victims. Several police agencies in Canada and the United States gave out Gene and Sandy's contact details if the initial search had been unsuccessful.

In the meantime, as the Ralstons waited to hear whether the Tyners could cross the border, they were going to look for the airplane. The working assumption was that the two pilots were unable to escape. Find the plane, find the bodies. This search took priority, because the water in the Fraser was rising as the snow melted in the mountains. Another couple of weeks and the river would be too high and too fast for the sonar to work.

I asked Gene what he thought the chances were they could find the plane. It had crashed into the Fraser in early June the previous summer at a spot where the river runs alongside a busy highway. One of the witnesses was driving when she looked out her passenger-side window and saw the tail sinking into the fast-moving water. The police had coordinated a massive search with boats, divers, helicopters, and lookouts stationed on bridges over the river downstream of the crash. No one had seen the pilots or the plane since the accident ten months back.

"My concern is that it may be partially covered up with sediment, but there are things you can look for," Gene said. "Let's say the current's going this way, and this is an object lying there." He placed a USB stick in the palm of his hand to model the airplane and then motioned with his other hand to show how the current of the river would split around the plane and create depressions in the bottom at the downstream end. "It causes a washout down below it. So you'll see those little plumes. Those little trenches, if you will. And we found what we think is an airplane, similar situation, in the Ohio River."

The Ralstons had received an email from a firefighter in early 2004 about a plane that had crashed into the Ohio River near Louisville, Kentucky, in the winter of 1977. The accident and the death of the pilot, Roland "Buck" Bellingham, were tragic. But something about the circumstances of the incident, how the plane and pilot just blinked out of existence, needled people in the community for years and then decades.

Tom Olympia, the firefighter, had researched and compiled a detailed, six-page report that included accounts from eyewitnesses and sent it to Gene and Sandy. One of the witnesses had compared the plane hitting the partially frozen river to something being dropped into a glass of water with ice cubes: "The ice cubes momentarily move to create an opening as the object enters the water, but close back over the surface once the object has been submerged." The river had swallowed the plane without so much as a splash. Gene and Sandy drove to Kentucky in November 2004 and spent several days searching with sonar. They found something that looked like a fuselage.

"But it was just too treacherous for divers to go down and check it out," Gene said. The current was too strong, and the visibility was terrible. It would have been like trying to scuba dive in chocolate milk.

"And it was right below a power line," Sandy added.

"Right below the power line that he supposedly struck," Gene said. A tugboat operator had seen the plane tangled up in the wires, like a bug in a spiderweb, before it fell and vanished into the ice.

In early 2021, the Transportation Safety Board of Canada released the results of their investigation into the crash on the Fraser River, or what the report euphemistically referred to as "the occurrence." A student and their instructor had been on a training flight. Fourteen minutes after takeoff, the plane began a controlled descent from 2,200 feet until it reached an altitude of 200 feet. It was flying east at 90 miles per hour over the Fraser. Less than a minute later, the plane struck a set of six aerial power lines that were strung between two towers 125 feet above the river. The report noted that the plane had been properly maintained. The weather that day would not have interfered with visibility or navigation. The student had no record of

trying low-level maneuvers before, and the chief flight instructor at the school had told his staff never to fly below an altitude
of 500 feet. "The investigation was unable to determine what,
if any, purpose there was to operate the aircraft at less than 500
feet above the Fraser River," the report stated.

No one came forward to say they saw the actual moment of
impact when the plane hit the wires. It was the power company
that later discovered damage to two of the lowest-hanging wires
and white paint residue that matched the color of the plane. I
asked Gene if he thought the current in the river was strong
enough that it could have moved an airplane. Maybe it was long
gone by now.

"It might have moved it a ways," he said. There had been
record-high snowfalls the winter before the accident. The
Fraser River had been rising so fast in the spring of 2020 that
people worried about flooding. The river was close to its peak
flow rate on June 6, the day the plane crashed, ripping along at
10,100 cubic meters per second. It was moving half that fast in
early April 2021.

"Let's see. This is upside down. No, right-side up." Gene was
looking at a map of the river on a laptop on the table in front of
him.

"Do you need to change your glasses?" Sandy asked.

Gene has one pair for reading and another for distance. He'd
had a checkup with an ophthalmologist just the week before.
The doctor gave him a new prescription for his distance glasses,
but he had trouble adjusting. So Gene, being Gene, ran a little
experiment. He tested each eye with the new glasses out in his
yard, covering one with his hand while focusing on an object
in the distance, like a tree branch or the wire between fence
posts. He discovered that his left eye with the new prescription
didn't cut the mustard. So he took the left lens out of his old

glasses and put it into the new pair. The hybrid set suited him just fine.

The local eye doctor has been suggesting cataract surgery to Gene for a few years now. But that did not square with his self-diagnosis. He didn't see any cloudiness in his eyes when he looked in the mirror and had no issue with seeing fuzziness or starbursts around headlights when he drove at night. He was wary about getting upsold. The ophthalmologist that did his eye exams ran a clinic for cataract surgery out of the same building. And going through with a surgery that felt unnecessary contradicted the Ralstons' general philosophy toward health: Leave it alone and it'll get better.

"Downstream a little ways. And I'm not sure where he pointed to. In here, it shallows up to like nine feet," Gene said, referring to a place on the map that one of the RCMP officers had told him about. It looked like it was a mile or so west and downriver of the power lines. "That would be a really good stopping place," he said.

Whether the plane had moved in the river depended on what happened as it sank. The engine, Gene explained, was so heavy that it would have pulled the plane to the bottom immediately. But then what? Did it get pushed by the water onto its back so the wings were flat on the bottom? If so, it might not be far from where the witness saw the tail sinking. But if the nose of the plane hit the bottom and it tipped right-side up, the rushing water would have generated the same type of lift forces on the wings and tail flaps as if it were flying through the air. The plane may have drifted aloft and unseen in the current for miles. Maybe even over that shallow bench and all the way out to the ocean.

"And rivers, they're a beast of their own," Gene said.

The Ralstons have had the most success on lakes when the

weather is calm. Ocean and river currents could surreptitiously transport bodies, even airplanes, vast distances. And moving water, whether in the form of waves on the surface or currents down below, made it harder to generate clear images with the sonar.

It was Gene's job to run the sonar and watch the computer monitor for potential targets. Sandy drove the boat. She had to go slow, no more than two miles per hour, and in a straight line. If the towfish moved side-to-side or up and down, the images got distorted. The pulses of sound needed enough time to transmit out, hit an object, and reflect back while the towfish was in the same position. Go too fast or allow too much rocking on the boat and you risked missing something. The Fraser added yet another layer of complexity, because the strength of the current was influenced by tides from the Pacific Ocean.

"As the tide's coming in, and it hits high tide, that'll probably be the lowest velocity downriver. As it goes out, when the tide is low, will be the highest velocity," Gene said. "All that water in the river is held back by the high tide coming in. And then all of a sudden it drops down, and here she comes." The Ralstons wouldn't be able to search crosswise on the river, only upriver and downriver. And when the current was really strong during low tide, then likely only going downstream with the moving water.

Of the all the searches planned for this trip to BC, the one for Bobby Aujla in Alouette Lake seemed, at least at first glance, like the most straightforward. The thirty-seven-year-old was with a group of seven friends on October 1, 2020, including a woman who was riding a Sea-Doo with him when it flipped. She was wearing a life jacket, but he wasn't. The rest of the friends were on a pontoon boat. They circled back and picked up the woman first. Several people saw Aujla go under, but they couldn't agree on where it happened. Some of the witness reports differed by more than a mile. Memory is flawed at the best of times, but more so during traumatic events. The brain zoomed in on certain details, which could be recalled vividly, but to the exclusion of the big picture. The Ralstons have run into this problem before. They sometimes found a body miles from where a witness felt certain the accident had happened.

So far Aujla's friends had spent about $40,000 on two commercial underwater search teams. Cold Water Divers, a company that specialized in salvaging boats, used a remote operated vehicle (ROV) and a sonar system to search the lake for several days. When they came up empty-handed, the friends hired Tim Bulman, another underwater expert from the West Coast. He'd spent a week and a half the previous fall scanning the bottom of Alouette Lake with sonar.

Bulman's company was called Indepth Marine. He did the kind of work that people usually associated with deep-sea exploration. He inspected infrastructure like underwater pipelines and hydroelectric dams, either as a diver or with an ROV, and also took part in higher-profile expeditions. Bulman was part of the team who supported James Cameron, the film director, to pilot a purpose-built submersible to the bottom of the Mariana Trench, the deepest point on Earth at 6.8 miles below the surface of the Pacific Ocean. Bulman also traveled the world for several years as the ROV expert and operator aboard the *Octopus*, a private research super yacht owned by Paul Allen, one of the founders of Microsoft. He helped discover the wreck of the Japanese battleship *Musashi* in 2015 at a depth of four thousand feet on the steep slope of an extinct volcano. The *Musashi* was the largest battleship ever built. It sank in 1944 in the Sibuyan Sea near the Philippines during the Second World War.

Most of the people I talked to who had access to this kind

of technology didn't go out of their way to help on drowning cases. They would go on searches that were close to home or if asked directly by the police. The typical person who was drawn to underwater exploration was more interested in maritime history, shipwrecks, and lost treasure. They had a taste for Indiana Jones–type adventures. The other underwater experts I spoke with told me that they were not averse to finding or even handling corpses. The part about drowning cases they found so difficult, the part they avoided if they could, was interacting with bereaved families. It's not that they were insensitive or callous but rather that drowning accidents were so terrible. Someone died suddenly and unexpectedly. And then vanished. Families were bewildered. They were desperate for answers. The other searchers told me that they didn't understand how the Ralstons had lived exclusively in that world for two decades, how they could go from one drowning search to the next to the next.

I asked Gene once if he ever thought about trying to find a sunken ship or some kind of lost treasure. "It's a lot like gold fever," he said, of what he called the shipwreck bug. "You're going to find the mother lode just over that ridge." He explained that he would rather invest time and effort in something more solid and less risky. Gene has never been a get-rich-quick kind of guy. The Ralstons lived modestly. Their newest vehicle was a 1991 pickup truck with crank windows. They didn't have kids, and the mortgage on their house and land was long since paid off. Gene told me more than once that he wasn't sure what they were going to do with the money that they already had. Sandy enjoyed buying what they needed when it was on sale, and Gene took pride in fixing and maintaining the things they already owned. "They're just people who aren't materialistic at all. There are no frills," said John Zeman, their longtime friend who often volunteered as a deckhand on the *Kathy G*.

The most Sandy was comfortable being away from home these days was about two weeks, and that clock started ticking yesterday morning. She had converted their second bedroom into a greenhouse several years ago and needed to get back to take care of her plants — all of which were by then drought tolerant, a lesson she learned the hard way after returning home from a longer-than-expected search to discover that her collection of African violets had all withered and died.

Gene, on the other hand, was in his element going from one search to another, forever riding off into the sunset. He often remarked how lucky he felt to have found someone who could put up with him and this unconventional life. The Ralstons have built up a network of friends across Canada and the United States, but they were not close with many people back home in Idaho, one of the costs of spending so much time on the road. The winters could get lonely.

CHAPTER THREE

The March of Rigor

The trip to Maple Ridge in April was not the first search for the Ralstons in 2021. They had spent a day in early March looking for an elderly man who had disappeared with his car in 2016. The retired postal worker had lived in Boise, not far from Gene and Sandy. His children suspected he had died by suicide. He struggled with health issues and missed his late wife. The son emailed the Ralstons at the end of January 2021: "It's been awhile since dad went missing and this loose end needs a more thorough investigation."

The boat launch near the dam on the west side of Lucky Peak Reservoir extended all the way to the bottom so people could use it even when the water level was low. The bank was steep enough that you could put a car in neutral and it would roll all the way down the ramp. The Ralstons picked up on a set of tire tracks on the sonar that veered off the launch not too far from shore. The treads cut two distinct furrows in the soft sand on the bottom of the lake. Gene and Sandy followed the tracks for two hundred yards, hoping they had been made by the missing man's 2003 silver Pontiac Bonneville. But then they abruptly vanished. Gene contacted the local county dive team. They told him that a different vehicle had been discovered by someone using a fisherman-style sonar system. The dive team had used airlift bags to float it back to the surface. "Another suicide," Gene told me.

Not quite a week after that day on Lucky Peak, the Ralstons got a call from the Malheur County Sheriff's Office in Oregon. Steven Nichols had been reported missing the day before. The forty-two-year-old was last seen on the Owyhee Reservoir tinkering with the motor of his boat. He had declined an offer by another boater to get a tow back to shore. Nichols was a welder. He built the boat and trailer himself and had gone to the lake to troubleshoot some mechanical issues. Later that evening, someone spotted his empty boat run aground on shore.

It was hard to know how Nichols got into trouble. One common way for a man to fall overboard was to lose his balance while he urinated. This has happened so often that the Ralstons called it zipper syndrome. Or maybe Nichols had leaned too far out off the boat while trying to fix the motor and lost his balance. His father told me that his son had lived for fishing and hunting. He was always outdoors. The Malheur County sheriff's deputies were the first people to ever use his custom-built trailer to pull his boat out of the water.

The authorities searched the surface of the lake and surrounding area with help from the local volunteer search-and-rescue group. Malheur is a small, rural county. The sheriff's office didn't have a dive team and had been relying on the Ralstons for years to help out on searches in the area's deeper lakes. Nichols drowned on a Saturday. Gene and Sandy got the call Sunday. They arrived Monday and found him Tuesday afternoon at a depth of 294 feet. They did the recovery Wednesday morning. Something unusual happened as they brought the body up from the bottom. Something Gene and Sandy had never seen before.

The Ralstons bought their own remotely operated vehicle, or ROV, in 2007 for $46,000. It was about the size of a carry-on suitcase and equipped with a ten-inch-long metal arm with a curved set of three interlocking pincers at the end. Gene called them grabber jaws. He used a black joystick to pilot the ROV, which had a video camera and connected to the boat with five hundred feet of umbilical cable. They invested in the submersible because they got tired of waiting for divers to arrive and do the recovery, which sometimes took days or even weeks. The Ralstons were nothing if not independent. They liked to do things on their own terms.

Back in the motor home on the afternoon I arrived in Maple Ridge, I asked Gene if he could show me the video of the recovery on the laptop. He edited a video of each recovery to give to the local police. He kept a copy to use in the training seminars that he and Sandy gave on how to search for bodies with sonar. As he looked for the file, Sandy sat down next to me. It was a tight fit because a large computer monitor, the one they used to display the images from the sonar on the boat, was covered in a protective cloth and took up the other end of the couch.

"This gorgeous little couple is on a post in our backyard," Gene said. He turned the laptop to face Sandy and me. The desktop photo was of a pair of birds with dark eyes and brown feathers nestled together on the top of a tall wooden post.

"American kestrels," Gene said.

"This is the smallest of the hawk family. They're about the size of a robin," Sandy added. The Ralstons both have graduate degrees in the biological sciences and a keen interest in the natural world. An ornithologist from Boise State University had set up some nesting boxes near their house, which was on twenty acres of land mostly covered by sagebrush and wild grass. The Ralstons watched the birds hunt and play from their back deck. They had become like pets — the kind you could leave at home for weeks on end and didn't have to ask a neighbor to look after.

Gene pressed PLAY on the video file. He explained that the propellers on the ROV had stirred up a cloud of soft silt from the bottom, which was why the water was so hazy. The only source of light was the robot, and it didn't penetrate the gray-green murk for more than a few feet. The depth read 272 feet on the screen, but Gene said it was actually about 20 feet deeper than that. He'd been in a hurry to get the ROV in the water and forgot to calibrate some of the instruments.

"Okay, you can see that we are approaching his arm," Gene said.

A hand and forearm materialized out of the gloom. The water was thick with swirling chunks of sediment, like flakes of ash from a bonfire. The grabber jaws were in the foreground and took up about a third of the screen. The ROV approached slowly. More of the body came into view. The man was on his back and wearing a white T-shirt and blue jeans. His arms were at his sides and bent at the elbow. His forearms and hands, which were balled in loose fists, reached up toward the surface.

Thomas Lynch, an American poet and undertaker, was ten years old when he saw his first corpse. His father, who owned a funeral home, had brought him to work. The body of an old man was lying on a table and covered by a sheet up to his neck. "There was a stillness about that body unlike anything I'd witnessed in nature before," Lynch wrote about the experience in an essay. "I wasn't frightened, but I was changed."

The feeling in the motor home turned solemn as we watched the footage. The mute, foglike water added to the strangeness of the stillness that Lynch associated with corpses. The man looked so out of place in that ghostly submarine landscape. The thrusters from the ROV made the hair on his arms billow like seaweed in an ocean current.

~

Water, especially deep water, has retained a sense of mystery despite the advances of technology and the detailed mapping of every square foot of land on Earth. Only a fraction of the world's ocean floors have been visited and charted, never mind all the lakes and rivers. Robert Macfarlane wrote about humanity's inherent fascination with the unknown — a simultaneous fear of it and attraction to it — in his book *Mountains of the Mind.* "Literature and religion are littered with stories of other worlds — uncharted oceans, secret realms, imaginary deserts, unclimbable peaks, unvisited islands and lost cities," he wrote. "The curiosity and attraction we instinctively feel towards the locked room, the garden over the wall, the landscape just beyond the horizon, the imagined country on the other side of the world; these are all expressions of the same desire in us to know somewhere apart, somewhere hidden."

Deep water is a parallel universe right under our noses. Things, sometimes giant predatory things, appear all at once at the limits of our field of vision, which is cut drastically short. Fundamental aspects of reality, stuff we take for granted like gravity, light, and sound, work differently at depth. Light is bent, absorbed, scattered, refracted, and weakened. Sound, a purely mechanical wave, is more powerful. Water is denser than air, the particles are packed closer together, so sound travels more efficiently. Some whale songs have been tracked for thousands of miles and across entire oceans.

A corpse on the bottom of a lake takes place at the intersection of two profound mysteries, the alien experience of the deep and the age-old question of what happens after death. What trace, if any, remains of the person in the body that is left behind?

For all of history, as far back as the archaeological record goes, humans, and even our humanoid ancestors, have invested precious time and energy on the dead. "This thing — this inanimate thing — that is always more than a thing has been the stuff of our imaginations since the beginning," wrote the historian Thomas Laqueur in his book *The Work of the Dead*.

Laqueur described how corpses have mattered for endlessly different spiritual, religious, and personal reasons throughout history. His main goal was to explore why they matter, and why they continue to matter into the twenty-first century, an era in which many societies have become increasingly secular. His book is "a story of the ways that the dead enchant our purportedly disenchanted world."

Some anthropologists and sociologists point to caring for the dead, to grave sites, as evidence of humanity's first forays into symbol making. The desire to honor the body of a deceased loved one may have propelled early humans to take the first steps toward creating more complex and sophisticated societies. It's possible, Laqueur wrote, that honoring the dead marks the beginning of civilization. The Ralstons use a powerful technology to satisfy a primordial instinct, an essential and enduring aspect of the human condition.

Almost every corpse that the Ralstons find is in the same position: back on the bottom, knees slightly bent, arms to the sides, forearms and hands raised up in the water column. It's almost like the person was sitting in a high-backed chair, arms resting on the armrests, and then the chair tipped backward onto the bottom of the lake.

Gene has tried to research why a corpse invariably ends up in this position, but there is not much science on the subject. Human taphonomy facilities, known informally as body farms, are located throughout the world and study how human remains decompose in various ecosystems on land. One of the primary goals of the research is to provide police with the information they need to determine an accurate postmortem interval, or time of death, when they discover a corpse. No such counterpart exists for aquatic environments. It's too expensive and complicated to carry out these kinds of experiments underwater. But Gene and Sandy have their own theory. The upper body is more buoyant than the lower body even when the lungs are mostly filled with water. So as a body sinks, the chest and head orient up. When the feet hit the bottom, the knees bend and the body falls back. The bent knees and raised arms create a telltale shadow with the sonar in the shape of an *M* or a *W*.

On the laptop in the motor home, we were looking at the 124th body that Gene and Sandy had found since they started using their sonar two decades before. That included both the number of people they imaged with the sonar and the corpses they reclaimed themselves with their ROV.

The robot hovered a foot or two off the bottom in the video. It moved from side to side until the grabber jaws lined up with the wrist and then it thrust forward, catching just below the hand between the pincers. If Gene was unable to snag the wrist, he would have tried for an ankle or one of the belt loops on the man's jeans.

"You can see, we have a hold of him here, but the jaws look kind of wonky," Gene said. The two pincers had not shut completely and interlocked. Then the camera angle tilted down to the bottom of the lake in a series of jerky movements. The ROV tipped forward because Sandy, almost three hundred feet up on the deck of the *Kathy G*, had started to pull on the cable plugged in at the back of the robot.

Gene never piloted the ROV up from the bottom. It was too ungainly to steer with a body attached. And the cargo was often fragile. So it was up to Sandy to pull the robot and the body, which together usually weighed about fifteen pounds in the water, hand-over-hand up to the surface. She had to go slow so the corpse's internal pressure could equalize with the diminishing pressure of the water.

"Okay, watch this real close as we're about ready," Gene said.

The ROV had lifted the body a couple of feet off the bottom. The robot was vertical in the water, but the man looked like he was still mostly horizontal. His arm was still bent ninety degrees at the elbow.

"Watch, watch, watch, watch, watch, watch, watch," Gene said in rapid succession. "Okay . . . boom!" The hand shifted suddenly. The top two knuckles filled the entire frame of the ROV's camera. The movement was too fast for me to make much sense of what I had seen.

"His arm slipped out of the grabber," Gene said. "His thumb is around the bottom of the bumper bar, and his fingers are over it like that." He made a hook shape out of his fingers on one hand. A metal rod, like a monkey bar at a playground, ran along the bottom at the front of the ROV to protect the propellers and other instruments from an impact. The man's wrist had slipped out of the jaws, but his fingers hooked onto the bar.

"It totally blew me away," Gene said.

He had not been watching the video feed when it happened. Gene had left the pilothouse to test the weight of the line himself after Sandy told him it was unusually heavy. The same sort of thing had happened a few years before on a lake in northern Idaho. Gene had let the corpse drift back to the bottom so he could investigate with the ROV. He found a rope tied to the ankle. He followed the rope and discovered a five-gallon bucket full of rocks. The Ralstons and the sheriff deputies aboard would later learn that the widow had discovered a suicide note, but in the moment they thought they had uncovered a murder. Gene had worried that the situation on the Owyhee Reservoir was similar, but one of the two deputies on the *Kathy G* took over for Sandy and managed to keep pulling. It took forty minutes to bring the body to the surface. Nichols was tall and muscular and so weighed more than usual in the water.

It wasn't until later that day, when Gene was editing the video back at the motor home, that he realized what had happened to the body and ROV just a few feet off the bottom. The corpse had independently hung on to the robot for the entire ascent.

The Ralstons were aware of the scientific explanation: Rigor mortis, the stiffening of muscle tissue after death, had made the muscles in the hand and fingers rigid enough to support the weight of the body in the water. But they also marveled at the unlikely turn of events. Gene said that the chances were one in a million.

"And the reason for all of this," Sandy said. "It was St. Patrick's Day, and St. Patrick, decided to help."

Gene closed the laptop on the table but continued to describe the recovery. He said he used a weighted fishing line clipped to the end of an extendable pole when divers were unavailable to secure the body from the ROV in the water. It was one of many job-specific innovations that he and Sandy have had to figure out on their own. Gene looped the line under the feet of Nichols's body, raised it up, and then cinched it around the chest and under the arms. One of the deputies on the *Kathy G* then passed the pole to other officers waiting on the sheriff's boat. They lifted the corpse out of the water onto a platform and then enclosed it in a body bag. The deputies returned to the boat launch where the family was waiting.

~

Every so often, the Ralstons find themselves on a remote lake without support from volunteers or the police. The sides of the *Kathy G* are too high to heave a body into the boat, so they wrap it in a bag in the water. They secure the bag parallel to the boat by attaching lines to the bow and the transom at the back. With the corpse securely fastened and resting on the surface of the water, they head for shore. The slow trip back to land can take hours. The Ralstons transport the dead at the same slow and methodical pace as someone rowing a boat.

I have come to think of Gene and Sandy as living out a modern-day version of the old story of the ferryman, the mythological figure who guides the souls of the recently deceased across a river or lake that divides the land of the living from the land of the dead. I always thought of the character as Charon of Greek mythology, but it turns out it's even older. The first written accounts date back to 2450 BCE and were found on the interior walls of the Egyptian pyramids, which some researchers say were built as tombs for royalty. The ferryman was called the man whose face is behind him, because he never looked in the direction he was rowing his boat. Some anthropologists go back even further, tracing the story to mortuary rituals from twelve thousand years ago.

Ronnie Terpening, in his book *Charon and the Crossing*, outlined how the myth cut across time and cultures. Norse mythology depicts a ferryman-like figure, as do the Hindu religion and legends from Babylonia. Anguta and Pinga help guide souls to the underworld, which is located beneath the land and the sea, in Inuit mythology. People were buried in canoes in southern Argentina, on ships in Scandinavia, and next to terra-cotta boats in Cyprus, all to ensure a safe journey to the hereafter. The cultural significance of an afterlife boatman is global. East and West, ancient and modern. "Universal aspects of the various phenomena concerning death (the barrier, the crossing, and ferryman) make any attempt to discuss specific origins of the boatman and, in particular Charon, futile," wrote Terpening.

The myth of the ferryman is one of those stories that somehow got lodged in the human psyche. Maybe it has that kind of resonance because it offers an answer to one of life's biggest questions. Death is portrayed as a beginning instead of an end. The recently deceased embark on a journey in the company of a skilled and compassionate guide, although there are also some grim and malevolent versions of the afterlife boatman.

You can draw a number of practical parallels between the cosmic role of a ferryman and the nuts-and-bolts work of an underwater search-and-recovery specialist, between rowing souls into the next world and pulling bodies up from the deep. The most salient comparison, however, is that of a shared purpose. Both the Ralstons and the ferryman help the bereaved to make at least some sense out of death, especially an abrupt and unanticipated one.

Gene and Sandy don't like the word *closure*. They have spent too much time in the company of families who have experienced sudden tragedy to believe in a clean finish line for grief. And yet there is no doubt they provide some kind of invaluable service. They help people get unstuck. They help them cross a barrier they could not cross on their own. The Ralstons offer a bridge between worlds.

Barb Boutilier described how she hated going anywhere west of Calgary after Kevin drowned and was still missing. "We went in November to Banff and the closer I got, because he was in the West, and the closer I got to those mountains, I just started to cry. I cried the whole time. I hated going to those mountains. Even though he wasn't in Banff, he was on the other side of those mountains," she told me. "It's funny what your mind does. He's home. He's with me now."

The Ralstons use a two-hundred-horsepower Evinrude outboard motor to power the *Kathy G* instead of oars, but they're doing the same job as their mythological counterpart. Gene and Sandy provide solace to the living by providing safe passage for the dead.

CHAPTER FOUR

Listen in the Dark

The next morning, April 8, 2021, I drove back to Pete Westra's house so I could get a ride to the boat launch. It was owned by some kind of metal fabrication company and had no public access or parking. The police officer's two-story home was on four and a half acres and included a rain forest in the back-yard. Pete lived upstairs with his wife, two kids, and two foreign exchange students, one from Thailand and the other Korea, who were staying with them for the entire school year. His wife's parents lived on the main floor. They had designed the house so all three generations could live together comfortably under one roof. Pete had encouraged Gene and Sandy to make use of the hot tub, which was at the side of the house and over-looked a streambed in the forest.

The Ralstons never knew what to expect in terms of the amenities and conditions of the campground or roadside or farmer's field where they parked their motor home for the dura-tion of a search. More often than not it was somewhere beau-tiful, somewhere people sought out for vacation. But they had endured the heat of summer in the middle of deserts and the all-night noise of run-down motel parking lots. They lucked out this time. Even the asphalt pad in front of the four-car garage was big enough to maneuver the unmarked RCMP truck with the *Kathy G* towed behind it. The Westra household felt like a refuge. It was tucked away from the highway at the end of a long gravel driveway lined with tall evergreens.

"I might get in trouble from my mother-in-law for that later," Pete said. He squashed some plants with the rear tire of the boat trailer as he pulled off the parking pad and onto the driveway. Gene sat upfront. Sandy was beside me in the back. Pete was bald and had an athletic build. He was forty years old and struck me as the kind of police officer you hoped to get if you were pulled over for a traffic infraction — someone with a sense of humor and an eye on the bigger picture. In addition to his role as the missing persons coordinator, Pete was responsible for cases involving domestic violence. He was part of his detachment's serious crimes unit, a team that handled the more complex and longer-term investigations. We were all dressed in warm clothes and rain gear in anticipation of the long, cold day on the water.

It was a short drive to the Fraser River. Dense trees and hedges obscured the residential acreages that lined the roads. I caught glimpses of mansions tucked behind ornate stone and wrought-iron gates. We passed a few ramshackle properties with an array of dilapidated cars parked on flat tires. We waited at a set of lights to cross the Lougheed Highway, one of the busy east–west thoroughfares that connected Vancouver with its myriad satellite communities. Pete parked the truck and trailer at the far end of the industrial lot. A line of yellow caution tape was strung across the entrance to the ramp that sloped down to the river.

A tall man with a beard the color of concrete was standing beside a white pickup truck with a modular canopy on the back. Gene recognized him as Tim Cucheran, the supervisor of the RCMP underwater recovery team's division in British Columbia. The Ralstons had worked with him on a few other searches. Cucheran was there to bring them up to speed on what had been done so far to find the plane.

A government agency regularly scanned this section of the Fraser River to ensure the bottom was free of debris for barges and other boat traffic. The sonar they used was designed to measure the depth of the water over large areas, so it was not good at identifying smaller shapes and objects. Cucheran told us that the surveyors had scanned the river within a week of the plane crash last June and detected something unusual off the tip of a small island across the river from where we stood. The RCMP divers had to wait until September before the current slowed down enough that it was safe go in the river. At that point Cucheran had approached the object from downriver, swimming against the current. The water was like liquid mud.

"I put my hands on it," he said. The visibility was so bad he had to search by feel, probing the bottom of the river in the dark. The object turned out to be two giant logs, one lying over the top of the other at a ninety-degree angle. The perpendicular shape was what had caught the eye of the survey team. After he ruled out that target, which had been their only lead on the location of the plane, Cucheran suggested to the Ridge Meadows RCMP detachment that they contact the Ralstons.

The underwater recovery team had a drop sonar, which was a type of scanning sonar. It created an image of a circular area of the bottom from a fixed position. The device was set up on a tripod and lowered to the bottom from a boat. You had to raise it, move the boat, and lower it again to scan a new area. Sidescan sonar, the system you towed behind a boat, was way more efficient for covering large areas. Cucheran didn't try to use the drop sonar to find the plane because the current in the river would have knocked the tripod over on the bottom.

Cucheran was one of only two full-time members on the division in BC. The rest of the twenty divers had other jobs within the RCMP. There was a total of about eighty members on the underwater recovery team across Canada. When a search came up, those officers had to get colleagues to cover their regular duties while they were gone. That part-time arrangement was similar for police agencies across Canada and the United States. If the police force was lucky enough to have a dive unit, then its members often had to balance any searches with an already full workload. Most police divers could not search for more than a couple of days if there was no suspicion of wrongdoing. The priority was aquatic crime scene investigation. It was this void in the public services that the Ralstons stepped up to fill when they bought their sonar back in the year 2000.

Cucheran asked Gene if they had any issues crossing the border into Canada. "But I guess you guys don't have to worry because you're vaccinated," he added. Americans got access to the Pfizer vaccine in late 2020, and the Ralstons, being in their seventies, were among the first people eligible for the shot. Gene told him that in fact they hadn't gotten the shots; they were not fans of these vaccines. The production and testing had all seemed too rushed.

"You don't have to explain yourself to me," Cucheran replied.

Gene had told me something similar, that he and Sandy were uneasy about this particular vaccination. But he added that they had not had any vaccinations, including the annual flu shot, for decades. Part of the reason was that they rarely got sick, so why try to fix something that's not broken. Gene attributed their good health to their relative isolation. Regular life for the Ralstons in the countryside was a kind of self-imposed lockdown. "We don't socialize a lot. We don't go to concerts. We don't go to movie theaters. We don't go to restaurants three times a week. We just stay away from other people," he said.

He also shared with me that Sandy had received a tainted vaccine for polio when she was six or seven years old. Idaho was one of five states to receive doses of the Salk vaccine made by Cutter Laboratories in the mid-1950s. The company's manufacturing process was flawed, and the vaccine contained live and infectious virus. An estimated 120,000 children were injected with the Cutter vaccine before the federal government ordered it withdrawn. Forty thousand contracted polio, leaving two hundred kids with varying degrees of paralysis. Ten died. Sandy got sick, and the virus paralyzed several muscles in her back, which caused health issues that she has dealt with ever since.

I was still surprised by the Ralstons' aversion to the vaccine given their education and sense of themselves as scientists. They often lectured about the value of empirical evidence over anecdotal information when it came to underwater searching. I wondered if there wasn't something else going on, maybe a political motivation, that he and Sandy didn't want to get into with each new person they met up here in Canada.

Mike Clement, a lifelong scuba diver and friend of the Ralstons, told me that most of the underwater people he knew leaned conservative; the nature of the work instilled a strong sense of self-reliance and a suspicion of government intervention. "A lot of people that are involved with hard, out-on-the-water working, having to do absolutely everything without help from anybody else, and having the government get in your way with permits and rules and regulations, it just makes it a lot harder and longer to get your work done," Clement said.

After Cucheran left, two men who worked for the company that owned the boat launch approached Pete. They wore grease-stained overalls.

"You guys are looking for that plane?" the older one asked. Various metal structures, like triangular lattices and tubes big enough that they could have worked as waterslides, were stacked in piles all over the lot.

"You know the guy who called that in was inebriated, right?" the younger one said. He was smoking a cigarette.

Pete ignored the questions and instead asked if it was okay to leave the truck parked on the boat launch. The older man said it was fine but to park it close to the water because some of the delivery trucks needed to use the top of the ramp to turn around.

"Even if it did crash in the river, the current would have taken it out to the ocean by now," the younger man said. The two men were intrigued by the sight of the *Kathy G* and the steel torpedo hanging over the bow. But they were convinced that any attempt to find the plane was doomed to fail. Either the plane had never crashed into the river — a drunk eyewitness had imagined the whole thing — or, if it had crashed, it was long gone by now because of the current in the river. They implied with a smirk that we were fools to try.

Their knee-jerk skepticism made me think of that firefighter from Kentucky who was so invested in finding the plane in the Ohio River decades after it crashed. His instinct had been to lean into the mystery. He was confident that with enough persistence and the right technology, it could be solved. Airplanes didn't just vanish. These two men had the opposite reaction: Life was a hell of a lot easier if you never acknowledged the mystery in the first place.

The sides of the *Kathy G* were about the same height as Gene when the boat was up on the trailer. He stepped onto the metal fender above the trailer wheel and swung one leg up and over the gunnel. The fluid movement reminded me of a cowboy settling onto a horse. Pete backed the truck and trailer into the water until the boat started to float and drift backward. Sandy and I walked down the steep gangplank to the concrete dock. Thick, dark clouds hung low over the river. The water was flat and smooth.

It was roughly at the location of that dock, according to the report on the crash, where the plane dropped to an altitude of two hundred feet and then lost radio contact. That was the height of a fifteen-story building. It would have been a shock to see an airplane, even a small one, fly by so low. I looked up the river and could discern the tops of the electrical towers poking out above clumps of brown trees on either side of the water. The metal lattices were faint, triangular wisps from this distance. I could only see them because I knew where to look. And all those trees would have had lush canopies of green leaves back in June. I couldn't see the wires at all. The river turned south not far past the towers. The backdrop for the wires from this vantage point was a forested mountain, not the kind of contrast you would need to notice something as subtle as transmission lines. The two towers and the wires, the report had noted, were clearly marked on the pilots' navigational charts.

The firefighter didn't mention any charts in his analysis of Bellingham's collision with the aerial wires back in 1977. An employee with the Federal Aviation Administration told Olympia that the crash was caused by "pilot error due to inattention and unsafe altitude." But he had his own theory. The week before the crash, the cables were lowered and laid out across the ice so the power company could do some maintenance. "It is my feeling that the pilot assumed that they were still missing," Olympia wrote in the report he sent the Ralstons.

"Okay, who needs a life jacket?" Gene asked as Pete and I climbed into the back of the boat from the dock. There was just enough room for the Ralstons to sit shoulder-to-shoulder in the pilothouse. Pete and I stood outside on either side of the door.

Gene asked me to keep an eye out for tugboats. "They can't move if they're towing a bunch of stuff," he said.

The job of lookout was usually up to John Zeman, the *Kathy G*'s veteran deckhand. He lived in Port Townsend, Washington, and has joined the Ralstons on dozens of searches, usually on lakes and rivers in the Pacific Northwest. He brought his own motor home so he could camp alongside them. Zeman met Gene and Sandy in the spring of 2002 when they were working with the FBI to recover the four homicide victims from a reservoir in California. He lived in the area at the time and volunteered as a boat driver for the local sheriff. Zeman told me that he had been amazed by the Ralstons' technology, the power to pinpoint a body on the bottom of a lake no matter how deep. He was also impressed by Gene and Sandy, an ordinary couple doing an extraordinary thing and not trying to get rich in the process.

Gene told me that Zeman decided against this trip because he didn't think he would be able to cross the border into Canada given the pandemic. Sandy said it was because his wife discouraged him from going. Zeman had recently turned eighty-two, and his wife worried when he drove long distances by himself these days.

We traveled downriver first. The banks widened as we moved west toward the ocean. It was a gloomy, industrial landscape. Railroad tracks flanked the river on both sides. The water was the same brownish red as the rust on the metal roofs of the factories and storage sheds that littered the shoreline. Gene slowed the boat to an idle about a mile and a half downriver from the dock, so three miles from the power lines. The depth sounder bolted to the ceiling of the pilothouse displayed a profile view of the river bottom. We had yet to see any rise or shallow bench. It was possible that Pete's colleague was right about the underwater ridge, and that it was farther west, but Gene said the search area was already too big to cover if they came this far downriver from the dock.

We sped back upriver and stopped several hundred feet past the power lines. The six wires were arranged in the shape of a barn roof and dipped substantially as they spanned the river. The accident report estimated the wires were 125 feet above the water when the plane struck them. They could hang as low as 90 feet. The tension on the lines between the towers depended on the ambient temperature and the electrical load. An assortment of buildings, including an immense heap of sawdust or mulch, on the north bank looked like a sawmill. The fresh smell of cedar was welcome relief from the intermittent doses of boat exhaust that wafted from the outboard motor.

Gene programmed a new search grid onto the black laptop on the dashboard above the steering wheel. It was held in place, like many things on the *Kathy G*, with a bungee cord. The computer displayed a series of parallel blue lines. A small circle with cross-hairs marked the position of the boat on the search grid. Sandy's job was to keep the boat headed straight on that line.

It was always tempting, Gene told me once, to rush from one area of high probability to the next in an effort to find the person as soon as possible. The problem was that you could never be confident that you thoroughly covered one area before speeding off to the next one. And people got discouraged quickly if they lurched from one new theory to the next without an overarching plan to organize the search.

The Ralstons embodied the philosophy of slow and steady. Gene picked the middle line of the search grid based on the best evidence for the point of last seen. And then they worked their way out in overlapping increments, like laying shingles on a roof, that covered and then mostly re-covered every square foot of the bottom. They called the technique mowing the lawn. Gene liked to say, borrowing an old adage from trench warfare, that underwater searching involved long periods of sheer boredom interrupted by brief moments of terror.

A computer program recorded all the search lines and overlayed the data onto a map. The Ralstons reviewed what they had covered at the end of the day and made adjustments to the plan if necessary. Gene and Sandy have found these maps just as useful in failure as in success. They were something tangible to show the family of the missing person. The orderly blue lines of the search grid added up to form neat geometric blocks that contrasted with the wayward contours of the lake or river. The act of searching, successful or not, was a way to honor the missing person. A map from the Ralstons was proof of their painstaking effort. It was a testament to the fact that someone was worth trying to find.

Gene fired up the generator on the deck near the bow, which powered the motor for the winch. He used a rubber controller about the size of a walkie-talkie to raise and lower the towfish by winding and unwinding the black electromechanical cable spooled on the winch. The cable was threaded through a system of pullies and then a metal ring on the top of the towfish before it plugged into the back of the device. The steel casing of the towfish had two long slits on either side. The apertures allowed the transducer to transmit and receive the pulses of sound.

Sandy climbed up and knelt on the bow. She moved more tentatively on the boat than Gene. He raised the towfish off its sheath, and she leaned out over the frigid river as she guided the torpedo past the front of the boat and into the water. That was another one of the jobs that Zeman usually performed. The six-foot-long steel torpedo, with its four sturdy fins at the back, vanished into the murky river. Sandy returned to the pilothouse and steered the boat onto the first search line. The bottom of the Fraser started to scroll down the monitor in front of Gene.

"Do you have sturgeon on the river?" he asked.

"Yep," Pete said.

Gene measured a thin, bright streak. It was half an inch on the screen, but using one of the program's tools he calculated that it was a six-foot-long fish. Gene had a mouse pad strapped to his right knee with Velcro. The sonar software displayed the images of the bottom in a monochromatic palette of bronze and yellow. The bottom of the river had a series of overlapping ridges. Gene explained that the current had created dunes with the sediment. They were between two and four feet tall and looked like the corrugated scales of a giant reptile on the monitor.

"I wish we could have been here on day one, or day two," Gene said. The chances of finding something were better the sooner you could arrive after the incident, especially when it had occurred in a fast-moving river. He set the sonar to search at a range of 131 feet out of both sides of the towfish. They usually scanned a shorter-distance and only out one side of the towfish, but a plane was a much bigger target than a body. The river was forty-nine feet deep. Gene flew the towfish about ten feet off the bottom so the sound pulses hit the floor of the river at a low angle. Gene liked to explain how the sonar worked by comparing the process to looking for a screw or pin that's fallen on the ground: "Take a flashlight and lie down and roll it on the floor. You'll see the shadow of the pin before you see the pin itself."

We chugged along for a mile and a half toward the dock and then moved sixty feet closer to the south bank of the river. We scanned the next line back up to the power lines. Down and back. Down and back. The bottom was mostly free of debris. We saw a few sunken logs. Some of them had root balls. I tried to make a plane out of everything that scrolled into view. A couple of tugboats passed us on the river. One was pulling a barge with piles of gravel and sand. A small electric heater was set up at Sandy's feet. It was cold enough outside on deck that I could see my breath.

And then, about two hours into the search, something on the screen caught Gene's attention. We were under the power lines and headed downriver toward the dock. He marked the object and saved its location so they could scan it again, but we kept moving. The object had been larger than any of the logs we had seen on the bottom so far. It also looked more angular. At the end of that line going west, I helped Gene bring the towfish back in the boat, and we sped upriver to scan the object again, but coming from the opposite direction. He measured it to be four and a half feet high off the bottom and eighteen feet long.

"If it did break apart then would that make sense, because we're actually quite close to the wires, for the fuselage and part of the plane to just go down?" Pete asked.

"Especially the engine compartment," Gene said.

Sandy turned downriver for a third pass on the suspicious-looking object. I thought of something else the firefighter had written in his report about the plane that crashed into the Ohio River: "My feeling is that this airplane probably settled to the bottom pretty quickly."

Pete had been getting texts all morning with more information about the crash. The witness had pulled over and parked at the sawmill on the north bank to make the 911 call. She was at about 287th Street when she made the call and then estimated that she had seen the plane disappear into the water at 280th Street.

"I would say that falls within that area," Pete said of the object we were scanning.

Pete got another text. "Turkey sandwich is waiting for you at the launch," he told Gene.

"What, they didn't have a helicopter?" Gene asked.

Pete laughed. "Exactly, just drop it into the boat."

Some of Pete's colleagues were waiting at the dock for the chance to meet the Ralstons. They had brought coffee and lunch.

"There it is," Gene said as we passed over the object a fourth time.

"It's funny how different it looks from every angle," Pete said.

"It sure isn't very interesting, except for the shadow," Sandy said.

"Could be a log," Gene said. And with that, after the fourth try, the Ralstons ruled out the possibility that it was the plane. They switched seats. Gene drove us back to the dock for a break. One of the officers told me that a day or so after the crash, searchers had found a satchel floating downriver from the power lines. It contained identification that belonged to one of the missing pilots. That bag, and the scuff marks on the aerial wires, were so far the only evidence that had been found related to the plane and the pilots.

The afternoon went a lot like the morning. We continued our slow march south across the river, moving toward the bank in sixty-foot increments. At some point, Pete pulled a sandwich from his gym bag.

"PB and J?" Gene asked.

"No. It's butter and chocolate sprinkles." Pete pulled the top slice of bread back to show Gene the unconventional contents of his sandwich.

"It's a hagelslag," he added, a traditional Dutch snack. Pete had unruly blond eyebrows that angled up toward the middle of his forehead, which made him look like he was always carefully thinking about something. His head was shaved close to the skin.

The sun started to break through the clouds. Gene lowered the black mesh blinds on the windows beside him and Sandy. It was hard to see the images on the monitor if it got too bright in the pilothouse. The river was calm, except for the wakes created by the occasional tugboat. There was a constant stream of traffic on the highway. We didn't see any objects on the bottom that warranted additional scans. We did see a giraffe, an alien spaceship, a variety of whales, and even a few dragons.

"You have to do something to entertain yourself," Gene said after pointing out a sand dune on the bottom that he thought looked like Snoopy smoking a vape pen. He described this type of late-in-the-day, search-induced giddiness as getting rummy. I had started to think of it as boat time. The growling of the generator up front and the rumbling of the motor in the stern created a wash of background noise that muted all other sounds. The boat rocked gently on the river. And then there was the monitor. Everyone, except Sandy, was transfixed by that waterfall display, an infinitely looping Rorschach test that ticked by in repeating ridges of sediment and shadow. Minutes dragged. Hours vaporized.

Gene zoomed in on something bright and square on the bottom. "That's like the objects we found on the Columbia River when we were looking for the two fighter jets," he said. And then he told us about the time two F-18s had collided over a river in northwestern Oregon while on a low-altitude training mission. One of the three pilots survived. One was found close to shore by a windsurfer. The Ralstons found the third on the bottom of the river, still strapped to an ejector seat.

The US Navy arranged for a crane to be set up on a barge on the river. The crane's boom had a GPS antenna so it could drop a basket right on top of the coordinates provided by the Ralstons. The visibility in the river was so bad that they had to use the crane to lower the divers, who were inside cages, to the bottom so they could hand-place pieces of the wreckage into the baskets. Gene distinguished one of the engine fuselages in a sonar image even though it was lying on a steep slope of riprap, a type of rock used to prevent erosion. He couldn't say what the object was by looking at it on the monitor, just that it looked out of place.

That was often the trick to finding a corpse. Gene had culti-vated a sense for what looked like it didn't belong. Other agen-cies from across Canada and the United States sometimes sent him their sonar images for a second opinion. He had found half a dozen bodies in images recorded by other search groups.

"How did you learn all this stuff?" Pete asked.

"Mostly self-taught," Gene said.

As the sun got lower in the sky, it got harder for Sandy to see the grid lines on the laptop. Sunlight reflected off the water, the metal deck, and flat polished surface of the gunnels. At about 5:00 PM, Gene turned to Sandy and asked if she was done for the day. "Yep," she replied, nodding emphatically.

A small airplane going upriver passed overhead. I had seen a dozen of the same single-engine propeller planes pass by that day. All of them hundreds and hundreds of feet up in the air. They looked like miniature toy aircraft from that distance.

As we left the dock the next morning, a big sturgeon, a flash of white and silver against the brown water, breached and then splashed back into the river near the bow of the *Kathy G.* Gene measured one yesterday on the monitor that was close to ten feet. Some grew to be twenty feet long and lived for more than a hundred years. Sturgeon as a species haven't changed much over the past two hundred million years. Their nickname is dinosaurs of the deep. Sharp, bony ridges along their backs add to the prehistoric mystique. Seeing one of these fish had the same sort of effect as going for a hike in the mountains. They are a reminder of the vast scale of geological time.

The highway buzzed with traffic. Train cars clanked and screeched. Small boats that looked like bathtubs poked and prodded floating logs into pens along the shore. And meanwhile an ancient type of fish hunted by smell and touch in the hushed, dark waters below. The Ralstons used pulses of sound to see through the turbid water of the Fraser River. The sturgeon used a set of highly sensitive whiskers.

It was another overcast and rainy morning. Sandy was all bundled up. She wore fleece gloves and a blue hat with a short brim and earflaps that were tied together with a string under her chin. Gene always wore a baseball cap, but Sandy had a variety of fisherman hats that added to the impression that she was a seasoned mariner. We picked up on the same search grid but started in the middle of the river and worked our way north toward the other bank. The current was stronger today. Sandy had a hard time keeping the boat straight when we traveled upriver. Gene decided to search only when we were going with the current. That meant we had to raise the towfish at the end of each line near the dock and then lower it back into the water upriver by the power lines.

I took over for Sandy, guiding the towfish in and out of the water. She had not asked for help, but I got the sense she appreciated not having to leave the relative warmth of the pilothouse. After guiding the towfish onto the sheath at the bow at the end of one search line, I turned and smashed the top of my head into the boom. My hood was pulled up over my toque, which had limited my peripheral vision. On another pass later that day, I cracked my shin against one of the horizonal supports at the bow. The cold somehow amplified the pain, like both the metal beams and my bones were stiffer and less forgiving in the freezing air. I learned to move more slowly and deliberately on the boat.

"If something floats and comes to the surface, it would eventually deteriorate and sink again," Pete said at some point that morning. The statement was really a question. We were huddled behind the door, using the pilothouse to protect us from the wind.

"You talking about a person?" Sandy asked impatiently. *Just call it what it is,* she seemed to suggest. I asked Sandy once if the work, retrieving corpses from water, ever bothered her. She told me that on several of their early searches, the coroners on the scene were women, and they had always conducted them-selves in a professional, business-like manner. Sandy adopted that same approach. Body recovery was just one of those jobs that needed doing.

Gene told Pete that Robert Teather, a pioneer in the field of underwater search and recovery, had a theory that a body would sink and then float and then sink again once and for all. Teather wrote a book called *The Encyclopedia of Underwater Investigations,* which was still the go-to text for law enforcement in Canada and the United States. Teather was the driving force behind the creation of the RCMP's underwater recovery team in 1977. It evolved into a national organization with divers stationed across Canada, but it started with Teather here on the West Coast.

Forty years ago and about thirty miles west of the dock where we launched the *Kathy G* that morning, Teather saved the lives of two fishermen after their boat struck a cargo ship near the mouth of the Fraser River. He had to feel his way underwater through the pitch blackness of the capsized boat until he found the two men alive in a pocket of air near the hull. He guided them through the submerged boat and back to the surface. He was the thirteenth Canadian ever to earn the Cross of Valour, the country's highest award for bravery.

Teather's theory was that a body would sink, then gases created by the decomposition process would bring it back to the surface, but then those gases would be released to the air and so the body would sink again. Gene's issue was that the theory had never been tested. It had never been proved.

"If someone sees a body floating, they go and get it," Gene said. No one sits there and waits to see if it would sink again.

"If the plane exploded or broke up and the people left the cabin, they might have floated out to the ocean and then eventually sunk again," Pete said, reframing his initial question. Gene agreed. Eventually, yes, a body was going to go down and stay down.

Teather, who died in 2004, wrote another book called *Merlin: Something Beautiful This Way Comes*. It was part memoir, part fantasy. The main character was a police diver haunted by his past body recoveries. He couldn't sleep and went for walks in the middle of the night and met a wise stranger who helped him to reconcile with the tragic elements of his job. Gene had told me that he saw a lot of himself in that story. He was a troubled sleeper. Like Sandy, the work didn't bother Gene in the moment. He was focused on what the recovery meant for the family. But unlike Sandy, he ruminated after the fact, particularly about the searches that involved kids. "I think what we do, having been around so much death, has to have had an influence on us," he told me. He mentioned an expression used by those in the emergency response community: *I wish my brain could forget what my eyes have seen.*

Later that day on the Fraser, another shape on the screen caught Gene's attention.

"Easter bunny," Sandy said, describing the object on the bottom of the river.

"It looks like a cat that's hissing," Gene said.

He zoomed in on the object. It sort of looked like a log but was wider than any of the others we had imaged. And the shadows were strange. They extended far out to the side and included crisp diagonal lines, but in a crumpled and disorderly shape.

Sandy swung the boat one way and then took a wide turn in the opposite direction. They called this maneuver a Johnson Turn. Sandy had to position the boat on track to scan the object again but with enough time beforehand for the towfish, which was extended below and behind us on fifty feet of cable, to start flying straight in the water.

The object scrolled onto the monitor again. The shadows were not as sharply defined, but the thing itself looked more interesting. It was long and narrow and had a texture of bright striated lines running from one end to the other.

Pete said, "We're at about 280th Street" — the landmark the witness used when describing where the plane sank in the river.

Gene was intrigued by the dimensions. The object measured nine feet high off the bottom and was thirty-two feet long. The plane that crashed, a Cessna 172 Skyhawk, was twenty-seven feet long and had a wingspan of thirty-six feet. The two scans were enough to convince the Ralstons they needed to get eyes on the object, which is the next stage in an underwater search. The shape on the screen didn't look much like an airplane, but it looked enough like the wreckage of an airplane to warrant further inspection. They couldn't operate the ROV in the river because its thrusters would be overpowered by the current. Someone was going to have to dive down and take a look. Pete said Cucheran and the rest of the RCMP dive team were out of town on a training exercise.

Whatever it was, whether it was the missing plane or a giant log or a scrap of old machinery from the sawmill, it was only thirty-three feet below us. Tantalizingly close. We could have peered over the gunnel and likely seen it if the water was just a little clearer. The object on screen, truth be told, could have been anything, some completely ordinary thing that I couldn't conceive of in the moment because I had already convinced myself it was the airplane. It must have been an ongoing challenge for the Ralstons to exercise restraint in the face of incomplete but provocative crumbs of information.

Gene and Sandy carried on with the search. They scanned a couple more lines toward the north shore to complete the first grid, which had covered most of the river between the power lines and the boat dock. We spent the rest of the afternoon searching a new grid downstream of the dock.

At about 4:30 PM, Sandy turned to Gene. "Well, I think this is my last line."

"I am surprised and impressed that you made it this long," he said, rubbing her shoulder. Gene often encouraged Sandy by squeezing her knee or massaging her neck and back. They spent the entire day within arm's reach of each other.

It had been more than eight hours since we launched the boat in the morning. The only thing I saw the Ralstons eat was a single-serving package of cheese and a handful of crackers. They shared one plastic water bottle between them. Gene had warned me to have only one cup of coffee in the morning or I would likely have to use the onboard bathroom, which was a plastic jug stored in the hatch by the motor.

Before I drove back to my hotel from Pete's house later that afternoon, I asked the Ralstons about their evening routine on searches. Gene often had a rum and Coke. Sandy prefered gin and tonic. They ate a light dinner, something like salad or soup. Then turned on the electric blanket, at least at this time of year, and went to bed.

"We're reasonably early go-to-bedders," Gene said.

"And early getter-uppers," Sandy added.

Gene said he would often wake up as early as three or four. He waited until five before getting out of bed so Sandy could sleep longer. He noticed his age the most first thing in the morning. It took awhile to feel limber enough to get going on the day.

"Didn't used to be that way. I could jump out of bed at four o'clock in the morning and go milk cows immediately," he said. Gene grew up on a dairy farm not far from where they lived now in the county of Kuna.

"Yeah," Sandy said. "Pretty hard to milk a cow when you don't got one."

CHAPTER FIVE

Heavens Gate to Hells Canyon

"Ask Sandy how long she's been married," Gene likes to say whenever the topic of relationships came up in conversation. It's one of his usual routines.

"Too long," Sandy replies flatly as if exhausted by both the joke and her marriage. The glint in her eye says differently.

The Ralstons were married at dawn on top of a fire look-out called Heavens Gate on the doorstep of the Seven Devils Mountains in western Idaho. The sun rose on a clear blue sky the morning of August 26, 1972. You could see into four different states from the panoramic viewpoint above the Snake River.

It was a small gathering, about twelve people. Most of the wedding party camped out at the base of the mountain the night before. Gene and Sandy slept on a mattress under a plywood shell that covered the back of their pickup truck. They woke before dawn and drove seventeen miles up the steep gravel road and then hiked the last few hundred yards to the top. A sliver of light traced the ridges of the mountainous horizon as the priest began the ceremony.

"We believe that in this union there is not a loss of individuality, but a gain in our cooperative pursuits of happiness," Gene said to Sandy. He looked lean and handsome in hiking boots, khaki pants, and a white collared shirt.

"We believe that this union will prove to be greater than

the sum of its parts: creativity, sensitivity, hope, appreciation, and love are just a few of those things which we expect to be multiplied many times in the sharing of our lives," Sandy said to Gene. She wore a flower-print dress that was pink, orange, and green. Her hair was dark and curly.

Someone brought a portable stereo that played "Morning Has Broken" by Cat Stevens. And then it was back down the mountain for cake at the campground. Gene and Sandy spent their first night together as a married couple in the back of the truck.

The Ralstons talk about that time in the early 1970s as their hippie phase, but they're quick to clarify that they were nowhere near as far gone as San Francisco–level hippies. Gene had sideburns. His hair covered the tops of his ears, so maybe an inch or so longer but still parted to the side in the same way. It never occurred to either of them to get married in a church. Gene was raised Protestant and Sandy Catholic, but they had drifted away from the formal aspects of religion.

In one of the handful of wedding photos that the Ralstons showed me, the photographer was crouched close to the ground and looked up at Gene and Sandy from behind. They stood holding hands against the luminous morning sky. They squinted at the light and traded bashful, I-can't-believe-my-good-luck kind of smiles. Gene was twenty-seven, and Sandy was twenty-four.

They had both studied biology at the College of Idaho and started dating in 1970 while on a school trip to Mexico. The group traveled throughout the country for two months, studying the vegetation and camping wherever they found a good place to pull off the highway. Gene was a farm kid, and Sandy was from the city. She grew up as an only child in Twin Falls. Gene helped her adjust to the rustic conditions of the trip. And she thought he was a hunk.

Sandy had originally wanted to be a doctor. She took a pre-med program in college and was accepted by several medical schools across the United States. She also applied for a master's in biochemistry and nutrition at Cornell University, which offered her a full scholarship and a grant for doing research. She decided on Cornell partly because she found the material more interesting, but partly because a medical degree would have been a financial strain for her parents. Fred and Jewel Odell were in their early sixties when she finished her undergraduate degree.

"It was quite an experience to end up in New York after being in Idaho all my life," she told me. She moved into a house with three other women that was walking distance from the campus near downtown Ithaca. She bought her first car, a Volkswagen Rabbit, and used it to go sightseeing whenever possible. She explored Montreal; Washington, DC; Boston; and New York City. Gene and Sandy drifted apart while she was in New York, but stayed in touch.

And then, during a trip back to Twin Falls to see her parents, she was offered a job as a lab assistant in the biology department at the College of Southern Idaho. Some of her friends at Cornell were working on doctorate degrees, and their difficult experiences disillusioned Sandy about a career in academia. She moved home after graduation and took the job. Sandy and Gene picked up right where they left off. "Oh, yep. This feels good," Sandy said, describing how natural it felt to rekindle the romance.

Gene earned a master's degree in biology from the University of Nevada and then went to work for the state of Idaho in the Bureau of Water Quality. He bought forty acres of land south of Boise in Kuna County at a public auction a couple years before the wedding. He sold a fifteen-acre parcel to a friend to help pay for the property. Not long after they were married, he and Sandy moved out of the small house they rented in Boise to a trailer they had delivered to the tract of land south of the city. They set to work building a house amid a sea of mint-green sagebrush and yellow desert grasses. It was like a scene from an old western movie. A young couple homesteading on the frontier. They watched the comings and goings of their new neighbors — antelope, deer, rabbits, and a kaleidoscope of birds.

The Ralstons hired contractors to dig the basement, pour the foundation, and frame the structure of the seventeen-hundred-square-foot, two-bedroom, ranch-style bungalow. They figured the rest out on their own. Gene would get home from work and then go to work on the house. He did the wiring, plumbing, roof, and most of the finishes. They collected the old chalkboards from a local elementary school that had closed down to tile the floor of the entryway. It took about six months until they could move out of the trailer and into the house. They watched the sun come up over the Boise Mountains out their living room window, then watched it go down across the scraggly desert landscape out the patio doors off the dining room. Sandy also got a job with the state of Idaho running a nutrition program for elderly people who lived in the city. She and Gene commuted together to the state government building in Boise. The road that branched off the two-lane highway to access their house was just a cattle trail for the first few years before they got permission from the county to build a gravel road. The ground would get soft as it thawed in the spring, and their four-wheel-drive Jeep would sometimes get stuck partway home. Gene and Sandy kept rubber boots in the back so they could walk the rest of the half mile or so to the house. The ground would freeze up again overnight, and they could drive the Jeep out of the hardened ruts in the morning. As the day warmed, the frozen mud would thaw and fall off the Jeep, leaving a telltale mess in the parking lot at work.

On the weekends they often visited either Gene's parents, who lived on the family farm about an hour's drive north in Fruitland, or Sandy's, who were in Twin Falls. It didn't matter how well you got to know Gene or how much time you spent with him, he still started every other sentence with, "I was born and raised on a dairy farm." It would be hard to overestimate the degree to which he was shaped by his experiences growing up on the Ralston farm. He'd wake up early to milk the cows before school and then milk them again when he got home. His parents, Sam and Nina, worked the farm until they retired in their midseventies and sold it. They'd been married sixty-eight years when Sam died at ninety-two in 2009. Nina passed away two years later.

Gene gave me a photocopy of a newspaper story published in the *Idaho Farmer* in June 1966 about how the land his dad bought along the Snake River in 1942 had been considered unfarmable. The article described how Sam transformed the 136 acres into "one of the finer dairy operations in western Idaho." He uprooted trees and leveled the sloped fields with a scraper and horse team. Sam had jumped on a freight train going west from Kansas when he was eighteen and worked on farms in the Fruitland area until he had saved enough to buy his own. The operation didn't make enough money to support his family for the first couple decades, so he worked the night shift at a sugar plant during the winter. The article concluded, "Hard work has never bothered Sam Ralston."

Nancy McQuiston, Sandy and Gene's niece, told me that Sam, her grandfather, was a very thin and muscular busybody. He was always painting or fixing something. He had a bushy, chin-strap beard of red hair. Nina was a redhead, too, and so were all three of Sam and Nina's kids when they were young. "They were known very well as the family of redheads," McQuiston said. Gene is the youngest. His sister, Linda Doman, lives in Huntington, Oregon. Samuel, the eldest and McQuiston's father, lives on a portion of the old family farm with his wife, Barbara. McQuiston is forty-six and a registered nurse. She's the only member of the family who stays in regular contact with Gene and Sandy these days.

"I always thought my aunt was just so beautiful. My aunt Sandy with her brilliant dark hair and her bright-blue eyes." McQuiston told me that Sandy had reminded her of Jackie Onassis, the wife of President John F. Kennedy. "She was just so classy and so soft-spoken. And my uncle was just really smart." McQuiston grew up next door to her grandparents, Sam and Nina, and was often there when Gene and Sandy visited for the weekend. She has fond memories of those family dinners. "Their relationship with my grandparents was really, really close," she said. Her grandfather didn't have much formal education, but he was an avid reader and outdoorsman. Sam and Gene would have in-depth discussions about nature and agriculture. "Just seeing them talk back and forth is a good memory for me." McQuiston told me that Gene and Sandy were a big part of what inspired her to go to college and get a degree.

Gene's mother was the youngest of nine and born on February 14, which inspired the name Nina Valentine. McQuiston told me her grandmother was talkative and social. Everyone who knew Nina loved her. She was always encouraging McQuiston to sneak away from her parents' house to come over and visit. Nina was an artist. She made clothes for the family, including Sandy's wedding dress, and painted with oil paints. She helped drive the tractor or grain truck at harvesttime.

The Ralstons keep McQuiston in the loop on where and

when they're going on searches. They sometimes invite her to join them, but she has three kids and a busy job as a nursing supervisor at a big hospital. She was able to go on a search near Eagle, a city northwest of Boise, in the fall of 2020. It was another tragic story. Gene and Sandy were asked to search the retention ponds in a residential neighborhood for the body of Rory Pope, a missing two-year-old boy. The toddler was in Eagle with his family to visit his grandparents but disappeared as they were packing up the car to return home to California. McQuiston's theory was that he wasn't ready to leave, that he wanted to go fishing with his grandpa instead, so he wandered off to look for a hiding place. The Ralstons searched the ponds with the ROV and sonar, but the visibility was terrible. The authorities ended up draining the pond closest to the grandparents' house and discovered the boy's body next to a fountain.

McQuiston told me that she has always respected her aunt and uncle for the work they do to help people. Knowing what they do, however, was different from seeing it firsthand. She was moved by how they counseled the family and by how everyone, even the police, deferred to their expertise. "Just seeing how kind they were to everyone and how accommodating everyone was to them," she said.

~

On the weekends the Ralstons visited Sandy's parents, they would sometimes meet in Jackpot, Nevada, a small town just across the border from Idaho. Jewel played the penny slot machines and was a champion pinochle player. The casinos featured touring bands and other live entertainment. Jewel ran a daycare out of the family home in Twin Falls when Sandy was growing up. Fred worked as a draftsman but went back to school to become a chiropractor when Sandy was around seven

years old. She told me that one of her dad's friends was a chiropractor and had convinced him to learn the profession. But
it seemed like Fred's motivation to return to school in his late
forties may have run deeper. He started his own practice in an
office next to the garage behind the house in Twin Falls. He was
one of the only people who could provide relief for Sandy from
the lifelong pain she endured after several muscles in her back
were paralyzed by the contaminated dose of the polio vaccine.

The topic of children is sensitive for Gene and Sandy. They
told me they had talked about having kids, which felt like a
roundabout way of saying they wanted kids, but had been
warned against it. Doctors worried it was too risky for Sandy
because of her scoliosis. "We were advised that childbearing
was not a good idea," Gene said.

By 1977, after eight years of working for the state, Gene was
restless. He'd been promoted into a managerial role and was
doing less fieldwork. He didn't like having to tell people what to
do. An opportunity came up in 1977 to start an environmental
consulting company with two associates he knew in the industry. That venture, however, imploded within six months as Gene
realized he was the only one interested in doing any real work.
He quit and decided to go it alone.

With his previous experience in government, Gene had a
detailed understanding of state regulations and a personal
history with many of the officials responsible for issuing
permits. He was a hot commodity in the private sector, and
business took off. He needed help, and Sandy had the right
background in the natural sciences. Friends and colleagues
warned them about working together. "There must be something special about our relationship," Gene told me. It's not that
he and Sandy don't disagree or argue and bicker, but they've
figured out ways to work through differences without feeling

too bruised or resentful. "At the end of the day, we're pretty much on the same page," he said.

Most of their projects in the early days were on the Snake River in southern Idaho. They were hired by industrial operations, like potato processing plants or municipalities, to ensure that any wastewater flowing into the river met environmental standards. The Ralstons strapped a canoe to the roof of their Subaru and stayed in motels for the first few years. Eventually they upgraded to a Ford pickup with a camper set up on the truck bed so they could haul bigger boats and sleep right next to the water.

Gene and Sandy got into a rhythm of spending two or three weeks on the road, traveling from one lake or river to the next. They got a contract with the Idaho Power Company to do hydrographic surveys of 150 miles of the Snake River, all the way from above Shoshone Falls down through Hells Canyon. Mapping the bottom of a river is painstaking work, and it was especially so before the advent of GPS technology. They had to pass over every inch of the river bottom using a survey-grade depth sounder. On another project, they partnered with a team of botanists from the College of Idaho to look for endangered plants along the corridor of a proposed gas pipeline. They walked close to five hundred miles, not counting the places where the right-of-way crossed through farm fields, from Stanfield, Oregon, to Burley, Idaho. They marked high-value plants with fence posts and flagging tape.

It was interesting to learn how similar life was for the Ralstons as environmental consultants and as underwater search-and-recovery experts. Work projects, like searches, meant long drives and long stretches away from home. It required careful planning, attention to detail, and then the patience and stamina to systematically analyze an aspect of the natural world. Someone had to paddle the canoe, or steer the boat, while the other operated all the gizmos. And the teamwork, the ability to anticipate what the other was thinking, was strengthened and refined year after year of working together on the water.

Tim Cucheran, the RCMP diver who met us at the boat launch on the Fraser River, told me that the RCMP used to have their own towed sonar system like the Ralstons but had lost the towfish on the bottom of the ocean. It had been only the second search they had ever tried using the equipment. The torpedo got snagged under some kind of debris, and then the cord that connected it to the boat snapped. The water was too deep for divers to go down to retrieve it. Part of the problem, Cucheran said, was that they didn't have the right boat to deploy the towfish. But another factor was the lack of coordination between the boat driver and the sonar operator.

The Ralstons have caught their towfish on submerged trees, rocks, and cables. They have plowed it deep into the soft mud of underwater embankments. But they have yet to lose one. They still use the same towfish they had custom-made back in 2000 because Sandy always reacts fast enough on the throttle to take the tension off the cord before it breaks. The Ralstons run the *Kathy G* with an almost telepathic degree of synchronization.

In the early 1980s, Gene bought a boat from a local company based out of the nearby town of Meridian for a job surveying fish populations. It had a flat deck across the bow, which provided an ideal platform to stand on and run the electrofishing gear. You can stun and attract fish with an electrical current, which is a handy and safe way to inventory the type of fish in a lake or river. Gene noticed that the same company also built a nifty little jet boat. It was fourteen feet long and had a sturdy steel hull, an ideal design for Idaho's shallow and rocky rivers. The Ralstons liked the boat so much, they teamed up with the company and started to build and sell them.

In March 1983, Gene was in Boise picking up parts for one of the jet boats when he heard on the radio that a woman had jumped off a bridge into the Boise River, which ran through the middle of the city. The river was at flood levels, and he knew the local authorities didn't have a boat that could handle the fast and unpredictable water. So he called the sheriff and offered to launch the jet boat. He piloted two police officers on the river most of the way through Boise. "Spotted her body draped over a log, a tree that had washed into the river off the bank because the water was so high," Gene said. "That was really the first body I remember recovering, and that started the whole process. Got a really, really nice thank-you from the family."

Gene has a vivid memory of the recovery. He emphasized how meaningful it was that the family of the woman reached out to thank him. But it seemed that the excitement of the search also made a strong impression. Gene told me how he met up with the police and paramedics near the bridge where the woman jumped into the river. There wasn't a place to launch his boat, so he had to bounce his truck and trailer down a set of concrete steps in a nearby park. One of the officers couldn't believe he was going to put such a small boat in such rough water. He dodged rapids and rocks as they sped downriver and then kept the boat steady in the rushing water after they found the body and one of the officers secured it with a rope around the waist. Gene was no doubt moved by the gratitude of the family. But I think he was also invigorated by taking part in a dramatic event where he had to think fast and put all his boating skills to the test.

Media reports about the incident included a description of Gene and his sporty jet boat. The Ralstons' home phone started to ring with the odd search-and-rescue request for people missing or in distress on the river. Sometimes the call came from police, sometimes from a volunteer with Idaho Mountain Search and Rescue. Most often it was someone who just needed help. Gene got a call one day about a horse that had fallen into the river. He and the woman who owned the horse came across the animal in knee-deep water. Its reins were tangled in some brush next to an island. "I nosed the boat up to the end of the bushes and she was able to get off and wade through the water to get to the horse," Gene said. The Boise Fire Department eventually got their own boat that could handle the fast-moving rivers in the area, but for several years Gene helped to fill a gap in the local emergency services — the same kind of gap that he and Sandy went on to fill across Canada and the United States.

Building jet boats was as much a hobby as it was a business venture. Gene took pride in the craftsmanship of each boat. They sold four or five a year, which was enough to cover costs. The Ralstons joined the Western Whitewater Association, which would hold monthly rallies where fifteen to twenty people got together on their boats for a weekend trip on a river or some kind of informal race. The boat the Ralstons built could go seventy to eighty miles an hour on flat water. It could climb over beaver dams and cross gravel bars in as little as four inches of water. You would hear the rocks click on the hull as you shot across the shallow sections.

Gene showed me a photo from the mid-1980s of him and Sandy on one of their jet boats. Gene was hunched forward, his hat pulled low. One hand gripped the low-profile windshield, and the other was on the wheel. Sandy was behind him. It was hard to tell if she was crouched or sitting, but she had one hand on the gunnel. They were mid-flight, four or five feet clear above the surface of the river, after crashing through the top of a rapid. Gene was tense and braced for impact. Sandy had a serene look on her face. She was smiling and gazing upward, like she was on a beach enjoying the sun instead of launching through the air over a turbulent river.

"You've got to be a very, very fast thinker, and very observant," Gene told me about driving a jet boat on an Idahoan river. There were often only a couple of safe passages through the trickier sections, with little to no room for error. The driver had to stay vigilant and read the river. You watched out for things like rock boils — subtle disturbances on the surface that hid boulders and debris that could flip or wreck the boat. The sport sounded gutsy. Races could last hours and cover more than a hundred miles.

The weekend rallies with the WWA evolved into more formal events. The Ralstons helped organize the US Jet Boat Championship in 1984 on the Payette River. The rivers in Idaho were ideal settings for the new and growing sport — shallow and winding waterways riddled with powerful and unpredictable rapids. And they were scenic. Spectators sat on rocky ledges next to the water and watched the boats bounce, slide, and careen past from only a few feet away.

A journalist from *Trailer Boats* magazine joined Gene for a ride-along and wrote about the growing popularity of the races. The publication had a global reach, and the WWA started hearing from boaters from New Zealand, South Africa, Canada, and Mexico. They organized the World Jet Boat Championship race in the spring of 1988. Gene codirected the event with his pal Ace Jones. It took place on three sections of river on the Payette and Snake, including a stretch through Hells Canyon. The team with the best cumulative time was the winner. They published a race program and sold advertising. The event was covered by local television stations. Gene estimated that something like twenty to thirty thousand people attended the races on any given day. He helped officiate from a helicopter.

During the part of the race on the Payette, one of the Canadian teams hit a rapid, went airborne, and crashed onto a log on shore. The crowd scattered in time, and luckily no one was hurt, but it felt like a wake-up call. "It had a potential of being a pretty bad disaster," Sandy said. The thought of having to deal with the fallout of a death or injury soured the Ralstons on the sport. They quit the WWA after 1988 and stopped making the boats. A few years after the boatbuilding and racing fizzled out, Gene and Sandy moved on to scuba diving. They started taking annual vacations to tropical dive locations, like Curaçao in the Caribbean, Fiji, and the Bahamas.

~

And then one hot afternoon in early September 1996, Gene and Sandy were finishing up a day of work on the Snake River. Their friend and colleague Rick Konopacky had asked them to help on a project to look for endangered and threatened species of mollusks on a section of the river east of the American Falls Dam. He had been hired by the Bureau of Reclamation, a federal agency that oversees hundreds of dams and power plants in the western United States. Konopacky was a fisheries scientist and an independent consultant, like the Ralstons. The three of them worked together when a project arose that required the other's complementary skill sets or equipment.

Konopacky was smart, outdoorsy, and a few years younger than Gene. He had a PhD in fish biology and was one of a handful of people in the world qualified to lead the study. Gene was one of a select few with the right boat, skills, and experience to navigate that section of the Snake River, which was riddled with rock outcroppings and considered dangerous.

They had worked their way up the river that day going east, stopping and evaluating any likely places for snail habitat. They were on the boat the Ralstons generally used for electrofishing. It had a flat bottom and a low profile. The gunnels only came up past your knees when you stood on the deck. Sandy and Rick were up near the bow. Gene was behind the waist-high console and steering wheel at the back. He asked them to kneel down and hang on as he turned the boat around to head west, down-river back toward the American Falls Dam. "It's always easier to go upriver than it is to go downriver," Gene told me. When you are going against the current, you can back off and hold your position in the water if it isn't easy to see how to get around an obstacle. You don't get second chances going downriver; the current shoves the boat forward.

Gene had boated this part of the Snake dozens of times. Rock ledges crisscrossed the river, some of which extended clear across from one side to the other. The sun was low and reflected off the water. Rick was on the right side of the boat. "And probably he was blocking my view, which is my fault. I shouldn't let him do that, but I did. I thought I could see around him or over him," Gene said. "I was probably three feet away from where I should have been, and hit a rock." It only stuck out of the water by an inch or two, but the rock launched the boat up in the air and it flipped.

Gene got pinned between the console and the back of the boat, but he could breathe in the pocket of air below the over-turned boat. He managed to wriggle free. Rick had helped Sandy get to her feet and to higher ground in the river. Gene could see them standing on an ankle-deep gravel bar about a hundred feet downriver. He went back under the boat and found the plastic bin with the life jackets. The river was only a couple of feet deep where the boat had landed, but the current was fast, and the bowling-ball-sized rocks on the bottom made it tricky for Gene to find his footing. He floated on his back to the gravel bar. By the time he got there, Rick had left. Sandy told Gene that he had gone ahead to try to get to shore. Rick had recently had surgery on an Achilles tendon. It was still sore, which made it difficult for him to stand in the rushing water.

Sandy helped Gene traverse the river. He had smashed up against the console when the boat hit the rock, and his stomach and upper legs were badly bruised. When they got to shore, the Ralstons met up with a few people who had been fishing from the banks. They had seen Rick float by, but didn't see where he had tried to make it to shore. It took half an hour or so for the police and ambulance to arrive.

The Ralstons figured Rick would turn up sooner or later. They imagined that every person they saw walking near the river from a distance must have been him, finally making his way back to their camp. But then the afternoon turned to night. The Ralstons had parked their pickup camper next to Rick's in a campground near the river. They didn't sleep. "We expected him to come knock on the door and want to get dried off or get warm or have something to eat," Gene told me.

The Bingham County Sheriff's Office had a dive team that searched the river the next day. They found Rick's body on the bottom of a deep section about a quarter mile downstream from where the boat flipped. It was a common spot on the river for people to drown. "It wasn't until they actually found him that it really sank in that he didn't make it," Gene said. "I take the blame for it because I was driving the boat and I should not have had him or anybody in the bow of the boat."

We were talking on the phone when Gene told me about

Rick and the accident. It had come up by chance. We had been discussing an upcoming presentation Gene had been asked to give at the Mid-Atlantic Public Safety Dive Forum in Chesapeake, Virginia. He told me about a bad episode of stage fright he had in high school, which led us to the topic of speech impediments. And then Gene said, "I had an attorney representing us in a case years and years ago who had a terrible stutter. Super neat guy. Extremely intelligent, but it was sometimes frustrating."

I asked him about the lawsuit, and the story about Rick started to unspool. Gene downplayed the significance at first, but then he got going unpacking what had happened. It sounded like the lawsuit was a formality, a way for Rick's widow, Lisa Konopacky, to receive money from the Ralstons' insurance company. She had two kids in elementary school when Rick died.

I had known Gene and Sandy for three years at that point and had asked several times, starting the first day I met them, if the inspiration for searching for drowning victims was personal. They never mentioned Rick. Whenever I tried to get a better sense of their origin story, the reason their lives veered off in such an unlikely direction, they would talk about how they had hoped to use the sonar for work, that they had stumbled into the realm of underwater search and recovery by happenstance. Gene's default answer, or at least the one that had worn itself into a groove after they were asked the same question by every news reporter who wrote about one of their recoveries, was that it was the gratitude expressed by the families of the people they found that motivated them to keep going.

I had never heard Gene say that part of the reason they searched for bodies was one person they knew they could never bring back, a person who drowned after Gene crashed a boat on a river. "I think in part it has led us to do what we do to help other people to get things resolved faster or get resolution, period. Because without that we know the consequences," Gene told me.

I had asked McQuiston why she thought her aunt and uncle had dedicated their lives to underwater search and recovery. "They didn't tell me this, but I know they felt really devastated by the loss of this gentleman and responsible and just horrible about it," she said, after describing what she remembered about the accident with Rick near the American Falls Dam. "That's what sparked their passion for recovering drowning victims and returning them to their family."

I reached out to Lisa Konopacky. She didn't know about the work the Ralstons have been doing to find drowning victims. She has no hard feelings about the events of that day. "I still view it as an accident and that these things happen," she said. She was impressed by how Gene and Sandy have taken the tragedy and turned it into something positive. "I'm very proud of them," she said.

Gene told me about another dimension to the fallout from the accident: He and Sandy never forgot that feeling of lying awake in the camper all night, expecting Rick to knock on the door at any moment. By the time the Ralstons arrive on scene in the aftermath of a drowning, the chance of any kind of rescue is long gone. And yet the friends and family of the missing person often hold on to the hope that their loved one will return, that they were somehow never on the lake or river in the first place.

Gene thinks it is an innate psychological defense mechanism that protects people from a reality they are not ready to face. That sleepless night near the banks of the Snake River in the fall of 1996 taught the Ralstons to handle such intense and contradictory emotions with respect and patience. Gene gave the example of the mother of a young woman who was in a car accident. Her daughter had been in the passenger seat of a truck that missed a curve and went off the road, rolling down a forested hill and into a river. The Ralstons and local divers searched the river but didn't find her body. Overwhelming evidence, however, pointed to the fact that the young woman had ended up in the river.

"The mother was there and she insisted that she was alive. And that she was thrown clear across the river and she's dazed and she's found a cabin and she's staying in the cabin and she has amnesia," Gene told me. The mother wanted the police to launch an extensive ground search through the forest. "I took her for a walk at the end of the day, one of the days we were there, up the roadway and held her hand. We walked and chatted." He tried to balance how he explained what he saw as the facts of the situation with the magnitude of her loss and grief. A group of fishermen ended up finding the body of her daughter on the river sometime later.

CHAPTER SIX

The Narrows

It was windy on the morning of April 10, a Saturday. Gene, Pete, Sandy, and I stood on the dock and looked up the Fraser River toward the power lines. The waves were about a foot high. The problem, Gene explained, was that the wind was blowing against the current. That kind of chop was normally not an issue if they could travel with the waves. But to go with the wind, they would have to go against the current. And going against the current meant the towfish would get jostled and the images would be distorted.

We walked back to the truck, which was still hitched to the boat and parked on the launch, to get out of the cold. I noticed another decal on the back of the boat next to the motor that read KATHY G. It was in the same pink, cursive writing as the one under the window of the pilothouse.

The Ralstons renamed their boat in 2008 after Kathy Garrigan, a twenty-four-year-old woman they found in Harding Lake, Alaska, in July 2007. She and two friends had drowned a month earlier while on a canoe trip. The Garrigan family made a donation to the Ralstons after the search, and they used the money to buy a new motor. "The motor is kind of the heart of the boat, so we decided to rename it after her," Gene told me once. Kathy was a volunteer for AmeriCorps and worked on a program that provided education and job skills for young Indigenous people. Her spirit of adventure and altruism resonated with the Ralstons. "There was something about her philosophy on life that we could feel a kinship with," Gene said.

It was the first sunny and cloudless morning of the trip, but only thirty-seven degrees. Pete suggested we drive the half hour to Alouette Lake, which is surrounded by mountains and might be sheltered from the wind.

"What do you think, kid? You're the driver," Gene asked Sandy.

"It's too lumpy for me," she said. The string on her blue fisherman cap was tied snugly under her chin.

Alouette Lake is part of Golden Ears Provincial Park, a protected tract of wilderness named after a mountain with twin peaks that look like the pointy ears of a fox. The mountain, and its craggy ears, tower over Maple Ridge from the north. The road into the park cuts through a lush rain forest. Pete told us to watch out for the stumps of old-growth trees. The squat hulks of ancient wood looked like half-buried shipwrecks jutting out from the ferns and moss that blanketed the forest floor. You could see the horizontal marks where lumberjacks inserted planks of wood to stand on as they hacked at the gigantic trunks with their axes. We lost cell reception after passing the park gates and tollbooth. When Bobby Aujla drowned the previous October, his friends rushed to shore and told a bystander to call for help. That person then had to run to their car and drive several miles down the road before they could call 911.

More than three million people live in the Lower Mainland, which include Vancouver and its neighboring municipalities in southwest BC. The few lakes in the area that have public boat launches are extremely popular — especially those like Alouette that you can drive to for an after-work swim.

Park staff had been gearing up for the summer rush. NO
PARKING signs, installed every twenty feet, lined both sides of
the road for the last mile before the turnoff to the boat launch.

The double-wide slab of concrete was deserted when we
arrived. The launch was tucked into the southwest corner of the
lake, which was long, narrow, and deep, over five hundred feet
in some places. It was a beautiful setting. Mountains, carpeted
in trees and dusted by snow, crowded the shores on all sides.
The round, forested ridges looked like the shoulders of muscular dogs splayed out in the sun. A rocky beach extended from
the launch toward the earthen dam that formed the south end
of the lake. I walked to the end of the dock and could see clear
through the turquoise water, probably ten to fifteen feet, to the
bottom. Yesterday, I lost sight of the towfish within inches of
the mud-brown river.

Finding Aujla, who'd drowned in early October, was the
top priority for the Ralstons' time on Alouette Lake, but Pete
wanted them to meet the witnesses before they began that
search. He wanted them to point out in person to Gene and
Sandy the spot on the lake where they last remembered seeing
their friend. It had been hard for Pete to arrange the meetup,
because the Ralstons were on standby to join the Tyner family
at Nicola Lake. Their schedule was a moving target. The search
for Aujla would remain on hold, leaving the cold cases on deck
for today's search. Pete had emailed Gene a synopsis of each of
the four cases back in early March.

They spanned from 1967 to 1977. All four involved men, rang-
ing in age from sixteen to fifty-six. Two had been fishing when
they drowned. The other two had been on canoes that capsized.
I had asked Pete about the cases yesterday while we sat at the
back of the *Kathy G*. I was curious why he'd decided to pursue
them now, so many years later. The Ralstons told me that Pete's

request was unusual. They sometimes got calls or emails about finding someone who has been missing a long time, but no police officer had ever asked them to work on a set of historical cases in the same lake. Gene thought it showed an exceptional degree of compassion. That was his highest form of compliment. He saw compassion as its own kind of currency. It was the primary metric by which he sized people up.

Pete told me that a missing persons file stayed open until the subject turned 110 years old or 92 years passed from the date they went missing, whichever came first. It was his job to review each file at regular intervals, usually once a year, to see if any new information had emerged or if a new type of technology was available that might help solve the case. Pete said one of his predecessors in the role of missing persons coordinator tried to arrange for a side-scan sonar team to search for the four men back in 2014. But that effort had fizzled out.

I wondered if the push to solve these historical drowning incidents was related to a broader shift in how the RCMP and other police forces around the world were dealing with cold cases. It seemed like there was a new story in the media every week about the body of a long-lost person being identified or a long-cold criminal investigation suddenly getting solved.

Major advances in DNA sequencing technology have given investigators new tools for solving cases that had been collecting dust for decades. Forensic genealogists work the same problem as the Ralstons, finding lost people, but they start from the opposite end of the equation. Gene and Sandy look for the corpses of known people. Genealogists began with the corpse and then try to track down the person.

The DNA Doe Project, for example, is made up of dozens of genealogists who volunteer their time on both criminal and missing persons cases. They compare a DNA sample from an

unidentified body with other DNA profiles stored in online data-
bases and then use any matches to start building a family tree.
A connection with even a distant relative, like a fourth or fifth
cousin, could springboard a police investigation into new and
promising directions. The Doe Project team has used this technique to put names to more than seventy unidentified bodies
since the organization was founded in 2017.

Pete consulted a coroner before the Ralstons arrived in
Maple Ridge. He wanted to double-check that there would be
something left for Gene and Sandy to find in Alouette Lake after
fifty years. The coroner told him that if the water was deep and
cold then, yes, the bodies would likely be well preserved.

Maybe these cold cases on Alouette were a sign of things to
come for the Ralstons. Now that Pete had seen firsthand what
they could do, he was already thinking about more cases for
other lakes. I wondered how the Ralstons would handle an
influx of search requests if other police agencies in Canada and
the United States started digging into their old files for missing people in deep lakes. Demand for their services already
outstretched the supply.

"It doesn't look too bad," Gene said as the first images of the
bottom of Alouette Lake ticked onto the screen. We had cut
across the lake from the boat launch and were scanning about
two hundred yards out from the east shoreline. The water was
290 feet deep. By *not too bad*, Gene meant the bottom was flat
and mostly free of debris — a good surface for spotting corpses.

We were looking for the body of sixteen-year-old James
Carmichael. His father dropped him, his younger brother
David, and the family dog off at the boat launch at noon on
March 30, 1977. The boys were experienced canoers and good

swimmers, but they never returned. The RCMP and search-and-rescue volunteers searched late into the night. The team came back early the next morning and discovered David's body, along with the capsized canoe, washed ashore about three miles north of the boat launch and on the opposite side of the lake. The dog was found alive a couple hours later. Dozens of police officers and volunteers scoured the lake and shorelines — by foot, in a helicopter, and with boats — for two days. They found James's life belt, but not James.

After a few passes parallel to shore, Pete suggested we try a different case. No one saw James drown, so there wasn't a solid point of last seen. The capsized canoe and the younger brother were found near where we were searching with the *Kathy G*, but the paddles were discovered on the other side of the lake. Alouette is ten miles long and about a mile wide. We were pretty much flying blind.

"Just in terms of using our time wisely, it might make more sense," Pete said. "Because then if I can go home and pinpoint this one better, then hopefully I can narrow the area down." He was learning more about the potential and limitations of the Ralstons' sonar system.

Pete ruled out two of the other cold cases for the same reason, no clear information on where the person drowned on the lake. He suggested that the Ralstons focus on finding Dennis Liva. He was twenty years old when he drowned on June 14, 1974. Liva was fishing with a friend when their boat sank. The two men swam for shore and were spotted by another boater on the lake. He pulled one man into his boat, but Liva slipped below the surface before he could reach him.

"That was the one where they said it was about four hundred yards from the narrows," Pete said. "There is a boat as well. The boat is also something that's easier to spot."

The narrows were a distinct geological feature about
two-thirds of the way down the lake from the boat launch. The
east and west shorelines pinched together and created a channel that was only about three hundred feet wide. The lake then
expanded out again into another long section of open water.
The rescuer estimated that he saw Liva drown four hundred
yards south of that spot, which was the best data point that Pete
had so far been able to glean from all four of the historical files.

I helped Gene raise the towfish back onto the bow. We then
sped north up the lake. Gene set up a new grid and started scanning about half a mile south of the narrows, which looked like a
green index finger and thumb squeezing the water down to the
tight opening. The forest almost extended right into the water,
except for a small beach strewn with boulders and driftwood.
The bottom of this part of the lake, which was 285 feet deep,
looked like peanut butter spread smoothly on toast.

And then, about fifteen minutes into that first line on the
new grid, Gene suddenly clapped his hands. "We have a boat!"
he shouted. A V-shaped object, about the size of my pinkie
fingernail, had scrolled onto the top of the monitor.

"Right on the center line," Gene said, shaking his head in
disbelief.

Pete laughed nervously. He couldn't tell if Gene was joking.
The Ralstons had pointed out dozens of imaginary shapes and
objects on the bottom to help pass the time over the past two
days. I had known the Ralstons for longer than Pete. They never
joked about a body or about a clue to the whereabouts of a body.
We were looking at the sonar image of a boat that matched the
dimensions of the one that had sunk in this exact spot forty-
seven years before.

"As soon as the motor showed up — bingo," Gene said. He

pointed to the bright-yellow square at the back of the triangular object.

"This kind of goes to some of those stories I told you about divine guidance," he said.

He'd chosen the line we were on, the center line of the new grid, by eyeballing the middle of the channel from half a mile away.

"Yep," Pete said. He laughed again, like he was still trying to process what that little shape on the screen meant.

"I think the price of our stock just went up a little bit, Sandy," Gene said.

"Aw, five cents don't count," Sandy said. She liked to play the curmudgeon but had perked up in her chair. We all had. A bolt of electricity had run through the *Kathy G.* It was easy to get lulled into a trance by the repetitive sights, sounds, and sensations of searching with sonar. You sort of forgot what you were doing out there on the water. But then, *bang*, a long-lost boat ticked into view.

I wondered if this part of the lake had changed much since Liva and his friend had gone fishing that afternoon. Alouette is part of a provincial park, and development has been restricted. I couldn't see any people, cabins, or docks on the shorelines. We might have been looking at a scene very similar to what Liva saw almost five decades ago. Stonerabbit Peak, a rocky snow-covered mountain, rose up in the distance beyond the northeast end of the lake.

Liva and his friend were the last people to see the boat that we were now looking at on the monitor. That fact somehow compressed the intervening years, as if June 14, 1974, and April 10, 2021, were dots on a map that you could now connect with a short, straight line. It almost felt like time was just another reading from one of the manifold instruments in the pilot-house. The surface temperature of the water was forty-two degrees. We were traveling at a mile and a half per hour. The water was 285 feet deep. The boat sank forty-seven years ago.

Gene zoomed in on the object. The gunnels were sharply defined and looked like an elongated wishbone. Something else, another square object that registered on the sonar image as a bright smudge of yellow, was resting inside the boat up near the bow. "Okay, so tell me the story," Gene said to Pete. He wanted every possible detail about Liva. Now that Gene had the boat, he wanted the body.

CHAPTER SEVEN

Sank Like a Stone

The weather was sunny and clear on the afternoon of June 14, 1974. The fish were biting, but Herb Silcock and Dennis Liva had yet to reel any into the boat. They were using trolling spoons with live worms to try to catch sockeye salmon. The metal lures gleamed as they fluttered in the pearl-green waters of Alouette Lake.

The day was warm but windy. The twelve-foot-long fiber-glass boat, with its fire-engine-red outboard motor, bobbed up and down in the waves. Silcock was in a fine mood, despite the bad luck so far with the fish. He felt like he was getting away with something, like he and Liva had somehow conjured up that afternoon on the lake right out of thin air. It sure beat the hot and dusty confines of the Hammond Cedar Mill. Silcock knew there would be hell to pay after the weekend, but Monday morning could not have felt further away on that Friday afternoon.

Liva worked as the headrig tail sawyer, the most dangerous job at the mill. He was twenty years old and had a mop of wavy brown hair. His father owned and operated a local golf course as well as a steakhouse and hotel. Most of his siblings and cousins worked easier gigs at the sundry family businesses, but Liva had an independent streak. He liked to row his own boat. Armed with only a pickaroon, an ax handle with a metal hook at one end, it was Liva's job to position the forty-foot cedar logs on the roll case after the head sawyer had made the first cut. Liva ensured that the log lay flat before it got to Silcock, who was thirty-one and had a decade of experience in the lumber industry. He worked in a small booth and operated another saw on the line. Liva had to wear hefty steel-toed boots that came up over his ankle because he was on the floor of the mill. Silcock's shoes had steel toes, but they were a low-cut, loafer style. The two men had worked side by side for months, but this was the first time they'd hung out together outside the mill.

They had hatched their scheme over the lunch break. The master coast contract for the thirty-two thousand members of the International Woodworkers of America (IWA) expired that night at midnight. Leaders of the IWA were in the middle of negotiations with Forest Industrial Relations, the group representing 120 mill owners and logging companies. The IWA had asked its members not to take any strike action as they tried to hammer out the final details of the new agreement. One of the sticking points was a proposed $1 an hour general wage hike.

Silcock and Liva arrived at 8:00 AM at the mill on the banks of the Fraser River in Maple Ridge for their usual shift. Then they got to talking. Maybe it would speed the negotiations along if they reminded everyone, including their own union leaders, who was really in charge. Plus it was one of the first nice days of summer, the kind of weather that makes a person itch to get outside. The two men had a case of spring fever. They convinced another two coworkers in the headrig, which is the point of entry for all the logs going through the main mill, to join them and book off sick after lunch. It only took four men to shut down the whole operation, except for the shingle mill, that afternoon. The facility, which was owned by B.C. Forest Products, employed close to five hundred people.

It wasn't until later, over a beer at the Haney Hotel, that Liva and Silcock decided to go fishing. It seemed like the perfect way to make the most of their unexpected freedom. They picked up Liva's boat, stopped to get some gas and a case of beer, and then headed for the launch at the south end of Alouette Lake. They were on the water by about 3:00 PM.

After an hour or so at the south end, Liva suggested they try another location. He had caught fish before at a spot near the narrows. He kept the boat close to shore as they made the six-mile trip down the lake.

Liva slowed back down when they were about half a mile from the narrows. The wind had picked up, and some of the waves crested into whitecaps. Liva said he had to pee. Silcock was getting his rod ready to cast when the boat suddenly dipped to the left. He turned around to discover Liva had fallen overboard. The boat had taken on water. Liva grabbed the edge of the boat next to the motor and tried to heave himself out of the lake. As he pushed down, a wave crashed over the back. Silcock stood up in the bow, and the boat fell away beneath his feet. It sank like a stone.

Silcock lost his glasses when his face hit the water. He was nearsighted, so the shorelines became a blur of green in the distance. It was freezing cold. He gulped and wheezed. The weight of his work shoes pulled him down. He reached under the water and managed to loosen and then kick them off.

"Don't give up! Keep going!" Liva shouted. He was fifteen feet ahead of Silcock as they started swimming. Liva swam on his stomach. Silcock tried the overhand stroke, but it had been years since he had been swimming. He soon tired and then rolled over onto his back and started to kick. Waves crashed over his face. He gasped and sputtered and swallowed mouthfuls of water. He lost track of Liva. At some point, the water no longer felt cold. In fact, he didn't feel much of anything. And then he heard Liva yell something. He lifted his head and saw a boat backing up toward him.

The man on board threw Silcock a life jacket. He then extended a pole into the water and guided him to the back of the boat next to the motor. Silcock clung to the transom with his fingertips. The rescuer, who worked as a prison guard at a camp on the lake, noticed that the other man, who was roughly ten feet away from the back of the boat, had not yet grabbed the life jacket. He used the pole to push the jacket right up close to him. That's when Liva extended both arms straight up over his head and sank, disappearing below the surface. The prison guard heaved Silcock into the boat and then grabbed his radio. Silcock collapsed facedown in the bottom of the boat and started throwing up lake water.

"Emergency! Emergency! I am picking up some people who are in the water. I require assistance. My position is the narrows," the guard shouted into his radio at 4:35 PM. The transmission was picked up by one of his colleagues in the office at the Boulder Bay Forestry Camp, which was located up the hill from the east shore a mile north of the narrows. A nearby jail ran the camp for young offenders. They spent four months living and working in a cluster of rustic cabins in the forested wilderness by the lake. The prison guard had borrowed one of the camp's boats for an outing with his wife and kids. They departed from the wharf at North Beach, which is next to Gold Creek and about three miles up the lake from the boat launch. They were two-thirds of the way to the docks at Boulder Bay, roughly four hundred yards south of the narrows, when he noticed the two men in the lake. They were only a couple hundred yards from shore, and he assumed they were out for a swim. But then his wife hollered at him that one of them had called out for help.

One of the awful things about drowning is that it often does not look like drowning. Or at least it does not look like we expect it to look. It can happen quickly and quietly. People die in crowded pools and in front of busy beaches. They don't shout or scream. They don't splash around dramatically like they do in the movies. A drowning victim does everything possible to keep their mouth and nose above the surface. There is rarely enough oxygen or energy left over to try to signal for help.

Drowning is a leading cause of accidental-injury-related death worldwide. About eleven people drown every day in the United States. The vast majority, 80 percent, are men. Studies suggest this is because men tend to go out on the water more often and are prone to riskier behavior. The biggest risk factors for drowning for adults are not wearing a life jacket and alcohol consumption. Gene can count on one hand the number of women that he and Sandy have found. The only body the Ralstons ever found wearing a life jacket was that of a man trying to ride his modified motorcycle at night across Canyon Ferry Lake, in Montana. When the bike stalled halfway across, the rider got tangled in it, and they went down together.

Frank Pia worked as a lifeguard at Orchard Beach in the Bronx during the 1960s. He studied film footage of drowning incidents to develop his theory of the instinctive drowning response, which he first described in a research study published in 1974. Pia observed that drowning people assume an upright position in the water. They bob above and below the surface. Their arms extend out laterally and press down in an effort to stay afloat. Sometimes people move their arms and legs as if they're trying to climb a ladder. It's difficult to travel even a few feet in any direction. Pia noted that this terminal stage at the surface lasts only twenty to sixty seconds before the person sinks and disappears from view.

A more recent analysis of video footage of drowning incidents, undertaken by twenty international experts in the field of water safety, confirmed many of the observations that informed Pia's theory. The team of researchers identified some new behaviors and also described some of what they saw drowning people do as mysterious and hard to explain. More than 70 percent of the Earth's surface is water, and humans have been drowning since the beginning of time. And yet we still don't have a firm grasp on what a person looks like when they're fighting for their life in the water. Bystanders, rescuers, and family members are often left with more questions than answers in the aftermath of a drowning.

Liva's last moments on the surface of Alouette perplexed the prison guard and the RCMP officers who investigated the accident. They didn't understand why the young man didn't grab the life jacket or the pole. Help was so close at hand. Corporal Beecroft, the officer who compiled the police report on the case, concluded that Liva's comatose condition was caused by hypothermia.

I asked Michael Tipton, a professor at the University of Portsmouth, to help shed more light on what happened that afternoon in 1974. Tipton studies how the mind and body respond to adverse environments. He has published dozens of articles and a few books on drowning and cold-water immersion. He also consults as a medico-legal investigator on drowning incidents that involve the police or the courts. He warned me that any theories he offered on what had happened to Liva were at the level of speculation. I summarized the information in the police report, but Tipton would normally have access to a much broader sweep of evidence before making a determination on how and why someone drowned.

My first question was about the steel-toed boots. Silcock told the RCMP that he doubted Liva could have taken them off in the water. Tipton told me that if the boots were going to drag him under, they would have done so soon after the boat sank. So either Liva had not been wearing his work boots that afternoon or he managed to kick them off. Or he was able to support himself in the water despite the extra weight. Tipton didn't think the boots would have suddenly caused Liva to sink if he had been able to swim with them for the twenty minutes leading up to his submersion.

Next, I was curious about alcohol. Silcock told the police that from the time they arrived at the Haney Hotel to when the boat sank — over the course of four hours — he drank five beers and Liva had six. Drinking is considered a top risk factor for drowning, right up there with not wearing a life jacket. And yet lots of us, surveys suggest 30 to 40 percent, drink while we're on boats. The CDC has reported that alcohol is involved in up to 70 percent of deaths associated with water recreation.

The connection between the risk of drowning and alcohol has largely been made by analogy. We know that many people who drown consumed alcohol. We know that drinking and doing other activities like driving a car increases the risk of an accident because alcohol impairs critical faculties, like judgment, awareness, and coordination. "You would point the finger primarily at people . . . making bad decisions and getting into the water when they wouldn't normally get into the water," Tipton said.

Tipton did a study in which people were given seven shots of vodka before jumping into cold water. He wanted to see how alcohol affected the body's immediate reaction to frigid water. "We found no change in those initial responses," Tipton said. He described another study that looked at the effect of alcohol on the rate of cooling during longer-term immersions. Alcohol is a vasodilator, which means it relaxes and widens the blood vessels. Drinking causes the body to cool down faster in cold air because more warm blood flows close to the skin. Water, however, is a more powerful vasoconstrictor than air. The body responds to cold water by shutting down blood flow to the skin, which counteracts the cooling effect of alcohol. "You don't really see a difference with alcohol in terms of cooling rate in cold water," he said. Tipton was cautious about drawing conclusions regarding the role of alcohol in this case. A person's level of intoxication depends on so many variables, like tolerance, food consumed, and body composition. It's possible Liva's balance was affected by alcohol, which contributed to his fall overboard. It was also a windy day. The small boat would have been rocking up and down in the waves.

The most telling detail for Tipton was Beecroft's description of Liva's diminished level of consciousness, what the officer described as a comatose condition. "There are only two ways you're going to be unresponsive in that situation," Tipton said. One is hypothermia, where the core and brain temperature has dropped several degrees. The other is hypoxia, or a lack of oxygen to the brain.

Humans are tropical animals. We evolved at sea level in East Africa, and so our physiology is best suited for a relatively narrow band of the planet near the equator. The body's thermoregulatory system works to maintain a deep body temperature of about ninety-eight degrees Fahrenheit. Any slip below that optimal baseline and the cold starts to inhibit cellular activity in the organs, tissues, and brain. The body has a few tricks to keep the core warm, but there is a progressive loss of function the longer someone spends in the cold. Hypothermia starts to affect brain function after a fall in core temperature to ninety-two degrees. People register that change as a feeling of confusion and sleepiness.

Alouette Lake is part of a mountain watershed. The police report included subjective descriptions of the temperature of the water, but no hard numbers. I found a government study that measured the warmth of Alouette Lake at various depths during 2014. The reading near the surface, which was taken at the south end by the dam, for mid-June was fifty-nine degrees. It's possible the lake has warmed up since 1974. A study published in the journal *Scientific Data* in 2015 compared the surface water temperatures of thirty-four North American lakes over the summer months from 1985 to 2009. The temperature in thirty-two lakes increased, but by no more than two degrees. It's reasonable to assume that Liva and Silcock were dumped into water somewhere between fifty and sixty degrees.

An average young, clothed, and healthy individual can survive for one hour in water at forty-one degrees. That jumps to two hours in fifty-degree water. "A general rule of thumb we use is that nobody in any water temperature becomes hypothermic in less than thirty minutes," Tipton said. He was confident to rule out hypothermia as the cause for Liva's comatose condition.

The RCMP calculated the time frame for how long the men spent in the water using the 4:35 PM distress call from the prison guard and Silcock's memory of the time they launched the boat as well as his estimate for how long they spent fishing at the south end. Even if we stretch the time of immersion from twenty to forty-five minutes or an hour, it's still nowhere near long enough for hypothermia-induced loss of consciousness. Liva did not pass out at the moment of rescue because of a drop in brain temperature.

However, people can be incapacitated by cold water long before they become hypothermic, which is defined as a drop in core temperature to below ninety-five degrees. A sudden fall into frigid water puts enormous stress on the body. Tipton helped define the term *cold shock* in the early 1980s to identify the set of physiological reactions to cold water. This initial response peaks within the first thirty seconds and lasts for two to three minutes. It includes a gasp reflex and hyperventilation, which makes breath-holding virtually impossible. Heart rate and blood pressure skyrocket. Cold shock is now considered the cause of the majority of drowning deaths following accidental immersion in open water below fifty-nine degrees. Tipton and his colleagues created the new term to account for a growing volume of evidence that contradicted the theory that hypothermia was the primary threat in cold water. One study found that 55 percent of open-water immersion deaths in the UK happen within ten feet of a safe refuge. Two-thirds of the people who died were regarded as good swimmers. Cold shock is dangerous because it increases the risk of inhaling water and puts immense strain on the heart and lungs.

Liva and Silcock survived this initial phase of immersion and started to swim. Silcock lost his glasses in the plunge, but both men knew that the shore wasn't far, about five hundred yards, or nine lengths of an Olympic-sized swimming pool. The body loses heat faster when moving in water. Blood flow is constricted to the skin and layers of subcutaneous fat and muscle. The body turns the outer tissues into a kind of jacket to insulate the vital organs. The trade-off is creeping sensory and muscle paralysis. The arms, which have twice the surface-area-to-mass ratio as the legs, cool the fastest.

Silcock was able to grab the life jacket, but the prison guard had to steer him to the back of the boat, which was only three feet away, with a pole. The guard described Silcock as deadweight when he pulled him into the boat. Liva was a strong twenty-year-old who worked a hard, manual-labor job. Silcock was thirty-one and operated a saw from inside a booth. It seems plausible that he carried a bit of extra heft and the additional insulation made all the difference in terms of preserving enough dexterity and function for him to grasp the life jacket and then the boat.

Tipton said the two men would have experienced significant loss of motor function after twenty to forty-five minutes of swimming in water between fifty and sixty degrees. However, the physiological response of peripheral cooling is designed to preserve the internal temperatures of the core and the brain. The body sacrifices strength and coordination to protect high-level functions like consciousness. It was something that affected blood flow to the brain that caused Liva's comatose condition. "That's either because you're not getting oxygen in through the lung or because the oxygen is going in through the lung and it's not being pumped around the system," Tipton said. "It's a lung or a heart problem."

Tipton compared the structure of the lungs to that of a tree in *Essentials of Sea Survival*, a book he wrote with his friend and colleague Frank Golden. The trunk corresponds to the main airway that connects the mouth and nose. Bronchial tubes diverge off the trunk into a canopy of branches and sub-branches. The leaves of the tree represent the alveoli, the air sacs where carbon dioxide is off-loaded from the blood and oxygen is absorbed. Adults have about three hundred million alveoli, with a total surface area equal to one side of a tennis court.

The CDC defines *drowning* as "the process of experiencing respiratory impairment from submersion or immersion in liquid." When water is inhaled into the lungs, it interrupts the diffusion of gas across the alveolar-capillary membrane. It washes away an oily substance called surfactant, which coats the

tiny air sacs and makes it easier for them to expand. "Without it
the lungs would collapse on expiration and, like a bubble-gum
bubble, be impossible to reinflate," Tipton wrote in the book.

The lethal dose for fresh water in the lungs depends on the
size of the individual but is roughly three liters. It's half that
for seawater because it's saltier than blood and so draws more
fluid into the lungs from the blood by osmosis. But drowning is
not an on–off switch. It's a process that can unfold over hours.
Inhaling as little as three hundred milliliters can damage the
lungs and affect the oxygenation of the blood. Silcock described
swimming on his back and waves crashing over his face. The
guard said he collapsed on the bottom of the boat and began to
vomit, retching for several minutes. Swallowing water and aspi-
ration go hand in hand. Inhaling even small amounts of water
can deprive the brain of enough oxygen to affect consciousness
— the lung problem that Liva was likely experiencing when the
prison guard stopped to help.

The other possibility, Tipton explained, is that not enough
blood was getting pumped to the brain by the heart. "I think
we probably, as a general rule, underestimate the number of
people who have a cardiac problem on immersion," Tipton said.
The physiological responses to sudden immersion in cold water
put enormous stress on the heart, which can cause ventricu-
lar fibrillation in people with a predisposing condition. Tipton
referenced a recent study that analyzed a decade of drowning
data from Canada. One-third of people who drowned had a
preexisting medical issue. Cardiovascular disease accounted
for 54 percent of the deaths in which a medical condition was
found to be a contributing factor.

One reason cardiac problems go unreported for drownings is that they're undetectable after the fact. Someone who
suffers heart failure still aspirates water into the lungs, and

the electrical disturbances to the heart are imperceptible in an autopsy. Another reason heart issues fly under the radar, Tipton explained, is that most people recruited for studies related to drowning are young and fit. They often have to pass a medical exam before they're allowed to participate.

But given his age, Tipton said, it was unlikely that Liva had an issue with his heart that reduced blood flow to the brain. "Most young, fit, healthy people dying on immersion close to a place of safe refuge, it's going to be cold shock and the gasp response stopping them from holding their breath and therefore aspirating water and drowning," he said.

Tipton noted that in the UK about 60 percent of the people who drown in open water, places like the ocean or a lake, die from the short-term responses associated with cold shock. Another 20 percent die from hypothermia. The remaining 20 percent die shortly before, during, or right after they are saved. Circum-rescue collapse was recognized as a unique cause of drowning during the Second World War as more reports emerged of sailors who suffered a sudden loss of consciousness during or following rescue. "What we believe is that relaxation, that relief — that vagal autonomic wave that goes across the body — can make their condition deteriorate," Tipton said.

The physiology of circum-rescue collapse is not well understood. It's impossible to study in a controlled experiment, but the theory is that the sensation of relief associated with being saved can be so powerful that it conflicts with and undermines the state of hyperarousal needed to stay afloat and keep the airway above water. Tipton said that rescuers should avoid telling a drowning victim to relax. They instead need to emphasize the severity of the situation so the person in danger remains alert and vigilant.

The prison guard told the police that he thought Silcock

and Liva were out for a swim when he first passed them in the water. It was seventy-two degrees and sunny. It likely felt like a relaxing afternoon to be on the lake. The guard would have kept right on going if his wife had not heard Liva call out for help. Silcock outlined in his statement that he had been oblivious to the rescue boat until he heard Liva shout. It's interesting that after twenty minutes, and maybe longer, the two men were still so close together on the lake. A strong swimmer could have crossed the full five hundred yards to shore in twenty minutes. Silcock had flipped over onto his back soon after the boat sank, but he had seen Liva swimming on his stomach. I wondered if Liva was a better swimmer. Maybe he chose to stick with Silcock instead of going ahead to the safety of dry land.

$$\sim$$

I spoke to Makenzie Ditto, a woman in her early twenties from Alabama, to learn more about the experience of drowning. She nearly died in the spring of 2020 but was saved by the quick response of bystanders. She had been kayaking on a small river that flowed behind her house. Her nine-year-old sister, Virginia, sat in her lap on the boat. It was the first sunny day after a series of heavy rainstorms. The water was high. They paddled up to a waterfall that flowed over a short rock wall not much higher than three or four steps on a staircase. The boat flipped.

Luke Johnson and his father, Larry, saw the whole thing happen from their backyard. Virginia was wearing a life jacket, and Luke pulled her to safety right away. Ditto got caught in the hydraulic created by the waterfall. She was unconscious in the water for two to three minutes before Luke was able to pull her to shore. The Johnsons performed CPR and rescue breathing for about ten minutes before the ambulance arrived. The paramedics got a weak pulse after the third shock with the defibrillator.

She was driven to a local hospital and then airlifted to a bigger facility. Ditto was hooked up to an extracorporeal membrane oxygen machine, which took over the job of her lungs and heart. She woke up the next day.

Ditto described what it was like underneath the waterfall. It felt icy cold. She fought against the undertow, but it was too powerful. It spun her around and upside down, like she was a sock in a washing machine. She felt a burning sensation like when you drink something and then laugh really hard and it comes out your nose, except that it happened backward. "It was shooting up my nose and coming out of my mouth, and I was spitting water out of my mouth that was coming through my nose," she said. "It was more of a gasp all in between." Then she hit her head against the stone wall, and the fight went out of her. "I eventually started to feel the water just go into my lungs and I started to really feel myself just giving up."

The amount of time a person can hold their breath under water is highly variable. Free divers, people who train their bodies to go without oxygen, can last longer than 10 minutes. The world record for someone holding their breath is close to 25 minutes. For most people in ideal conditions, as in warm and calm water, that time is more like forty-five to sixty seconds. Cold temperatures reduce that interval because the nervous system ramps up the heart rate and oxygen consumption to keep the body warm. The average breath-hold time in water at forty-one degrees for someone wearing normal heavy clothing, as in more than a swimsuit, is nine and a half seconds. Physical exertion, like swimming or fighting against a strong current, rapidly depletes oxygen stores and again reduces breath-hold time. Whether it's two seconds or ten minutes, though, we all reach the break point, the moment when carbon dioxide and oxygen concentrations reach critical levels and the brain triggers an involuntary gasp. Water, and anything else in the water, gets inhaled.

Fluid in the throat can provoke laryngospasm. The vocal cords slam shut and prevent anything, whether it's air or water, from entering the lungs. The latest understanding of this involuntary response, however, is that a dearth of oxygen will eventually cause the vocal cords to relax again and water will still get aspirated into the lungs. The theory known as dry drowning has been discarded.

Most adults reach the break point before unconsciousness. So we're awake and alert to the fact that death is close at hand. Much of our understanding about the mechanisms of drowning comes from inhumane experiments on dogs in the 1950s and early '60s. Researchers observed a cessation of struggling at seventy-one seconds after submersion. That lines up with later studies estimating the time for loss of consciousness in humans at seventy-five seconds after going under. That leaves a window of time below the surface between when people first breathe water into their lungs and when they pass out. One of the last things Ditto remembered before everything went dark was hearing the enveloping roar of rushing water. "It was blurry and it was really bright and really pretty," she said.

Tipton and a colleague published a study on the subjective experience of drowning. They dedicated the paper to Oscar Montgomery, "a very fine young man and lover of the sea." The seventeen-year-old drowned at the end of May 2020. He was snorkeling in the English Channel and testing his ability to hold his breath.

The two researchers scoured the internet for reported experiences of drowning and then assessed the veracity of each account. They included thirty-four cases in their analysis. The subjects reported a sequence of events similar to Ditto's. They struggled to breath-hold and then described a burning and painful sensation when inhaling water into the lungs. Fifteen of the thirty-four drowning victims then experienced a feeling of tranquillity. "I felt at peace," commented one. "I just started breathing. It was quite peaceful and not painful," another wrote. The paper included a firsthand description of drowning from 1791 by Sir Francis Beaufort, a British naval officer: "A calm feeling of the most perfect tranquillity succeeded the most tumultuous sensation . . . Nor was I in any bodily pain. On the contrary, my sensations were now of a rather pleasurable cast."

I asked Tipton if he was surprised that so many people in his study reported feeling calm on the brink of death. "The terminal event for a lot of people is hypoxia, whether that's caused by disease or trauma or drowning or whatever," he said. A lack of oxygen to the brain affects cognitive function. People see flashing lights and colors. Their field of vision attenuates the same way as an old television after it's shut off. The light narrows until all you see is a pinprick in the expansive darkness. "It didn't really surprise me that it was quasi-pleasurable," Tipton said. I wondered if being underwater, a sensation of weightlessness in a hushed and ethereal realm, added to the feeling of serenity.

Submersion of four to six minutes, without immediate resuscitation, leads to brain damage and ultimately heart failure and then death. Ditto survived because everything went right during her rescue. Luke worked as a whitewater rafting guide, and Larry was a volunteer firefighter and search-and-rescue technician. They both knew first aid and CPR. And the river in spring was frigid. It's likely that the cold water Ditto aspirated rapidly cooled her blood, which in turn cooled her brain. The drop in temperature slowed brain activity and reduced oxygen demand, extending the window before permanent damage.

People sometimes survive after prolonged submersions in cold water. These remarkable recoveries typically happen to children and young adults. One of the most dramatic incidents involved teenagers who drowned while on a school field trip during the winter. Their boat capsized into an inland sea in southern Denmark. They tried to swim for shore. Seven of the thirteen students were clinically dead when the paramedics arrived on scene two hours after the boat had flipped. Doctors revived all of them using the same kind of machine that saved Ditto.

I asked Gene once why he thought people drown. It was one of those big, general questions that is hard to answer. And people drown for vastly different reasons in different parts of the world. But I was curious if Gene had thought about the why after arriving at so many of the same kinds of accidents across Canada and the United States. He answered by telling me a story.

A dilapidated wood structure extended out over the Snake River and housed an old irrigation pump behind the family farm where Gene grew up. When he was around nine or ten, he would run down to the river and climb on the rickety beams during big rain- and windstorms. "I'd just love to go down there and walk out on a couple of planks, clear out as far as I could get. It was kind of wobbly. And I'd shake it. Wobble it back and forth, like I was in the ocean. And just look out across the river into the storm. Here I am rocking this structure, totally oblivious to what could happen if that thing collapsed. Totally oblivious, but it was such great fun."

Water is a ubiquitous aspect of our environment. Lakes, rivers, and oceans offer the kinds of beautiful settings we seek out for adventure or when we want to relax. It's easy to forget that we're only a matter of seconds, or inches, from mortal danger. "Sometimes we get complacent and take a risk when we don't even realize we're taking a risk," Gene said. "Like crawling out on the bow of the boat to hang the pulley on the front of the boom — of course, I always try to wear a life jacket when I do that."

Ditto was walking again within three days of waking up in the hospital, but it took months to fully recover. She broke three ribs, cut her foot, and damaged her right lung. Doctors used a suction device to remove all the rocks and gravel she had inhaled along with the river water. She lost muscle mass and felt like a frail and elderly woman during those first few weeks after she drowned. She still has the occasional nightmare about rolling around in circles.

Ditto had kayaked that river behind her house countless times before the accident. She would paddle up to the little waterfall and put her hand under the water as it flowed cold and clear over the rocks. A few days of heavy rain transformed that peaceful ritual into something perilous. "You need to respect the water," she told me. "It not only brings life, but it can take it away."

CHAPTER EIGHT

Pay It Forward

The prison guard circled the area where he last saw Liva on the surface. A milk carton and an orange plastic container bobbed in the rough water. Silcock asked for a cigarette. He struggled to speak but managed to relay that Liva was wearing a light-blue T-shirt and jeans. Two more boats from the camp arrived. One took Silcock to the launch at the south end, where an ambulance was waiting. He spent the night in the intensive care unit at the hospital and was released the next morning.

Beecroft described how the remaining two boats and prison guards immediately started dragging operations. Additional dragging efforts were carried out the next day "at a medium level as the lake sinks to its deepest point of 420 feet in this area," the police report read.

Towing hooks along the bottom of a lake was the go-to method for body recovery back in 1974. It sounds grim and clumsy, but the technique is still used today. It can be effective if the water is relatively shallow and the bottom is smooth and flat. A well-organized drag search includes several boats moving side by side and along a preestablished grid pattern. Five or six treble hooks, fish hooks with three bends and sharp points, are attached with short chains to the base of a triangular metal frame. It looks like a big rake with dangling tines.

Someone on the boat holds the rope that's attached to the rake so they can react quickly if it snags something.

The police report suggested that the searchers pulled hooks through the water at various depths but didn't reach all the way down to the bottom. Beecroft described how that part of Alouette Lake was littered with stumps, exactly the kind of debris that would interfere with a drag search. The earth-fill dam at the south end of Alouette was built in 1929 and had flooded a massive area of the river valley. The original lake was only a mile and a quarter long. Alouette now extends for more than ten miles.

"It has been my 8-year experience with this body of water that bodies lost have never been recovered," Beecroft wrote. That sense of fatalism, that Alouette does not give up its dead, was shared by other officers in other sections of the police reports on the four missing men that Pete had asked the Ralstons to help find.

The Liva family did not share the RCMP's sense of resignation back in 1974. They used their own boats to perform dragging operations. They hired commercial and amateur divers, although no description about where or how those underwater searches unfolded was included in the police report. "The Liva family are extremely upset and frustrated that the body of their son has not been located," Beecroft wrote. He concluded his report on Liva's case with a note about how the family was going to advocate for the creation of a publicly funded program to assist in the location of bodies.

I read the police reports on the four cold cases because I was curious how the RCMP handled them over time. There was no good way to look for bodies in deep lakes back then. The cases went dormant after the original searches failed. Most of the annual reviews after that included just two short sentences by a rotating cast of officers: "Nothing further to report. No new information since initial investigation."

And then, after decades of those cursory reviews, the four cases were suddenly rebooted by Constable Chris Wilson in July 2014. The catalyst was his discovery of Legacy Water Search and Recovery, which he described as a local nonprofit society that searched for the bodies of drowning victims with side-scan sonar.

Wilson carefully reviewed all four files in an effort to track down any surviving witnesses and provide Legacy with information about the point of last seen for each of the men — or, as he called them, "the quartet of missing people." His investigation culminated in a meeting in Maple Ridge on a Tuesday afternoon in July 2015 when he provided a report on each case to the members of Legacy and to volunteers with Ridge Meadows Search and Rescue. The plan was for the Legacy search team to scan the lake over the next six months to a year, going out for short trips when they had the time and then reporting back to the RCMP on what they found.

Wilson was transferred in 2016, but he left detailed notes on the renewed efforts to find the quartet. Other officers came and went in the role of missing persons coordinator. It took three years before someone followed up with Legacy. Corporal Christine Day sent an email in February 2019. The contact at Legacy replied and explained that they'd encountered some challenges in getting their boat set up with the sonar. They requested another six months to complete the searches on Alouette. Day followed up at the end of August. And then again in October. But she never heard back. She noted that Legacy's website had not been updated in a long time. She concluded that they were one of those well-meaning volunteer groups that never managed to get off the ground. Pete took over as the missing persons coordinator in August 2020. One of his jobs was to find out if another side-scan sonar team could be hired to search for the quartet.

～

"It's still going and it's still going to go," said Anna Ward, vice president of Legacy Water Search and Recovery. Her husband, Jim, the president, was also on the call. I phoned the Wards at the end of September 2021. They had recently taken the boat and sonar out for its maiden voyage on Pitt Lake, another popular destination in the Lower Mainland. They had a setback, a glitch with the wiring. The towfish didn't transmit any data to the onboard computer, so they didn't see any images of the bottom. "It was 50 percent successful," Jim said, taking the glass-is-half-full perspective on Legacy's trial run.

"We were actually hoping to be fully functional a couple of years ago," he said. The biggest challenge has been finding the time. The Wards, who are in their early fifties, run a busy automotive repair shop in Langley, a small city south of Maple Ridge. It's not uncommon for them to work ten-hour days, seven days a week. They have a teenaged daughter. "This is life. Life in general," Jim said, summing up why the boat was not yet operational. Legacy was incorporated as a nonprofit society on June 17, 2013. It had sounded to Constable Wilson that they would be ready to search Alouette Lake for the missing quartet sometime in 2015. I had assumed, like the RCMP officers who took over the cases after Wilson, that the organization must have fizzled out, a classic case of good intentions getting outmatched by reality. But maybe that was the glass-is-half-empty interpretation. I spoke to the Wards for two hours. It's clear they're still passionate about the cause.

Jim told me that if you went out today and bought all the equipment that Legacy has put together — the boat, the sonar, the electric winch, the thousands of feet of electromechanical cable, the ROV — it would cost about $400,000. Some of the gear was donated. Some of it was provided at steep discounts. Legacy also raised hundreds of thousands of dollars in donations. They organized charity golf tournaments and ran two annual dances, one at Halloween and another on Valentine's Day, for several years in a row. And the fundraising was ongoing because the group is building a contingency fund. They will only charge for expenses to go on searches, but they also want to cover those costs in the event a family is unable to pay. "We never want to say no," Anna said.

Jim was able to diagnose the wiring issue. Moisture had infiltrated a control panel for the winch while the boat was in storage, and one of the connections had become loose. Once he finds the time to reconnect the wires, they'll get the boat back on the water. And then comes the training phase. Legacy was launched with fifty volunteers. About twelve remain. "This is 100 percent volunteer time. Nobody gets paid a dime. Nobody will ever," Jim said. "You've got to be in it with all your heart or not at all."

The Wards envision running the boat with a crew of three or four. One driver, another to run the towfish and onboard computer, an ROV operator, and ideally a deckhand. Some volunteers have boating experience, but none have ever worked with a sonar or ROV. The more volunteers Legacy can train, the better chance they have of responding quickly to a search request. Everyone on the team has a family and a day job. The plan is to have enough capacity to sub people out for shifts on the boat, maybe two to three days, so they can keep a search going with as little downtime as possible.

The more I talked to the Wards, the more sympathy I had for why it has taken Legacy so long to get going. First, they had to raise the money. Then they had to figure out what type of gear to buy. And as a nonprofit society, they made every decision by consensus, which meant herding a bunch of already busy people together for meetings. Jim then had to modify the boat, which they got at a discount but was not designed for running a sonar system. And the next step, after assembling everything, was to figure out how to use it. Starting an underwater search-and-recovery nonprofit from scratch was a monumental task. Eight years and one 50 percent successful test run later, the Wards are still keen to realize their vision.

"Our nephew and his best friend drowned in Nicola Lake," Anna told me. Several photos of Austin Kingsborough and Brendan Wilson, who were seventeen years old when they drowned, are posted on Legacy's website. The teenagers each have an arm draped over the other's shoulders in one photo. They're wearing jerseys for opposing ball-hockey teams. The young men are lanky and angular. They look like goofballs, like the type of teenagers who are popular not just because they're athletes but because they're fun and kind.

The Wards told me about the night of April 21, 2013. It was a Sunday, and the boys were late returning from a weekend at the Wilson family cabin in the Nicola Bay RV Park. Connie Wilson, Brendan's mother, called the RCMP after a neighbor at the lake checked on her cabin and found the truck all packed up and ready to go. The cabin was unlocked and the lights were on, but there was no sign of the two young men.

Jim drove the three hours to Nicola Lake with Curtis, Austin's father, and Barry, Brendan's father. They searched through the night, driving back and forth across the lake to visit campgrounds and walk along the shorelines. Early the next morning,

Jim spotted a V-shaped impression at the edge of the water near the cabin, as if a canoe had been dragged into the lake. He then noticed a canoe-shaped outline in the snow next to the fence.

They launched the Wilsons' motorboat. Not long after they got on the water someone radioed from the RCMP helicopter that had taken off at first light that morning. One of the searchers had spotted an object in the water near shore at the far end of the bay that extends north of the community. The cluster of mobile homes, trailers, and small cabins at the RV park occupied a finger of land that curled out from the east shore near the north end of Nicola Lake.

Jim, Curtis, and Barry sped over in the boat and discovered the overturned canoe. They got it on shore with the help of volunteers from Nicola Valley Search and Rescue, who had also been searching since late Sunday night. They flipped the canoe over and a work boot that belonged to one of the boys tumbled out. Someone else found a tin of chewing tobacco. One volunteer saw a headlamp underwater near shore. It was still on and cast an eerie glow beneath the surface of the water. The search team would eventually piece together what had happened. Austin and Brendan had not packed up the truck on Sunday to get ready to return home to Langley. They had never unpacked in the first place. They got to the cabin Friday evening and took the canoe out that night.

A community of friends, classmates, family, and neighbors — Anna estimated somewhere between 100 and 150 people — gathered to help with the search. The Wilson cabin became the headquarters. Connie set up a whiteboard in the front yard where volunteers kept track of where and when they were searching. Everyone had to team up with a buddy. The RCMP dive team arrived and spent several days with their drop sonar, searching the bay where the canoe was found. The Upper

Nicola Band, a Syilx Indigenous group, prepared meals for the growing ranks of volunteer searchers. The RCMP called off their search on the afternoon of Friday, April 26. Scott Lebus, a friend of the two families, called the Ralstons later that same day.

"We heard through a friend of a friend of a friend about this couple from Idaho who could find people who had drowned," Anna said. The Wards assumed that hiring a private sonar team would cost serious money. They talked about remortgaging their house to pay for it. "You can't put a price on bringing your family home," Jim said.

Gene and Sandy had just returned to their house in Kuna after an unsuccessful search for a thirteen-year-old boy in a lake in Colorado when they got the call from Lebus. They took a few days to regroup. And then, while they were gearing up to leave, Gene got a call about a missing fisherman on Shuswap Lake, a three-hour drive east of Nicola Lake. The plan when they left their house on the morning of May 4, 2013, a Saturday, was to try to find Brendan and Austin, then search for fifty-nine-year-old John Poole.

The Ralstons arrived Sunday evening. The small lakeside community was a whirlwind of activity. So many people wanted to help but didn't know how. Gene and Sandy provided a sense of calm. "He was so professional, and so . . . I don't even know the words. He was just so knowledgeable," Anna said.

The Ralstons were more personable than the police. Gene didn't hesitate to hug strangers. He knew if and when to deliver a joke. They showed up in the middle of the storm and gently took the wheel. Gene and Sandy explained to the Wilsons and Kingsboroughs how their sonar system worked and walked them through how they were going to conduct the search for their sons on Nicola Lake.

It was only later, when the Wards looked back on that first night they met the Ralstons, that they realized how Gene and Sandy investigated the drowning as they talked to people. Their tone was conversational and empathetic, but they managed to collect all the details they needed to set up the search grid on the lake. They launched the *Kathy G* that same evening they arrived and searched until dark.

The Ralstons were back on the water by seven o'clock the next morning. Gene set up a new search grid farther out into the lake from shore. Not long into that first line on the new grid, they imaged the bodies of the two young men. They were 150 feet apart. Gene figured that one of them must have held on to the canoe a little longer after it capsized. The Ralstons waited for the RCMP to arrive with a boat before they recovered the bodies with their ROV. The Wards had been prepared to remortgage their house. Gene and Sandy charged $800 for the search and recoveries.

Anna described how later that day more than a hundred people gathered along the main road out of the community. They clapped and cheered as the coroner drove away with the bodies of Austin and Brendan. "It's the weirdest thing," she said. "You can see the joy that they bring to people. And I don't even know if they truly understand how much they bring back to the family when they bring those loved ones home. It's a body and there's no life left, but they bring them home."

After the coroner left the RV park with the bodies, members of the Upper Nicola Band served chili and bannock for dinner. Anna and Jim sat with Gene and Sandy outside the Wilsons' cabin. The Ralstons told them about other searches. "We saw the compassion that they had and just how dedicated they were," Anna said. "We were just like, *You know what? We want to do that. We want to help people and pay it forward.*"

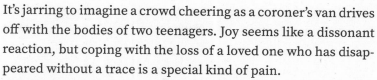

It's jarring to imagine a crowd cheering as a coroner's van drives off with the bodies of two teenagers. Joy seems like a dissonant reaction, but coping with the loss of a loved one who has disappeared without a trace is a special kind of pain.

"That is a gift to these families that allows them to begin the grief process," Pauline Boss said after I told her about the Ralstons and the work that they do. She is a professor emeritus at the University of Minnesota and has spent her career in the field of family social science. Boss pioneered the theory of ambiguous loss, which explores how grief can be interrupted, or even frozen, if the body of a loved one is never recovered. She has counseled the families of people who vanished in a variety of conflicts and natural disasters, such as the Vietnam War, the 9/11 terrorist attack in New York, and the 2011 tsunami in Japan that caused the Fukushima nuclear disaster.

Grief is extremely personal. It affects people in myriad ways. Boss told me that many people have a much harder time letting go if they don't have access to at least some evidence of the transformation from life to death. Without recovering a body, without that physical proof, people inevitably wonder. Some report catching glimpses of their lost loved ones in everyday situations, like in the aisles of a grocery store, for years after they go missing. Others convince themselves that the person decided to leave. They disappeared so they could start a new life in a new place. "You need to see that the person is no longer breathing," Boss said. "Or you need to see the bones."

Finding the body, bringing it home as the Wards described, is helpful for closing the gap between knowing that someone is gone and feeling that someone is gone. The Ralstons experienced their own version of ambiguous loss for one sleepless night in a campground by the Snake River as they waited for a knock on the door from their friend. The Wilsons and the Kingsboroughs lived in the shadow of that uncertainty for two weeks, between the Monday morning that searchers found the overturned canoe in the lake and the Monday morning when the Ralstons imaged Brendan and Austin on the bottom.

CHAPTER NINE

Master of a Thousand Skills

Legacy Underwater Search and Recovery is not the first group that the Ralstons inspired to follow in their footsteps. A similar set of circumstances led to the creation of another nonprofit, but on the opposite side of Canada, in Newfoundland.

Nineteen-year-old Stephan Hopkins was canoeing with a friend on a small lake near his hometown of Deer Lake in early July 2007. The boat flipped. The friend managed to swim to shore. No one saw Hopkins again. Police, search-and-rescue volunteers, and community members searched almost every day for more than two months. The lake was only two and a half miles long and half a mile wide, but the marathon effort proved fruitless. The Ralstons arrived in mid-September. Gene and Sandy found the body of the young man within twenty-nine minutes of launching their boat. They had driven a thousand miles, including a trip on a ferry, from another search in Maine to get to Deer Lake. And that lake in Maine was twenty-eight hundred miles from their house in Idaho.

The people of Deer Lake, like the crowd at Nicola Lake, were enormously grateful. The Ralstons had done what no one else could do. The community decided to start a foundation in Hopkins's honor. They raised close to $300,000 (CAD) in six months and used the Ralstons' boat, sonar, and ROV as a blueprint to assemble their own search-and-recovery system.

I talked to Dave Lewis in the fall of 2021. He is the leader of the search group formerly known as the Stephan Hopkins Memorial Foundation. The group merged with Deer Lake Regional Search and Rescue in the spring of 2020 as a way to expand their pool of volunteers, which had dwindled to five. Joining the local search group expanded their ranks to thirty. Lewis has been taking the new recruits out on Deer Lake for regular training sessions. They run their boat with a team of four: a sonar operator, a driver, and two deckhands.

I spoke to Lewis just after he got home from a search in the North Atlantic for two fishermen and their thirty-foot-long boat, the *Island Lady*. Lewis and his team had arrived on scene a week after the men vanished. The potential search area was immense, and the bottom was riddled with peaks and valleys. The locals called them ribs. The depth changed suddenly from three hundred feet to five feet and then back down again. "So basically a sheer wall that you're trying to search," Lewis told me. It was difficult to keep the boat going straight because of strong winds, ocean currents, and powerful tides. "Very, very challenging to say the least. We did give it 100 percent," Lewis said.

These types of thorny open-ocean searches have been the norm for the group since its inception in 2008. "You're basically looking for a needle in a haystack, and you're not even quite sure of where the haystack is," Lewis said. The nonprofit set up in Hopkins's honor had better luck than Legacy in terms of getting up and running. Their big challenge has been that most of the drownings on the East Coast of Canada happen in the ocean. Their sonar system, which was modeled after the Ralstons', is best suited for lakes. Lewis estimated that the boat had been used on fifteen or so searches since it was purchased. Only two of those were on lakes. Lewis described how he would plan a search and budget a certain number of days and then arrive and get grounded by storms and rough seas for half the allotted time. It takes a broad base of volunteers to support an ocean search because people need to sub in and out to keep it going. "We all have families and day jobs," he said.

Dozens of police agencies have also purchased a sonar after seeing the Ralstons at work. On the drive up to Maple Ridge in April 2021, Gene and Sandy stopped at their friend Crayton Fenn's place near Seattle. He runs a company that does underwater work for clients like the US Navy, Air Force, and the National Oceanic and Atmospheric Administration. Gene told me that Fenn's boats are more like ships. Fenn mentored the Ralstons when they were starting out and manufactured their towfish. Gene and Fenn are both gearheads. They often swap equipment and parts or troubleshoot finicky mechanical issues together.

The Ralstons dropped off an electric winch with Fenn that needed a modification before they could deliver it to the Cascade County Sheriff's Office in Montana. Cory Reeves, the undersheriff, was putting together a side-scan sonar system. He has been shadowing the Ralstons on searches over the past few years.

Many of the police agencies who get their own sonar go on to have success. Others keep calling the Ralstons. Side-scan sonar is a perishable skill. It's a use-it-or-lose-it kind of thing. Most jurisdictions only get the occasional drowning, one or two a year, so the authorities don't get enough hours on the water to become proficient. And police officers often rotate through different positions. Someone the Ralstons train one year might get shuffled into a new role the next year.

Gene and Sandy considered starting a nonprofit society, something akin to Legacy or the Hopkins Foundation, back when they first got their sonar. One option was to team up with Idaho Mountain Search and Rescue. The Ralstons worried about getting bogged down by bureaucracy. "We wanted to be able to tell the family, yes we could come. It's just a matter of when we can come. We didn't want to have to go to a board of directors to get approval to go do something," Gene told me.

He frames their decision to go it alone in terms of what was best for the families of the missing people. No foundation meant no intermediary steps. They were free to respond at the drop of a hat. I think their decision had more to do with how much they value autonomy. The Ralstons like to be the captains of their own ship. Gene's highest compliment is calling someone compassionate, but his worst insult is labeling someone a joiner. Joiners suffer from an outsized ego that fuels no end of uninformed opinions. Joiners want all the credit but none of the responsibility. They lack the cardinal search virtue of stick-to-it-ive-ness. Gene and Sandy didn't want to take the chance they would get saddled with a joiner in their nonprofit.

The experience of the Wards and Lewis, people who tried to emulate the Ralstons, underscores how difficult it is to start and run a nonprofit underwater search-and-recovery outfit. The gear is expensive. The work is complex and time consuming. Despite these headwinds, several groups in Canada and the United States have had success doing this kind of work. Bruce's Legacy from Wisconsin is a volunteer-run group funded by donations and sponsorships. The Hutterian Emergency Aquatic Response Team, or HEART, is based out of the Canadian province of Manitoba but travels widely to find and recover drowning victims with sonar. It was started by two brothers who are scuba divers and Hutterites, a religious group who live in agricultural communities.

The Ralstons have worked with the Canadian Canine Search Corps on a number of searches. Karen Somerville, a firefighter, started the nonprofit in Calgary in 2016, but it has grown to include a dozen volunteers from across western Canada. Somerville told me that her original plan was to use search dogs to help with rescues, to locate people lost in the wilderness or trapped in the rubble of a collapsed building. "We ended up doing almost all recovery work even though we had live-find dogs," Somerville said. She pivoted the organization to meet the need she discovered in the community. The search dogs are now trained to find cadavers on land and in water. The team has their own towed sonar system. The Ralstons reach out to Somerville to help on cases without a solid point of last seen. The dogs can detect the gases released by a decomposing corpse on the bottom of the lake and so help to narrow down the area to scan with the sonar.

Tom Crossman, a friend of Gene and Sandy, travels internationally for searches. He dedicated himself to underwater searching full-time after he retired from the Federal Bureau of Prisons in 2008. Crossman is in his early sixties and from Hermantown, Minnesota. He is a high-tech version of the Ralstons. He works with the latest and greatest sonar transducers and ROVs and sells the gear through his company, Crossman Consulting. He funds the searches for drowning victims, which he performs at cost, with the commercial side of his business, which includes salvage, underwater surveys, training seminars, and shipwreck exploration.

Nobody besides Gene and Sandy bankrolls their own equipment and searches. That financial independence has allowed the Ralstons to gain an unrivaled amount of experience. Gene and Sandy describe themselves as frugal, but not wealthy. They live modestly. And yet they didn't hesitate to spend $100,000 on a sonar system and then another $46,000 on an ROV a few years later. Not to mention the brawny motor home that tows the boat and all the winches, cables, and computers. Gene told me that his father, Sam Ralston, never spent money on things that didn't make him money. Gene inherited that parsimonious sensibility, except he never spends money on things that don't help him to find and recover bodies.

Mike Clement, a friend of the Ralstons, told me that a person needs to master a thousand skills to get good at finding and recovering bodies in water. Clement is from a small town on the coast north of Vancouver and runs a consulting company called SAVI Marine. He has done a few body recoveries, most of them with the Ralstons. His main business is salvaging boats or inspecting underwater infrastructure like pipelines and conduits. His passion is marine archaeology.

You need to understand wind and weather, Clement explained. You need to know the mechanics and limitations of scuba diving so you can support divers from the surface. Success depends on an excellent boat driver and coordination between the driver and sonar operator. You have to be mechanically inclined, have to understand how your boat and engine work in case you have to repair something when you're in the field and days away from access to spare parts. You need discipline and organization to know what you've covered with the sonar and what parts of the bottom are left to scan. You need to know how to tie knots and deploy and retrieve anchors. You need to cooperate with the local authorities. "They may not be the best in the world at any one of those kinds of things, but they're the best people I have ever, ever come across that have all of those skills," Clement said.

The Ralstons spent decades working as environmental consultants before they found their first drowning victim. They're fluent in the science of limnology, the study of inland waters. The field draws on elements of geology, physics, chemistry, and biology to explain the dynamic properties of water in lakes and rivers. Their understanding of these complex systems informs how they search and helps them to rule out assumptions about if and how a body will move on the bottom.

Gene and Sandy have clocked thousands of hours in the *Kathy G*. Each of the hundreds of cases they have worked on, whether a homicide or an accidental drowning, presented a unique set of challenges. The Ralstons became adept at investigations as they honed their technical skills with the sonar. They learned how to talk to witnesses in a way that made them feel relaxed so they could remember crucial details about the point of last seen. The Ralstons are creative problem solvers. They often notice or think of something that everyone else overlooked.

Finding a body with sonar is occasionally easy. You shine a bright light into the dark and see what you're looking for. It's when things get complicated, when there is an unusual topography on the bottom or no point of last seen, that the years of experience pay off. Most searches have some kind of plot twist, some puzzling factor that the Ralstons don't learn about until they're on the scene.

Back in May 2013, Gene and Sandy spent the night at the RV park on Nicola Lake after recovering the two teenagers. The next morning, they drove three hours east to Shuswap Lake. John Poole's motorboat had been discovered a week earlier, empty and run aground with the engine still going. He had been fishing by himself on the lake. No one saw him fall into the water. One of the devices on board recorded the location of his boat, but Poole had disconnected the power at some point to wire in new equipment. The Ralstons only had a partial picture of where Poole had been on the lake. A sizable chunk of data was missing between his last recorded position on the water and the spot where the boat ended up ashore.

The Ralstons set up a grid using what little information they had. After a few long days of searching, Gene got an idea. The boat was found with two fishing rods set up for trolling, the lines trailing off the back and into the water. Poole used manual downriggers, small weights that look like miniature cannonballs, so he could control the depth at which the lures and hooks were suspended in the lake. Gene realized that those weights would have started to drag on the bottom as the boat moved into shallower water. The RCMP dive team was also at the lake looking for Poole. Gene pitched his idea to them during a lunch break on shore. He asked the divers to search the bottom around where the boat was found for anything that looked like drag marks made by little cannonballs. He told them to follow the tracks along the bottom and then mark the spot where they disappeared with a buoy at the surface.

Once the spot had been found and divers had deployed a buoy, the Ralstons built a small tower on shore using driftwood and flagging tape at the spot where the boat was found. They tried to make it as big and bright as possible so they could see it clearly from way out on the water. Gene and Sandy drove out into the middle of the lake and lined up the makeshift tower on shore with the buoy at the surface. Gene figured the boat had to have traveled along that line. They used their navigation program to extend another line based on the last GPS coordinates recorded by the device on Poole's boat. They found the body on the bottom of the lake not far from the intersection of those two lines.

I sometimes describe the Ralstons as having an uncanny knack for finding bodies. It's a way to suggest some kind of unusual connection to the dead, an extra sense for detecting corpses in water. I was drawn into their orbit because of that mystery at the heart of their story. The more time I spent with

Gene and Sandy, the easier it was to explain their remarkable track record in terms of knowledge, experience, and the stamina to endure stiff joints and long days on the water. They have a natural aptitude for the thousand skills required for underwater work, and they have spent an incomparable amount of time on searches. Describing their ability in practical terms doesn't diminish the mystery. It only shifts the frame. The magic is less in the how and more in the why. The Ralstons are exceptions in a rarefied field because they made an extraordinary investment of their own time and money.

CHAPTER TEN

The Path Not Taken

Not long after Gene and Sandy imaged Dennis Liva's long-lost boat on the bottom of Alouette Lake, a snowstorm blew in from the south and put a stop to the search for the day. The trees that lined the road through the rain forest next to the lake were so tall and grew so close to the pavement that the sky attenuated to a ribbon overhead. It felt like dusk, regardless of the time of day, when we drove through the provincial park. A couple of small, unassuming signs along the road read HORSE CROSSING in white letters on a brown background. Gene couldn't resist making a joke about the sign every time he noticed one. "I wonder if the horses know they're supposed to cross here," he said that afternoon on the drive back to Pete's place.

The conversation in the truck that afternoon turned to the pandemic. Our voices were muffled by masks. We had been listening to CBC Radio, a public news agency in Canada, every morning and evening in the truck. The number of cases of COVID-19 was rising again because of the emergence of new variants. The BC government had recently reinstated several lockdown policies, including shutting down gyms, churches, and indoor dining at restaurants. I saw signs on my drive out to Maple Ridge warning that BC was closed to nonessential travel. I got in the habit of backing into parking spaces to hide my Alberta license plate. I had heard stories about vehicles with out-of-province plates getting vandalized. The Ralstons were grateful they could keep their motor home at the Westra household.

"They probably won't let us back in the country because they're doing a lot better there," Sandy said.

"In the US?" I asked.

"In Idaho. All the restaurants are open. Bars are open," Sandy said.

We were in the back seat. Pete and Gene were upfront.

Pete told the Ralstons that his wife and in-laws wished they could have been better hosts. "It's just killing my family that they can't have you inside," he said. He asked the Ralstons if there was a particular drink that they could get for them. Gene liked brandy with ginger ale. Sandy asked if Pete had heard of Empress Gin. It was made on Vancouver Island with a type of flower blossom that turned the alcohol a brilliant shade of purple. She'd had it once on another search in Canada.

And then Sandy said that tonic water worked as a cure for both malaria and the coronavirus. Gene said that they didn't put quinine in tonic water anymore, or at least not in high enough concentrations to prevent malaria.

"It's anti-malarial and anti-covid," Sandy repeated. She sounded frustrated. The conversation ended in an awkward silence.

~~

Former president Donald Trump promoted hydroxychloroquine, a synthetic form of quinine, as a cure for the coronavirus in the early days of the pandemic, but that theory had been debunked pretty quickly. The idea persisted in conspiratorial corners of the internet. It's an appealing notion that a household remedy, something as benign and readily available as tonic water, can keep you safe from a new and deadly strain of virus.

By April 2021, 81 percent of Americans over the age of sixty-five had at least one dose of the vaccine. By October 2022, the CDC reported that 95 percent of Americans in that cohort had at least one shot. The Ralstons were a part of a small minority of people their age who didn't get vaccinated.

Gene and Sandy have graduate degrees in the biological sciences. Their disciplined approach to underwater search and recovery, and their ability to differentiate fact from conjecture out on the water, is a big reason for their success. I didn't understand how those contradictory elements coexisted, how they could identify as scientists in one context but then distrust science in another.

I asked Gene one afternoon over the phone why he and Sandy became so opposed to the vaccines for COVID-19. He told me that he discussed the issue with his niece, Nancy McQuiston, a nursing supervisor at a hospital in Idaho. The Ralstons respect her opinion, especially when it comes to their health. She was suspicious of the vaccines and had regularly shared information with Gene about potential risks and side effects.

I then asked Gene if he had any thoughts on why organizations like the CDC or the FDA would lie to the public about the safety of these treatments. "I guess you could put it into one word — money," he said. "And political support and those kinds of things." Gene saw the vaccine, and the vaccine mandates, as part of a conspiracy to enrich government bureaucrats and pharmaceutical executives. These same powerful groups colluded to squelch dissent, to discredit anyone questioning the narrative that the vaccines are safe and effective.

Gene told me a story about his former cardiologist who prescribed him a blood thinner that made him feel terrible. "My entire body was aching, and even after spending the night, a good night of rest in bed, I'd get up in the morning, I could hardly move," he said. Gene wanted to switch drugs, but the doctor assured him that it was doing more good than harm. Gene had noticed several photos in his doctor's office of him playing in a variety of golf tournaments. Some of them took place in tropical locations, like the Caribbean. The events were sponsored by the same company that made the blood thinner. "It's right there on the placard. And his walls were plastered with these pictures," Gene said. "And when you see little clues like that, you wonder. This guy was going on paid vacations for golfing all over the world." Gene read up about the drug online and discovered that muscle pain and fatigue were among the major side effects. He found a new cardiologist who took him off the drug. His symptoms improved within a week.

It was hard to argue with Gene's point that the pharmaceutical industry influences the medical system to make money, and that sometimes happens at the expense of people's health. I asked Gene how he and Sandy decided who to trust after they lost faith in the public institutions responsible for providing unbiased information about health. "That's a tough one to answer," he said. "It really is. I guess I trusted my nurse niece." He also relied on his instincts. "I'm suspicious. And being a biologist, I always question everything. Or a scientist, I should say, I question everything."

I was surprised by the Ralstons' perspective on the vaccine because of their rigorous and evidence-based approach to search and recovery. Gene and Sandy, however, felt that it was precisely because of their scientific training and outlook that they ended up rejecting the mainstream view. They were skeptical of the advice from public health institutions and so looked into the issue themselves. "We made that decision, day one, after learning it irreversibly alters your RNA, had never been tested for efficacy, and was rushed to market," Gene wrote to me in an email. I didn't try to debate him on the validity of the science. I had trusted the Canadian health authorities that reviewed the studies and then deemed the treatments not only safe and effective but also essential for minimizing the harm of the pandemic.

Even after learning more about what informed the Ralstons' decision not to get vaccinated, I still found it hard to make sense of their susceptibility to what I think can be fairly characterized as misinformation. I didn't understand what made them receptive to theories that I would have expected them to disregard given their scientific backgrounds. Gene and I did not spend much time discussing topics like the COVID-19 vaccine. We're on opposite sides of the political spectrum and plugged into different sources of information about the world. It's hard to talk about something when you don't have any common ground to stand on. We learned to move on.

The Ralstons returned to the Fraser River the next morning, April 11, 2021. Pete had the Sunday off. We were joined by one of his colleagues from the serious crimes unit at the Ridge Meadows RCMP. Nate Olson had short, dark hair and a small birthmark under one eye. He was keen to learn more about the sonar. He told Gene and Sandy about his metal detector on the drive to the boat launch.

Olson liked to search beaches and parks for lost treasures but had mostly found old nails and other souvenirs from the lumber industry's long history in the area. He found a silver ring once, which he gave to his daughter. Olson was excited to watch the Ralstons work with a similar but more powerful type of technology. Devices like metal detectors and side-scan sonars seemed to appeal the most to people with energetic imaginations, to those with an intuition that the world was full of secrets, that untold riches and artifacts lay in wait just below the surface of things.

The past Friday, the last time we were out on the Fraser, Pete asked the Ralstons to scan a section of the river near a pallet factory on the south bank a few miles downstream from the boat launch. He had received an unsolicited tip about the location of the missing plane by someone who had used a dowsing rod on a map of the river. The sonar registered only more blank river bottom, more dunes of sediment. Pete seemed a little embarrassed that he had asked the Ralstons to follow up on the tip. "Now at least we can say that we checked," he said.

Dowsing rods have been used for centuries to find, or at least to try to find, all manner of subterranean and submarine valuables. One of the primary goals was to locate freshwater sources underground so people knew where to dig a well. Proponents claimed that the technique could also locate precious metals, buried utility lines, and missing corpses. The rods were made from sundry materials, including tree branches and various kinds of metal. They could be pendulums made from wire wrapped around a coin or a small bottle of mercury at the end of a string. Dowsing was done in person or using a map. It was also known as divining, doodle-bugging, and water-witching. The dowser didn't direct the rods but rather channeled the

power of the spirit world to guide the rods toward the invisible
objective. The dowser was a medium, an intermediary, who had
cultivated a sensitivity to unseen forces. The American Society
of Dowsers has about two thousand members.

The Ralstons had encountered manifold dowsers, psychics,
and clairvoyants who claimed various mystical powers that
could direct them to the location of a missing person. Gene
and Sandy got frustrated when they were diverted from a carefully planned search grid to follow up on someone's hunch or
prophecy. I had noticed, however, that they were not immune
to magical thinking. The Ralstons wondered about the unlike-
lihood of some of their own recoveries. They were astonished,
for example, by how the body they found earlier that year had
held on to the ROV after the wrist slipped from the grabber
jaws. The scientific explanation, the stiffening of muscle tissue
postmortem, felt unsatisfying to them in the face of such an
improbable event.

The Fraser was calm that Sunday morning. It looked more
like a narrow lake than a river. The Ralstons started by scanning farther north into a gradual bend that arched between
the power lines and the concrete dock. Pete had a theory that
the current might have pushed the plane out of the main channel and then lodged it somewhere in the shallower water near
shore. It took all morning to cover the area with the sonar. The
closer we got to shore the more detritus — piles of gravel, logs,
and branches — cluttered the bottom. I noticed that Sandy was
smiling as she steered the boat. It was a subtle but persistent
expression. She looked relaxed, like she had found her rhythm
of how to handle the boat on the Fraser. I thought about what

John Zeman, the *Kathy G*'s veteran deckhand, had told me when I asked him why he thought the Ralstons devoted so much time to searches. "That seems to be their happy place," he said. Zeman had observed how they got into a kind of zone with Gene watching the screen and Sandy steering the boat. They were physically close, shoulders less than an inch or two from touching, and absorbed in individual but complementary tasks.

Pete had invited me over for dinner with the Ralstons and his family the night before. The snowstorm that had surprised us on Alouette Lake never reached his house in Maple Ridge. We sat on his patio in the evening sun and ate fried chicken from a nearby take-out place. I learned that Pete and his wife met at a Christian university in Hamilton, Ontario. She played for the varsity volleyball team, and he played for the soccer team. Pete got a job in a group home for people with developmental disabilities after he graduated with a bachelor of arts degree. He had never planned on becoming a police officer. It was some of his wife's relatives who were police officers, an uncle and two cousins, who introduced him to the idea. Pete told me that joining the RCMP had been a means to earn a better income so they could start a family. I looked him up online when I got back to my hotel later that night and learned that he had been given an award for valor by the provincial government a few years back. He was part of a small team of officers who had risked their lives to rescue hostages from a group of armed assailants during a home invasion.

The Westras' seven-year-old daughter was on the move all evening. She whizzed by us, doing laps around the yard, first on a push scooter and then riding on the shoulders of the exchange student from Thailand who was living with them. She steered the galloping teenager by turning his head with her hands. Their son, an almost-teenager, made only a brief appearance. He was tall and had a sharp triangle of blond hair that covered one side of his face. He stuck close to Pete, sitting on the arm of his deck chair, when he joined us outside.

Margie and Luke, Pete's in-laws, looked like they were a decade or so younger than the Ralstons. They had a million questions for Gene and Sandy. Gene answered with long, detail-rich stories. Sandy chimed in to correct him about names and dates.

One of the stories Gene told that night was about their search on Dubawnt Lake, which is only a hundred miles from the Arctic Circle. They got a call in August 2013 from the wife of a man from Detroit who had gone missing, along with his father, while on a fishing trip on the remote lake. It took two floatplanes to transport the sonar gear and ROV from an airport in Flin Flon, a town at the end of the highway in northern Saskatchewan, to Dubawnt Lake. July was the only month of the year when you could safely travel to and from the lake. Any earlier and the weather was too dangerous and unpredictable. Any later and you ran the risk of getting stranded until the following summer. The Ralstons had only managed to complete a few hours of searching before they were radioed to get off the lake and pack up in a hurry. A big storm was brewing. All the equipment had to fit in one plane for the impromptu return flight.

At some point that evening, Pete and his wife had carried a gas fireplace from the side of the house and set it up in the middle of our circle of chairs. Margie, who took pride in mothering guests, had wrapped Sandy in several flannel blankets. We all listened to Gene, the reflection of the flames flickering in our eyes, as he described the sensation of bouncing off rough water in an overladen single-engine airplane. He said the plane felt like a stone getting skipped across the surface of the lake as the pilot struggled to get enough lift to take off.

The Ralstons soaked up the hospitality. They were clearly running on fumes, though. Sandy struggled to keep her eyes open not long after we finished dinner. Her head would droop forward and then snap back up only to fall forward again. The vibrancy of Pete's family was a striking contrast with the worn-out-ness of the Ralstons. It was, in many ways, an unfair comparison. Gene and Sandy were living out of their motor home and had been up early and out on the water running the sonar for three days by then. They had on the same set of rumpled clothes that they had worn on the boat that day.

But the comparison between the liveliness of the Westras and the tiredness of the Ralstons that night hinted at a more significant difference: the one between a life on the road and a life rooted at home. Pete's family, three generations under one roof, was a pronounced example of the path not taken by the Ralstons.

At the end of the night, Gene stopped me before I got in my truck to drive back to the hotel. "This is what it's all about," he said, holding my gaze. He didn't want me to miss the significance of the moment, to miss how much a night like that in the company of new friends meant to him and Sandy.

We drove back to the dock by the boat launch at around 12:30 PM for a break. Sandy left to see if she could find a bathroom. She took slow, careful steps up the steep gangplank that connected the dock to the industrial lot at the top of the riverbank. Gene had helped zip up her fleece jacket earlier that morning in front of Pete's house. Her hands, the joints swollen with arthritis, hung at her sides as he fit the small interlocking pieces of metal together.

Olson sat on the gunnel of the boat with his feet on the dock and brought up a map on his phone of the missing plane's flight path. He pitched Gene on a new theory. Olson had been on duty the day the plane crashed. He worked through the night, helping to coordinate the massive initial search to try to rescue the missing pilots.

The flight path, represented by a blue line on the map, continued straight over the middle of the river from the dock. The point of impact with the power lines was depicted by a gold star. Olson wondered if the plane could have continued upriver a considerable distance after hitting the wires. He thought it was possible that the tail of the plane clipped the wires. The aircraft could then have traveled for several hundred more feet in the air before crashing into the river.

"As far as I'm concerned today, you're the boss," Gene told him. He was happy to try something new. After two and a half days, the Ralstons had searched the entire river, from the south bank to the north bank, and from the dock all the way up to the power lines. They had also covered a significant part of the middle of the river for another mile and a half downstream. They were running short of places to look.

"I don't think it hurts," Olson said.

"It's got to be somewhere," Gene agreed.

I spent the next few hours leaned against the doorframe to the pilothouse, watching the monitor over Gene's shoulder. The uniform ridges of the river bottom marched down the screen, one after the next. The trees lining the riverbank had recently started to bud, creating an almost imperceptible sheath of green over the scraggly limbs and branches. We found no sign of the airplane upriver from the power lines.

"How far to the bunny?" Sandy asked after they had ruled out Olson's theory. Something about the object had been nagging her since they first scanned it two days ago. It was roughly the right size and located on the bottom at about where 280th Street met the river, which was the landmark given by the witness.

"Not far. You want to do the bunny?" Gene said.

It took three passes and about half an hour, but the Ralstons got another clear image of the cylindrical object with a bunny-shaped shadow. It lay parallel with the flow of the current. And it was big, long and wide enough to be a fuselage or set of wings. The array of shadows cast on the bottom dwarfed the object itself.

We all stared at the shape on the screen in silence. And then, after a minute or so of gently bobbing along on the river, Gene said, "I don't think it's an airplane." He sounded discouraged. No one responded. He rubbed Sandy's shoulders. "You done?" he asked.

She nodded.

And then Gene took a deep breath through his nose. He raised his shoulders and lifted his body up and off the back of the chair. He let the air go in one long, exaggerated sigh and deflated back down into a hunch over the monitor.

"Bummer, bummer, bummer, bummer, bummer," he said. It felt like the end of the search for the plane and two pilots. The anticlimactic conclusion seemed reminiscent of their search for the aircraft in the Ohio River in 2004. Back then they had imaged something that looked a lot like a fuselage, but the water was too swift and murky for the divers to confirm whether it was the airplane and tomb of Buck Bellingham.

The tide was out when we got back to the dock. The water level had receded to reveal a soupy layer of muck at the bottom of the concrete ramp. So we had to go back out on the river and keep searching. It took a couple hours for the water to rise up enough that Olson thought he had a fighting chance to get the boat out of the river. The front tires of the truck spun on the pavement and started to smoke while the back ones turned uselessly in the mud, but Olson managed to drag the *Kathy G* out of the Fraser. It was after 6:00 PM. We had been on the river for more than ten hours.

CHAPTER ELEVEN

A Body in Water Tends to Stay in Water

We went back to Alouette the next morning, a Monday. The mountain lake was a welcome change from the drab atmosphere of the Fraser River. The water looked like one enormous pane of glass. I could see the outlines of individual trees that lined the tops of the mountains in the reflection off the lake. It was hard to tell what was up and what was down, like I could step off the end of the dock and fall through sky instead of sink in water. The air was cold. The sun felt warm.

Gene squeegeed the mud off the windshield of the *Kathy G* that the truck tires had kicked up the night before. The plan that day was to look for Dennis Liva. The Ralstons heard from the Tyner family last night that they had left their ranch in Wyoming and started the twenty-hour drive to Nicola Lake. They were going to spend the night somewhere in Montana and then try to cross the border the following day at Osoyoos, a lakeside town on the Canadian side. The Tyners were taking a chance that they would meet a sympathetic border agent and be allowed into the country.

Gene told me that Richard, the missing cowboy's father, had applied to the Canada Border Services Agency on the grounds of compassionate entry, but was denied. The border had closed to nonessential travel at the end of March 2020 as a precaution against the spread of coronavirus. The regulations for the closure included an exemption for people to attend a funeral or visit a dying spouse or relative, but not to search for a missing family member.

The Ralstons qualified as essential workers and had been to Canada on several searches since the border closed. The Tyners planned to use the Ralstons and their search for Ben in Nicola Lake as justification for getting into Canada. They would make their case to the border agent that they were needed in Merritt, the small city west of Nicola Lake, to provide gas and other resources to the Ralstons to keep their boat and the search going. The gist of the Tyners' strategy was to argue that they were essential to the essential workers. An FBI agent was going to meet the family at the border to try to bolster their chances of making it across.

Jen, Richard, and Jack, who was three years younger than his brother, had not been to the Nicola Valley since the winter of 2019, when they arrived soon after Ben was reported missing. They had stayed for close to a month back then, helping with the initial search-and-rescue mission and then with the homicide investigation. The Tyners returned to Wyoming in mid-February and brought Ben's truck, horse trailer, three horses, and two dogs back home with them.

Richard, a retired airline pilot, had never stopped trying to find his son. He was determined not to let the investigation go cold. He enlisted the support of a US senator from Wyoming, who helped to get the FBI involved. Richard had been in regular contact with the RCMP officers and FBI agents investigating the murder. And then, on January 26, 2021, the second anniversary of the day Ben vanished, the Tyners announced a $15,000 (CAD) reward for any information that led them to their son and to the arrest of those responsible for his death. John Liu, the owner of the Nicola Ranch where Ben worked, said he would match that sum. The total of the reward was now $30,000 (CAD).

The short video the Tyners made to announce the reward was heart wrenching. The three of them sat on a couch in their living room. Photos of Ben hung on the wall behind them. He was on horseback in one photo and in a canoe in another. He had a round face that was often half covered by a woolly mustache or scraggly beard.

Ben's disappearance had been international news. I'd learned more about him from the many newspaper stories published in early 2019. He was well over six feet tall and weighed more than two hundred pounds. A family friend of the Tyners told a reporter that Ben was the archetype of an American cowboy: tough and dependable but also mannerly and shy.

Richard read a statement in the video from a piece of paper. Jen held his hand. The brim of Jack's baseball hat was pulled low over his eyes. Richard talked about his son, about how Ben had grown up around horses, cattle, and dogs and gone on to study animal production in university. He worked for cattle operations in Montana, Idaho, New Mexico, and Russia. I didn't know much about what it meant to be a cowboy in the twenty-first century, but it seemed like a job that was also a way of life. "He was always going to be a gentle giant with an incredible bear hug that made you feel needed, wanted, and loved," Richard said. "To have to live with Ben's loss is the most painful, excruciating thing ever. The loss we feel is immeasurable." Richard read the statement quickly — the syllables of some words ran together and sounded muffled — in an effort to get to the end without breaking down.

Even though Ben had traveled extensively for work, he was obviously tightly bound to his parents and brother. They were a close family, a team of four trying to get by with three. "Our hope is that we'll be able to find Ben and be able to determine what happened," Richard said.

It was not uncommon for Gene and Sandy to field requests to search a lake or river that was somewhere in the vicinity of where a missing person was last seen. They usually declined to take on these types of long-shot searches. The Ralstons had learned that their efforts were better put to use on the cases where there was solid evidence that the person was in fact in the water. They sometimes made exceptions for homicides and for cases that involved missing children. The Ralstons were more willing to take a chance that they would get lucky if it meant they could play a role in serving justice or help a family reeling from the loss of a child. "There's just something that inspires me to really do the absolute best, which we always do anyway, but you want to go that extra mile for those two types of cases," Gene told me.

When the Ralstons got the call to search for the teenagers on Nicola Lake in the spring of 2013, they had just gotten home from a trip to Colorado. They had tried to find Dylan Redwine, a thirteen-year-old boy who disappeared under suspicious circumstances in November 2012. Dylan had been visiting his father, Mark Redwine, for the Thanksgiving weekend. The Ralstons had no clue where to look except that the prime suspect, Dylan's father, Mark, lived a few hundred yards from a lake and was not thought to have had access to a boat. So Gene and Sandy scanned all the places on the lake where someone could have dumped a body into the water from shore. They told me they were going to try a similar approach to find Ben Tyner in Nicola Lake. They would follow the contours of the shoreline looking for a cliff or sections of the bottom that were deep enough to trap a body for the past two years. Some of Dylan's remains were eventually found on land. His father was sentenced in October 2021 to forty-eight years in prison for the murder of his son.

~

Pete drove the empty boat trailer up to the parking lot above the launch on Alouette and then walked back down the hill on a dirt footpath through the rain forest. His black jacket had Velcro patches on the shoulders where he could stick a variety of police badges, but he had so far left them blank. I think he wanted to avoid drawing any more attention from bystanders about the odd-looking boat with the steel torpedo.

Pete stepped on the gunnel of the *Kathy G* with one foot, held on to the boom and mast near the bow, and pushed off the dock with his other foot. Gene steered toward the middle of the lake and waited for Pete to find his spot behind the pilothouse before hitting the throttle. The front of the *Kathy G* flicked up with the initial thrust of the propeller. You had to hang on to something when Gene accelerated or you risked falling backward and off the boat. The *Kathy G* leveled out again as it gained speed and started to plane on the water. We shot across Alouette Lake at thirty-five miles per hour.

"The image in the water is almost clearer than above the water. How is that possible?" Pete shouted into the wind and grinned. He was proud of this area, of his home. He had told us all about his favorite hikes and other outdoor adventures near Maple Ridge.

"That's unreal!" Gene yelled back. The flawless water and sunny weather had made the crew of the *Kathy G* almost giddy this morning. Sandy had the hood of her oversized fleece jacket pulled up over her head, but I imagined she was smiling at the stunning view along with the rest of us.

And then I saw something curious out in the middle of the

lake. A single log stood straight up, reaching fifteen to twenty feet out of the water like some kind of rough-hewn wooden monolith. Gene slowed down so we could take a closer look.

"Well, you just messed it up," Sandy said to Gene. The waves from our wake had propagated out in all directions, ruining the perfect inverted image of mountains and sky.

The depth sounder read 275 feet. The tree, which looked like all the branches had been hacked off, was suspended vertically in the blue-green water. One tiny shoot with flat needle-like leaves sprouted out sideways about halfway to the top. Pete gently pushed the cedar log. It rotated slowly but stayed upright. It seemed somehow caught between sinking and floating. Maybe the lake had risen and eroded the soil away beneath the root ball. A tangled mass of wood at the bottom could have weighed the log down enough to hold it vertical in the lake. But it had been cut with a diagonal slash across the top, and all the branches were gone. It was unlikely the root ball would still be intact. It must have been some kind of unlikely geometry that held the log aloft and prevented it from tipping over and lying flat like the other driftwood we had seen on the lake. It made for a peculiar sight regardless of the forces at play beneath the surface. The reflection off the water made it hard to see how far down the monolith went.

Archimedes, a scientist from ancient Greece, first outlined the physical laws that govern buoyancy more than two thousand years ago in a treatise called *On Floating Bodies*. He observed that the upward buoyant force exerted on an object immersed in a fluid is equal to the weight of the volume of fluid that the object displaces. Another way to think of the law is that objects that are more dense than the fluid sink. Those that are less dense, float. The human body is close to the same density as water, which is what makes swimming so pleasurable. It's a vacation from gravity.

Gene once tested Archimedes's principle in his shop next to the house in Kuna. He ran the experiment with a concrete block, a bucket of water, and a fish scale. The block weighed around forty pounds in the air and only six in the water. "It's a pretty graphic example when you actually do it yourself," he told me. It was not that Gene distrusted Archimedes, or ancient Greek scientists in general, but rather that he liked to see how things worked for himself. And the weight of a body in water is a common source of confusion on searches. People tend to assume that if the person is big and heavy then they would sink to the bottom and never resurface. The average adult drowning victim weighs between eight and sixteen pounds in water. Body composition, the ratio of muscle to fat, affects the weight of a person underwater, but the gases produced during decomposition drastically alter the density of a body and can bring any corpse, regardless of weight, back to the surface.

It didn't take Gene long to discover the blind spot in the scientific research regarding what happens to a corpse underwater. "I got the idea early on that, well, somebody needs to do this," he told me. "And it's going to be a really, really, really long-term project. It's not something that you're just going to go out there and do it for two or three days." Body farms, the research facilities that study human decomposition, focus on the decay process in terrestrial ecosystems. The same kind of comprehensive studies but done underwater have so far proved prohibitively complex and expensive.

Gene saw an opportunity in 2002 to launch his experiment after reading a newspaper story about two men who were missing and presumed to have drowned in Crescent Lake, Oregon.

One had been on the bottom for two years, the other for a year and a half. Gene drafted a letter to the Klamath County sheriff. He outlined, as tactfully as possible, how he would first find the bodies of the two men but then leave them in place so he could return every six months and scan them again with the sonar. Gene explained the value of learning how the sonar image of a body changes as the body goes through the stages of decomposition. He wanted to know what to look for on the monitor if they were searching for someone who had drowned ten years ago versus ten months ago versus ten days ago.

Before Gene had the chance to mail the letter, they got a call about a search on Odell Lake, which was ten miles from Crescent Lake. After they found the missing man on the first day, the local sheriff asked them to search for another two corpses in a nearby lake. "By the way, we've got two guys just down the hill from here," Gene said, paraphrasing the sheriff. "We'd sure like to get them out of there." The Ralstons found both men in Crescent Lake. They were recovered by divers.

And so Gene never sent his letter. He never got to create the world's first and only deep-water body farm. Instead, he and Sandy have had to learn search by search, recovery by recovery. They have not discovered any hard-and-fast rules for what a body would look like on the sonar given how long it has been in the water. They have cultivated a sensitivity, an internal radar of sorts, for shapes and shadows that look like they don't belong at the bottom of a lake.

Another key question for underwater searchers, besides what to watch out for on the sonar, is if and when a corpse will float back to the surface. The decay process creates gases that make a body more buoyant. The time it takes to resurface depends on water temperature and depth. Gene and Sandy provide a handout at their training seminars with some rough guidelines. If the water is cold, less than forty degrees, then the corpse will not resurface unless the water warms up. A body will rise in two to three weeks in water at fifty degrees. If it's warmer than eighty, then the refloat time is measured in hours, not days. People who drown in deep water, below a hundred feet, may never surface because the pressure of the water pins the body in place.

Robert Teather, in his textbook about underwater recovery, warned against trying to predict an interval for when a body will develop enough buoyancy to float. "The variables are many and the possibilities endless," he wrote. Some of those mitigating factors include when and what type of food the missing person last consumed. Foods high in carbohydrates, like beer and hot dogs, produce gases faster. A person's overall health also influences the volume and type of bacteria on and inside the body.

It takes an amazing degree of coordination to keep the human body in good working order. It takes next to no time for it all to fall to ruin. The body decomposes from the inside out and from the outside in. Autolysis, a term derived from the Greek words for "self" and "splitting," begins at the moment of cellular death. Cells rely on a type of protein called enzymes to help with the heavy lifting of molecular work. The mechanisms that keep these potent chemical reagents in check go offline when the cell is starved of oxygen. Legions of enzymes are set loose. They break down cell membranes and spill the contents of individual cells and entire organs. The first sign of autolysis, a whitish appearance of the corneas, happens within hours of death. The body's final act, the breaking back down into elemental parts, is baked into each cell from the beginning.

Billions of bacteria make a home inside and on the surface of the body. They outnumber human cells ten to one. We have microbiomes in our gut, lungs, mouth, nose, skin — pretty much anywhere that comes into regular contact with the outside world. These bacterial civilizations coexist with their human hosts for mutual gain in healthy individuals. They're set free after death.

Teather, maybe unsurprisingly as a career police officer, compared bacteria in the body to prisoners in jail. When all the guards (the immune system) walk off the job, the prisoners riot and burn the jail to the ground. His analogy missed the helpful role that bacteria play in human health. They break down many types of proteins, lipids, and carbohydrates into nutrients that the body is then able to absorb and put to use. Microbes also produce beneficial compounds, like vitamins and anti-inflammatories.

But Teather was not wrong about the rioting. The stomach is home to the most populous microbiome. The mucus that protects the stomach lining from getting dissolved by gastric juices, like hydrochloric acid, is no longer secreted after death. Bacteria seep out of the gut and encounter new sources of sustenance. Putrefaction, the consumption of tissue by bacteria, begins within an hour of death. The by-product of bacterial metabolism is gas, which causes the abdomen, and other microbial hot spots in the body, to inflate. The makeup of bacteria is unique to each person, and therefore so is the profile of putrefactive gases generated during decomposition — one last expression of our individuality. These gases include varying concentrations of hydrogen sulfide, ammonia, carbon dioxide, and methane. Advanced stages of putrefaction can be seen in as little as twenty-four to thirty-six hours in the heat of summer on land. The body bloats and swells until something gives way and the gases are released.

John Wallace is a professor at Millersville University in Pennsylvania and a forensic aquatic entomologist, which means he is one of a handful of people in North America qualified to help police on cases with evidence involving aquatic ecosystems. He once helped exonerate a man who had already served fifteen years in jail for the murder of a three-year-old girl by proving that the marks on her body had been made by crayfish and not human teeth. Police later found and arrested the real killer.

Wallace told me about another case he worked on in which a woman had been murdered, chained to a pair of seventy-pound cinder blocks, and then dropped into a lake in Michigan. "And so she went to the bottom. I don't remember how deep this lake was, but she did end up floating to the surface. And that was primarily because of the gases produced during decomposition," Wallace said. Gene and Sandy have never witnessed a body surface, but they have heard similar stories about the surprising power of the buoyant forces generated by putrefactive gases. Put in terms of Archimedes's principle, bloat increases the volume of a human body and thereby decreases its density.

Autolysis and putrefaction don't take place in a vacuum. Scavenging, which is called anthropophagy when the carrion is a human body, is the third primary mechanism by which bodies break down and decay. Wallace called the cohort of creatures that feed on carrion in a particular ecosystem the players. You can't predict the duration of decomposition, whether it takes place on land or in water, unless you know all the players involved. Most people think that a forensic entomologist helps police figure out how long it has been since the person died, the postmortem interval. "What we really do is determine time of colonization," Wallace said. And in most cases, at least on land, time of colonization coincides with time of death because the critters involved are so ubiquitous.

The team of players on land is big, diverse, and organized. Insects and animals like blowflies, flesh flies, rove beetles, and vultures have evolved to feed on carrion. "They need dead things," Wallace said. Fish and aquatic insects, by contrast, can eat dead things, but they don't rely on them as their only source of food. They have lots of other ways to get by. The appearance of carrion in a lake or river — maybe a caribou falls through the ice in early spring — is such a rare occurrence that aquatic insects and fish have had little incentive to specialize in that type of food.

I asked Wallace about the players on the bottom of a lake like Alouette. He listed several species of fish and insects that likely live in that kind of ecosystem but explained that the lack of sunlight at the lower depths means few nutrients are available to support a large and varied population. "That doesn't mean there's nothing that lives there. It just means that maybe there's a lot that's excluded. And if you start excluding the players, then you change the rate of decomposition," he said.

Wallace mentioned a colleague, Gail Anderson, and her work observing the decay of pig carcasses on the bottom of the ocean off the coast of Vancouver Island. Anderson is also a forensic entomologist and works at Simon Fraser University. She has used a deep-sea monitoring station to observe how pigs, which are an effective substitute for human cadavers, decompose at various depths on the ocean floor.

You can watch footage from one of her studies on YouTube. The short video is aptly called *Dead Pig Forensic Experiment*. The carcass was lowered a thousand feet to the seafloor on a small platform with a metal grate to protect it from large predators. The two-minute video condenses a span of nine days. The pig is encased in a febrile mass of sea lice by the end of the first day. The swarm of inch-long crustaceans make quick work of the carcass, reducing it to a pile of white bones in less than a week. The video concludes with footage of a curious octopus that threads its tentacles through the grate to investigate the scattered remnants of a pig skeleton.

"And so she's the only one that's done that," Wallace said. And that's for a coastal ocean ecosystem, which is teeming with players compared with a deep, freshwater lake. "So you've got this black box still, but we can speculate." Someone has yet to run the type of study that Gene outlined in the letter he never sent to the Klamath County sheriff more than two decades ago.

Water is the most dense at thirty-nine degrees. Warmer than that and it becomes less dense. Colder than the thirty-nine-degree threshold and water again becomes less dense, which is why ice floats and forms from the top down on a lake instead of from the bottom up. This unique property of water is what allows aquatic plants and animals to survive under the ice in cold environments. The bottom of a deep lake like Alouette, which is part of a mountain watershed in a northern climate, stays at about the temperature of a fridge. "I suspect at five hundred feet that water temperature doesn't change a whole heck of a lot," Wallace said. Water that is thirty-nine degrees sinks and stays at the bottom year-round. Temperature is like the volume knob for the metabolism of bacteria and insects. Turn it up and these critters feed and multiply exponentially faster. Turn it down and both scavenging and putrefaction are inhibited.

Teather outlined in his book how most of the gases produced by bacteria during putrefaction are highly compressible and soluble in water. So not only is the initial volume of gas produced in deep water diminished because bacteria become sluggish in the cold, but the gas that is formed might also be dissolved and carried away by the surrounding water. "Bearing this in mind, it is easy to understand that depth has a great effect on the time to refloat," Teather wrote. "It is believed (but not proven) that bodies that come to rest in depths greater than two hundred feet will not refloat."

That number, based on the Ralstons' experience, is more like one hundred feet. And that's not the only discrepancy between what Gene and Sandy have learned on the job and what the conventional wisdom has to say about decomposition in deep water.

Rigor mortis, the stiffening of muscles, begins hours after death. Muscle cells contract and harden when they run out of ATP, the energy molecule. The stiffness is gradually undone by bacteria during the putrefaction phase. The march of rigor unfolds over a period of about thirty-six hours at room temperature. It's thought to proceed in a similar way at the bottom of a lake, except slower because of the cold.

That assumption, however, doesn't ring true for the Ralstons. "In our experience, they've always been pretty doggone stiff," Gene told me. He estimated that he and Sandy have had to personally handle more than half the bodies they have imaged with sonar, so a conservative sample size of doggone-stiff bodies would be sixty. The corpses would have been found at various depths and water temperatures. The amount of time in the water also varied considerably, from a matter of days to several years. "I don't ever remember recovering somebody where it wasn't difficult to get their arms and legs squeezed together enough to get them into a body bag," Gene told me. He would be the first to admit that his observations about rigor mortis in water are more anecdotal than scientific, but it's still a striking difference to note. The Ralstons have unparalleled firsthand experience with the decomposition of corpses in freshwater lakes and rivers. They have seen it all.

I called Gail Anderson to talk about her work on pigs in the ocean. She told me about another experiment where they placed the carcasses on the bottom of a glacial fjord. It was an intolerable environment for most critters because the oxygen levels were extremely low. "It just sat for months and months. It got covered with a film. I'm sure if you tried to pick it up, it would have been pretty slimy," she said. Anderson would turn on the deep-sea camera over the pig whenever she had a free moment, which was sometimes in the middle of the night. "So I would come on at two in the morning, anytime I was awake. I would put my camera on and see what was going on." She said it was like watching paint dry, no observable changes from one day to the next and then one month to the next. But then the currents shifted, and the oxygen levels in the water suddenly shot up. She saw a fish nosing around the pig. And shortly after the fish arrived, a cloud of invertebrates stormed onto the scene and skeletonized the carcass in short order.

I asked Anderson if a corpse could theoretically be preserved forever if the water was deep enough and cold enough. She told me about a chemical process that sometimes takes place in wet environments during putrefaction whereby fatty tissue is transformed into a soaplike substance called adipocere. The waxy tissue is inedible for bacteria and scavengers. Saponification is one of the few ways, like getting frozen in ice or mummified in a desert environment, by which a body is preserved in perpetuity.

Anderson told me about the tragedy of the *Kater Radez I*, a motorboat carrying Albanian refugees that sank in the Mediterranean Sea in March 1997. The boat was rammed by an Italian warship late at night and then sank swiftly. Only 34 of the 120 people aboard survived. Many vanished along with the boat.

A marine engineering company used a remotely operated submarine to find the wreck. They discovered it lying flat on a sandy seafloor at a depth of twenty-six hundred feet. They spotted two bodies near the ship. They were completely skeletonized four months after the incident. The boat was brought back to the surface and towed to a nearby port on October 18, seven months after it sank.

A team of experts was assembled to identify the bodies. The group consisted of forensic pathologists, forensic anthropologists, a forensic odontologist, and autopsy technicians. They were shocked by what they discovered in the cargo holds of the boat. "With great surprise, most of the victims were in good condition," read a 2012 report about the *Kater Radez I* published in the *International Journal of Legal Medicine*. It took the team three days to remove all fifty-two corpses (twenty-eight women and twenty-four men) from the boat.

The refugees had attempted the crossing to start a new life in a new country. They wore multiple layers of heavy clothing, which protected most of the surface area of their bodies from the smaller scavengers, like mollusks and crustaceans, that could still find a way into the cargo holds. The forensic pathologists noted that some bodies were almost perfectly preserved. Most of the corpses showed signs of decay only where tissue was not protected by clothing. The water was thirty-nine degrees on the bottom. The pressure, eighty-one atmospheres. "Initial adipocere formation (soft with a greasy consistency) appeared on most covered areas of the bodies, explaining the preservation," the report read.

The emergence of adipocere is hard to predict. Saponification requires moisture, some kind of protective barrier from scavengers, and a period of several months, but the chemical process doesn't unfold every time all those variables are in place. I asked Gene if he had ever found a body that had turned to soap. The Ralstons are often surprised by the relatively good condition of the corpses they find, but he couldn't recall if they had ever encountered adipocere. It's hard to register those kinds of observations in the heat of the moment when the priority is to secure the body and get it to shore.

In late June 2013, the Ralstons were several days into their search for Sid Neville, a thirty-five-year-old man who drowned a few weeks earlier, when they scanned one of the sharpest images of a corpse they have ever captured with the sonar. The body was under 570 feet of water in François Lake, BC, and matched the dimensions of the missing man, who was more than six feet tall. Neville had drowned while fishing with his nephew. A storm suddenly swept across the lake and capsized the boat. He helped his nephew climb up onto the overturned hull but then slipped below the surface.

Gene and Sandy reported back to the family, including Sid's widow, Marley Neville, about what they had found. The couple had been married for thirteen days when Neville disappeared. The Ralstons and the family were camping together by the lake. Gene and Sandy showed them the sonar image but expressed caution that they had not yet confirmed that it was in fact Neville. Gene told me that it was hard not to feel optimistic, though.

The Ralstons' ROV has five hundred feet of umbilical cable, and so it couldn't reach far enough down to retrieve the body. The family had to hire a commercial underwater team. It took the ROV operator a couple of days to arrive. Gene and Sandy took him and his robot out on the *Kathy G.* The Ralstons watched the video feed over the operator's shoulder as the robot approached the body from the feet. It took somewhere between five and ten minutes of careful scrutiny with the ROV before they realized that they had the wrong guy. Most of the body was relatively intact. Then they saw what looked like a small branch lying across his chest. "Wait a minute, that's a long arm bone,"

Gene said, telling me the story of the recovery. Neville had been underwater for less than a month, nowhere near long enough for that degree of decomposition in such deep water. "He was in remarkable shape," Gene said of the body they would later learn belonged to John Mowat, a thirty-three-year-old man who had drowned twenty-nine years earlier.

"It was difficult to go back and tell the family that it wasn't him — devastating," Gene said. He compared the feeling to what he guessed a police officer would experience when knocking at the door of a family home to relay the news that their teenage son or daughter had died in a car accident. "It's like all hope was lost at that point," he said.

The Ralstons spent close to a month on François Lake that summer on two different trips. They returned again the next summer and spent two more weeks searching the lake. They found two fishing rods that belonged to Neville, but not Neville. I asked Gene why he and Sandy kept going back, why they spent so much time on that search. Two and a half years before he drowned, Neville had been working at the local sawmill when it exploded and burned to the ground. Gene told me about how Neville had escaped but then ran back into the burning building to help rescue his friends and coworkers. He was severely burned and spent weeks in the hospital undergoing surgeries for skin grafts. Neville seemed like the type of person you wanted to help, Gene said. The Ralstons became close with his family. "We get attached to a lot of families, but there just seemed to be something about this family and we still stay in contact with them," he said.

Sandy told me about how when Marley was aboard she would often pester them with variations on the same question: *Have you found him yet?* Sandy said she would have found that extremely irritating coming from anyone else, but somehow from Marley, or Bob as they called her, it helped to lighten the mood. "A sweetheart of a lady," Gene said. "I mean, I just, I could just hug her to death."

Back in the spring of 2021, the Ralstons had talked a lot about François Lake and Sid Neville after finding Dennis Liva's boat on the bottom of Alouette. The similar timelines, the duration of the bodies on the bottom, was likely what had kept that particular search front and center in their minds. John Mowat drowned on July 13, 1984. The Ralstons imaged him in June 2013, so twenty-nine years later. Dennis Liva drowned in the summer of 1974, almost forty-seven years before they imaged his boat. Mowat's body had decayed at a glacial pace. The sonar image featured the same telltale contours of someone who had drowned weeks, not decades, previously. I think it was their experience on François Lake that made the Ralstons so hopeful that Liva might appear on the monitor in the *Kathy G* with the same startling degree of resolution.

It's really anyone's guess, however, what kind of shape a body will be in after almost five decades on the bottom of a cold, deep lake. "The fate of human remains in water is not well understood," Anderson wrote to introduce one of her research papers on how decomposition unfolds on the seafloor.

CHAPTER TWELVE

A Body at Rest Tends to Stay at Rest

Robert Teather wrote *The Encyclopedia of Underwater Investigations* for public safety divers, the people who work with the police to find evidence and corpses in water. The book included an entire chapter about postmortem physiology. It's crucial for these divers to understand how the human body decays because they're often the first to arrive at a potential crime scene. They need to know the difference between natural decomposition and any injury or artifact that is a sign of something criminal.

The sights and smells of putrefaction often inspire a deep-seated sense of revulsion. It's hard not to react, but that's precisely the job of public safety divers. It's up to them to report on submerged bodies in detail and with objectivity. Teather coached his readers to "look beyond the sometimes horrific appearance caused by nature" by reminding them that decay is a natural stage in the cycle of life. Even scavengers, Teather wrote, play an honorable role by speeding the process up and minimizing the spread of bacteria.

Something about the care that Teather took in his book to guide and counsel his colleagues deepened my appreciation for the different ways that the Ralstons have to think about corpses. Like public safety divers, they rely on a detailed understanding of how a body behaves like an inanimate object in the water.

And searches can sometimes take on the feel of a treasure hunt or a quest to solve a mystery. But Gene and Sandy develop close bonds with the family of the missing person and learn all about who, instead of what, they're trying to find.

Mary Roach wrote about the dual nature of corpses in her book *Stiff*, which is about the manifold ways that human cadavers have contributed to advances in medicine and other fields. The dead of science, Roach wrote, are always strangers. Anonymity is a precondition for the doctors and scientists who work with and study corpses. "I would not want to watch an experiment, no matter how interesting or important, that involved the remains of someone I knew and loved," she wrote. "I could not, emotionally, separate that cadaver from the person it recently was. One's own dead are more than cadavers, they are place holders for the living. They are a focus, a receptacle, for emotions that no longer have one."

The historian Thomas Laqueur worked to answer the seemingly simple question of why bodies matter in his book *The Work of the Dead: A Cultural History of Mortal Remains*. Laqueur sets his book up as a challenge to the ancient Greek philosopher Diogenes and his argument that corpses are no more valuable than a worn-out piece of furniture. Diogenes told his friends that in the event of his death, they should toss his still-warm body over the city walls to be devoured by wild animals without ceremony or delay.

We can respect the logic of Diogenes's argument, Laqueur wrote. It rings true, at least in a superficial way. We understand on a rational level that whatever it was that was so invaluable about the body — the person, soul, spirit, consciousness — has departed or evaporated or been extinguished. And yet for all of human history, we have cared for the dead. "Some irresistible

power of the imagination, independent of any particular religious beliefs, blinds us to the cold reality of what a corpse really
is," Laqueur wrote.

And that cold reality is that a lifeless body is no more, or no
less, than an assemblage of organic tissue on its way to becoming dirt and then dust. The human instinct to honor the dead
runs deeper than any of the spiritual justifications offered
throughout the millennia. We are compelled by what Laqueur
described as "deep structures of intuition and feeling" to care
for the dead.

The authors of a study published in the *Journal of Cognition
and Culture* in 2015 examined the mortuary rituals of fifty-seven
cultures, which were determined to make up a representative
sample of contemporary human societies. Their results sided
with Laqueur and not Diogenes. The majority of the rituals in
the study, more than 90 percent, included some way for people
to view or touch the body. Corpses were washed, embalmed,
anointed, pickled, dismantled, painted, adorned with jewelry,
clothed, wrapped, placed in a container, moved, viewed,
embraced, wept over, shouted at, danced over, and force-fed
food. The researchers found no comparable practice to throwing the recently deceased over a city wall.

The authors concluded that seeing and touching the body of
a loved one must have some kind of therapeutic value, such as
helping people to accept the loss and then move on to make
new social connections. They noted that many cultures place
enormous importance on finding missing bodies and returning
them to relatives.

No one ever asks Gene and Sandy *Why bother?* when they're
on a search. It would be an absurd and insensitive question in
the moment. And yet the answer to that unaskable question
— Why go to such great lengths to bring back a dead body, an

empty vessel? — is at the heart of why life for the Ralstons veered so far off a more conventional path.

I arrived at one search ten days after the person drowned. David Gavin, a twenty-six-year-old man from a small village in Ireland, had jumped into a narrow river just before it flowed into Kinbasket Lake, a massive reservoir on the east side of British Columbia. He had been on a road trip with a few of his teammates from the Irish Sporting and Social Club in Vancouver. They were on their way to Calgary for a Gaelic football tournament when they decided to pull off the main highway and go for a swim. He was the first to take the leap off the bridge. His friends saw him surface briefly and then go under again. David had moved to Canada with his partner, Ciara O'Malley, just a few months before the accident.

The bridge connects a gravel logging road and crosses the river next to a small campground with a few dozen plots for tents or motor homes and a handful of rustic wood cabins. I arrived at that wedge of forest between the river and the lake on the evening of July 10, 2017. I found Gene and Sandy finishing up dinner, seated on lawn chairs on a ledge with a view of Kinbasket Lake from the south. Gene and I shook hands. He was wearing jeans and a long-sleeved flannel shirt. I gave Sandy a hug. Her hair was pulled back in a ponytail under her baseball hat.

A set of wooden stairs led down a rocky embankment to a dock where the *Kathy G* was moored. The bridge was only two hundred yards or so upriver to the west. The deck of the bridge was made of broad wood timbers and supported by two concrete pillars. It didn't look that high, maybe forty or fifty feet, above the surface of the river. The water was blue and opaque, like the milky consistency of a gemstone.

Kinbasket Reservoir is a 134-mile-long slash of water that cuts between rows of low, rumbling mountains. The lake was created on the Columbia River in the 1970s by the construction of one of the largest earth-fill dams in the world. Several small towns were submerged when the valley was inundated.

It was hot and dusty that summer. Smoke from nearby forest fires cast the evening in an eerie orange glow. The Ralstons had arrived a couple of days before I did. They introduced me to Ciara and David's family. His father, Mick; mother, Angela; sister, Aoife; and a couple of close friends and relatives had taken the first available flight to Canada after getting the call about David's accident. We set up a semicircle of chairs next to the gravel road that led down the hill and around the corner to the boat launch. The family was living in two camper trailers set up next to the road and with a clear view of the bridge, river, and lake. The Ralstons' motor home was parked not far up the hill from the trailers.

Some of David's teammates from Vancouver had set up tents. Angela warned me to arrange my tent so the door faced away from the gravel road; otherwise my stuff would get covered in dust. She had fine blond hair and kind, soft features. David was a tall and handsome athlete. You could see the resemblance in both of his parents. Mick had curly gray hair and wore glasses. He worked for the county government back in Ireland but looked like the affable coach of a kids' sports team.

Someone was cooking hamburgers and chicken skewers on a barbecue. Angela asked me several times if I was hungry. "You wouldn't be an Irish mother if you didn't keep offering people food," Ciara said. She had pale-blue eyes and an intense, direct gaze. She and David were teenagers when they started dating.

Gene told me that they had tried searching near the bridge, but he was starting to wonder if David had moved. He pointed to a mass of driftwood on the surface of the river. A tangle of logs passed under the bridge. The wet wood glistened as it spun and twirled in the current. The water level had already risen twelve feet since David had drowned, as the last of the snow melted in the mountains. The depth of the river and lake fluctuate dramatically over the year because of the meltwater and the operation of the dam.

I had talked to Gene on the phone before they left for Kinbasket. He had sounded optimistic about the search. The river was a relatively small area and the witnesses, David's teammates, had provided good information on the point of last seen. It had not taken the Ralstons long, however, to scan those sections of the river. And if the body had moved, if it had been flushed by the current along the bottom and into the open expanse of the reservoir, then the search area had expanded exponentially.

The RCMP's dive team had already come and gone. They called off their search four days after David drowned. The Gavins then hired a commercial diving company. Those divers searched for another three days. The river wasn't that deep, but the visibility was terrible. The divers searched by feel on the bottom while trying to dodge driftwood and other debris that whooshed through the water like silent, slow-motion missiles. They tested the strength of the current by attaching a buoy to one of the divers who then lay on the bottom of the river. It took twenty minutes for the submerged diver to drift along the bottom from the bridge and out to the lake. The commercial team told the Gavins that David's body could have already drifted for several miles into the lake.

Gene and Sandy were always having to debunk the common-sense or superstitious ideas people had about currents and how they could carry, or not carry, bodies in lakes and rivers. The Ralstons had seen time and time again that bodies were found close to where the person was last seen on the surface. Teather noted in his textbook that the average human body is heavy enough to resist water flows up to 1.5 miles an hour. The fastest sustainable swim speed for a strong diver is 1.8 miles an hour. So Teather's rule of thumb is that if the diver could swim against the current, then it was unlikely the body had moved. Corpses can be transported vast distances in rivers, but those cases generally involve shallow, fast-moving water.

The evidence in this instance, it seemed like Gene was saying, had started to weigh in favor of the fact that David had moved. And if he had moved, then this search was going to be much more complicated and labor-intensive than the Ralstons had anticipated.

I didn't spend much time with Ciara or the Gavins after that first night on the rocky ledge overlooking Kinbasket. Ciara told me the next day that they would rather not have someone around taking notes. The family didn't appreciate the feeling of being observed during such a vulnerable ordeal. Everyone was friendly and hospitable, even funny at times. But they were in shock. Their world had been turned upside down. They had left home in a panic and had been camped out next to a lake for close to two weeks.

I got the feeling, in the few interactions I had with Ciara and the Gavins in early July 2017, that they were not so much trying to find David's body as they were trying to find David. They wanted him back. He was loved and missed and lying somewhere on the bottom of that godforsaken river or lake. And he was out there all alone in the cold and the dark.

A team of researchers from England observed some of the ways in which a body can retain its social meaning and identity after death in a study published in the *British Medical Journal* in 2010. The authors noted that the boundary between the living and the dead is often blurred when someone dies, especially if the death is sudden and unexpected.

The researchers conducted in-depth interviews with eighty people who had a spouse or close relative suffer a traumatic death. They set out to test the conventional wisdom, which they noted had never been backed up by any empirical evidence, that it's unhealthy to view a body if it's been injured or disfigured. The underlying assumption was that viewing a corpse in an unsightly condition subjects the bereaved to a lifetime of harmful, uninvited memories. *You don't want that to be how you remember so-and-so* is often the form that this type of counsel takes. I had heard the Ralstons say something along those lines on searches when the person had been missing several months or years.

Many of the study participants who chose to view the body said that it had been helpful for them in the long run, even if it was shocking and painful at the time. They provided different reasons for why they wanted to view the body, but many expressed a powerful instinct to get to their deceased loved one as soon as possible. Mothers, in particular, wanted to be at their child's side. "I just wanted to get to her straightaway because I felt that there was something I could do, you know, that's what every mother feels, isn't it, you can always do something to make it better," said a woman whose daughter died in a car accident. Others wanted a chance to say goodbye or didn't want their loved one to be alone, to have to go through something so difficult by themselves. One mother brought the body of her daughter a coat. Another woman sang to the body of her husband in the hospital. "I reassured him that he wasn't on his own," she said.

Lucy Hone, an expert on resilience and a professor at the University of Canterbury in New Zealand, wrote an article about her decision to keep the body of her twelve-year-old daughter at home for a few days after she had been killed in a car accident.

"It gave my poor, traumatised brain time to start to believe that she'd really gone," she wrote. Hone described how she could not bear the idea of her daughter lying alone and cold in the morgue. Hone spent time with her daughter in her bedroom. She read to her, plaited her hair, and put her favorite lotion on her legs. Hone said it was terrible. And beautiful. It was a game-changer in terms of helping to manage her grief.

Laqueur wrote about how his research for *The Work of the Dead* took him in a surprising direction. He thought he would write about an evolution of sorts, a history of how the body, at least in Europe and North America, was once considered sacred and imbued with all kinds of religious significance, but gradually became more ordinary and profane. He had expected that as Western societies became less religious, so, too, the body would lose some of its special and revered status. "Instead I found a continuity," he wrote.

The West, by and large, seems to have embraced the first half of Diogenes's argument: We are a temporary constellation of atoms. But not the second: A dead body is no more than a rich source of nutrients for scavengers. Corpses don't matter today for the same sorts of religious reasons that they used to, but the intense degree to which they do matter has not changed. And that is not to suggest that religion, or a belief in the soul, is somehow incorrect or not relevant, but rather that those kinds of metaphysical beliefs are not a necessary condition for feeling a powerful connection and sense of duty to the body of a loved one.

Two of the writers that Laqueur discussed in his book stood out in terms of explaining something I had noticed on searches with the Ralstons. William Godwin, a writer from the early nineteenth century, and Robert Hertz, a sociologist working in the early twentieth century, both tried to articulate aspects of what Laqueur called the deep structures of intuition and feeling that oblige us to care for the dead.

Hertz was only twenty-seven years old in 1907 when he wrote *A Contribution to the Study of Collective Representation of Death*, a research paper about the ritual of double burials in Indigenous groups, mostly from Indonesia. The customs he studied included an initial temporary burial that was followed up some time later — weeks, months, even years in some cases — with another ceremony and burial that then concluded the funeral rites.

The physical changes that the body undergoes during decomposition, like autolysis and putrefaction and bloat, symbolized for the cultures Hertz studied the changes taking place in the soul. The spirit of the recently deceased was liberated in increments as flesh rotted away to reveal the skeleton, which was considered a purified physical form worthy of permanent burial. Hertz described how one society believed that the ancestors of the recently deceased arrived each night and removed parts of soft tissue from the bones, carrying them to the center of the Earth to assemble a new body for the soul to inhabit. "While the old body falls to ruins, a new body takes shape," he wrote.

These types of mortuary rituals, Hertz theorized, allowed families and communities to draw out the process of death, to give people more time to acclimatize to the shock of losing someone:

> The brute fact of physical death is not enough to consummate death in people's minds: the image of the recently deceased is still part of the system of things of this world, and looses itself from them only gradually by a series of internal partings. We cannot bring ourselves to consider the deceased as dead straight away: he is too much part of our

substance, we have put too much of ourselves into him, and participation in the same social life creates ties which are not severed in one day.

The evidence of death, an insensible corpse, is often no match for the potency and persistence of feelings. The flood of memories and emotions overwhelm the reality that someone was here one moment but then gone the next. And without the body, without what Hertz called the brute facts, it's that much harder to accept that someone who still feels so present has somehow become irrevocably absent.

William Godwin, a journalist and philosopher, wrote a pamphlet in 1809 called *Essays on Sepulchres* in which he argued that honoring the dead, by maintaining gravestones and other monuments in perpetuity, would help make people, and society in general, more virtuous. Laqueur wrote about how Godwin's personal history with loss informed his ideas about the mysterious power of corpses.

Godwin wrote the collection of essays twelve years after his wife, Mary Wollstonecraft, died from complications of childbirth. His daughter, who was named after her mother, grew up to write *Frankenstein*, a novel about an inert corpse brought to life. Godwin felt a strong connection to his wife's body after she died, and then by extension to her gravesite. "And, yet, strangely, the corpse still remains the person it was, lacking only what seems so little yet so immeasurably great—the breath of life, the 'rosy hue,'" Laqueur wrote, paraphrasing Godwin as he tried to make sense of his feelings about his wife's body. Many of her belongings, such as jewelry or a favorite book, also held new meaning for him after she died.

Laqueur described Godwin as being as close to an atheist as a person could get in the early nineteenth century, and yet his ideas about the value of the body resembled those of Catholic theologians. St. Thomas Aquinas defended the worship of relics of the saints, which could be a body part or a possession, in similar terms as Godwin used to explain his attachment to Wollstonecraft's body and her personal effects. A corpse is a physical object, but it was the physical object most closely tied to the ethereal substance of the person or soul. "The dead body carries with it a quality of having been something material that had an intimate relationship with the soul, just as a beloved father's ring or clothes had with his person," Laqueur wrote.

Godwin was caught between what he thought was rational, Diogenes's argument that a body is no more than food for worms, and what he felt emotionally. "He wants the presence of his beloved Mary Wollstonecraft and believes that proximity to her dead body is, sadly, as close as he can get," Laqueur wrote.

Hertz and Godwin believed that the value of the body was derived from the fact that the person who inhabited that body lived on in those who are left behind. "We live with and care for the dead because of a seemingly universal and long-standing commitment to the existence of a person after death," Laqueur wrote. Or as he put it in another and more succinct way, "the dead matter because we cannot bear to give them up."

Biological death is too fast, too sudden, for us to absorb. The speed and finality of death is at odds with how we form attachments. The people we love become a part of us, and that part persists even in the absence of its source. So we need evidence, time, and the guidance of communal rituals to realign our internal world with the external one. Anything tangible associated with the person, like a necklace or a fishing rod, carries an imprint of their inimitable existence. But the body most of all.

CHAPTER THIRTEEN

The Ferryman

The Ralstons searched for two weeks straight on that first trip to Kinbasket Lake in July 2017. And then they returned in late August for another three weeks. They spent thirty-seven days that summer and fall looking for David, the most time ever on a single search. They never found him.

Brian Harmes, a volunteer with the Canadian Canine Search Corps, and his dog Koda, who has jet-black fur and pointy, wolflike ears, found his body on Saturday, April 28, 2018. It was buried by a layer of snow and mud about a hundred feet toward the lake from the base of the bridge. David had been close at hand all along. The layer of sediment would have camouflaged the body as a boulder on the sonar. The water level in Kinbasket dropped significantly over the winter. The spot on the exposed riverbank where Koda detected the remains in late April had been under sixty-five feet of water during the summer and fall.

Ciara, Mick, and Angela were already in Golden, a town about an hour's drive east of the campground on Kinbasket Lake, when David's body was found. They had arrived in Canada four days earlier to coordinate the next phase of the search. The Gavins and Ciara decided to leave the campground the previous September and go back to Ireland without David's body on the condition that they would return again in the spring. They had seen photos of what the lake looked like after winter, how it drained all the way down to a narrow channel, and figured the low water levels would offer new options for where and how to look. A team of volunteer divers from Ireland were scheduled to arrive on Monday. The Gavins had also talked to Gene and Sandy about returning to Kinbasket Lake.

I drove the three hours out to Golden from Calgary in early May after hearing from Gene that David had been found. Ciara, Mick, and Angela were staying in a bungalow that looked like a summer cabin. It had brown wood siding and a welcoming front porch. The four of us settled into the living room. I asked how they were feeling now that they had found David. I'm not sure what I was expecting them to say. I knew how hard and how long the search had been, and I was happy for them that they had succeeded against such unlikely odds. I guess I thought that the question would be a chance for them to talk about that sense of perseverance. But the feeling in the room shifted down, like I had cut the power to a stereo that had been playing music in the background.

Angela spoke first. "Initially it was elation. We were elated." She was sitting on a couch by the wall to my left. Mick and I were on either end of a big leather couch facing a large window with a view of the houses across the street. Ciara sat across from us in a chair. "But then obviously on Sunday when we had to go and . . ." She paused for a moment and then seemed to change her mind about what she wanted to say. "When he was being removed from the lake it went to the other extreme. Very mixed emotions," she said.

"It's kind of scary now that it's real," Ciara added. "We knew David was gone, but now it's very real." She talked about how everything over the past ten months had revolved around finding and bringing David home. "And now we've done it," she said.

"It's a roller coaster of emotions," Mick said.

It seemed that finding the body had helped to bring the reality of their loss home, for better and for worse. The search for David had been all-consuming. Even when back in Ireland, they were counting down the days until they could return to Kinbasket Lake. The search, the logistical challenges of scouring the bottom of the river and lake, along with the fact that it was so far from home, had provided a distraction.

So they were relieved and grateful to have found David's body, but they were unsure about what lay ahead. The fog of their prolonged search was starting to lift, but it was lifting on an unfamiliar landscape. Ciara and the Gavins were free to move on from the shores of Kinbasket Lake, but they had to move on in a world without their beloved partner and son.

Gene and Sandy sometimes talked about the families of drowning victims as belonging to an exclusive club. It was only the other people who had experienced something similar who could understand the bittersweet quality of that moment, the contradictory emotions. Finding the body was a necessary step, but it didn't blunt the hurt of the loss.

Ciara, Mick, and Angela told me about something else that only the families of drowning victims could truly appreciate, at least in Canada and the United States. You were all alone. It was up to you to raise the money and rally the resources to keep a search going. "It's just something that you never could have imagined would have been the situation," Angela said.

They didn't blame the RCMP. They knew the underwater recovery team was stretched thin, and they were grateful to the divers who did what they could to help. They were thankful to all the people who showed up with boats, the staff at the resort, volunteer groups like the Canadian Canine Search Corps, and everyone who donated money to cover the cost of hiring commercial divers, helicopter searches, and other professional help. Friends from the Irish Sporting and Social Club set up a GoFundMe account that raised more than $300,000 (CAD) from over five thousand donors. The response to that kind of tragedy in Ireland, however, was radically different. Angela told me that if David had drowned over there, hundreds of volunteers would have showed up in addition to the authorities. "And we were just down there on our own," she said.

They told me that in March 2017, three months before David had drowned, Rescue 116, an Irish Coast Guard helicopter, crashed into the sea while supporting a rescue mission off the west coast, not far from the Gavins' home in Breaffy. All four crew members were killed. Two of the bodies were never recovered, but the search effort was one of the largest in Irish maritime history. Volunteers in fishing boats worked shoulder-to-shoulder with the coast guard, military, and police to execute a coordinated sweep of thirty-three hundred square miles of water.

"The whole community around the area were bringing in sandwiches, and tea and coffee, and soup and everything. And everything was coming from everywhere just to keep the rescue services going," Mick said. "If there's a tragedy in Ireland, the whole community, as they say, comes together, and not just from a rescue point of view or a recovery point of view, but from a support point of view."

David's drowning and the search for his body was national news in Ireland. "Unless someone was living in a hole in Ireland, they'd know about David's situation," Ciara said. Whereas in Canada, the Gavins had to visit the local newspaper office in Golden in person to get the story out about the drowning and the ongoing search for his body.

The family realized, with the benefit of hindsight, that it wasn't realistic to expect the same sort of approach to search-and-recovery operations in Canada. Kinbasket Lake is almost as long as Ireland was wide. Their home country is so much smaller, so much more densely populated. "There's always somebody that knows somebody, that knows somebody, that knows somebody," Mick said.

But that contrast, the feeling of being left to fend for themselves in a crisis, provided a glimpse into the mind-set of the Gavins and O'Malley when the Ralstons pulled into the campground on a Saturday evening in early July. It would have been eight days since David drowned. Seven days since Mick, Angela, and Aoife dropped everything to travel halfway around the world and move into a trailer next to a dusty road overlooking the lake. The RCMP were long gone. A commercial dive team had also tried searching and then told them it was a lost cause, that David was likely out of reach forever.

"Once we met the Ralstons, it was different," Ciara said. "They were very professional, but they were also very empathetic." She liked how Gene knew when to tell a joke to lighten the mood.

The Ralstons called on their extensive network in the search-and-recovery community, organizing teams of search dogs to come to Kinbasket from eastern Canada and the United States. And as the days turned into weeks, they arranged for divers to investigate any suspicious objects they detected on the bottom with the sonar. But it was something else, too, something above and beyond those practical skills that drew the Gavins and the Ralstons closer together during the summer and fall of 2017.

"They looked after us so much. I mean without them for that period of time . . ." Mick drew a sharp breath through his teeth. "Do you know? I mean, we were lost souls."

"Yeah," Ciara said softly.

"We really were," Mick continued. "It was like as long as they're here, we have that hope. They gave us that. They were guiding us through."

~

Mick's use of the expression *lost souls caught my attention during our conversation in Golden*. It's associated with the myth of the ferryman and the idea of purgatory. The focus of the myth is on the recently deceased and their journey to a new realm. The purpose of the story, however, is to comfort the bereaved. Death is envisioned as a voyage, not a vanishing act. It's a beginning, not an end. There is a similar dynamic with the Ralstons. Their skills and equipment are all geared toward the person who drowned, finding the body, but their ultimate goal, their vocation, is to provide relief to the family.

Francis Sullivan was a priest and theologian who wrote about the evolution of Charon, the name of the ferryman in Greek mythology, in art and literature for an article published in *The Classical Journal* in 1950. The story of the boatman first appeared in Greece around 500 BCE, but Sullivan acknowledged that the character has much deeper roots. "He seems to belong to those far-off days when men began to think of the dead as living on, no longer merely in the grave but in the depths of the earth."

Some of the earliest surviving representations of the ferryman in Greek art are painted on a type of slender vase that was used during funeral rituals. Some are still on display in museums. An aged but hardy boatman, usually bearded, steadies his small wooden boat with an oar in one hand and reaches out with his other to receive someone into the craft. "It is a serene sorrow, mingled with a grave tenderness, simplicity and reserve," Sullivan said of the countenance of Charon in these ancient illustrations.

The portrayal of Charon in the art and literature of so many different cultures is by no means uniform. For example, the ferryman that Michelangelo painted on the front wall of the Sistine Chapel during the 1530s is downright gruesome. He swings his oar like a baseball bat to banish a desperate-looking crowd from his boat and into hell. This boatman has patchy gray hair, green skin, wild eyes, and talons on his toes. He is more of a vengeful demon than a sympathetic shepherd. The Italian painter based his image of Charon on Dante's portrayal of the mythical figure in the *Divine Comedy*. And Dante based his understanding of the boatman on Virgil's description in the *Aeneid*, which was completed in 19 BCE. Virgil described Charon in Book 6 of his epic poem:

> *Grim ferryman, stands sentry. Mean his guise,*
> *His chin a wilderness of hoary hair,*
> *And like a flaming furnace stare his eyes.*

Sullivan wrote that Charon is described in radically different ways depending on how he fits into the religious and metaphysical framework of the day. As attitudes toward death and the afterlife change, so do the demeanor and physical attributes of the ferryman.

There is a general consensus among the variations on the myth that spending eternity in the company of the dead rubs off on a person, even a supernatural one. And added to that morose environment is the fact that the job is never done. Regardless of how fast you row, more lost souls always await your return. "Never ends" is sometimes all Gene writes when he forwards me another search request that he has received by email.

A few years ago, the Ralstons got into watching a science-fiction crime drama called *Person of Interest*. The series featured an artificial intelligence program that could predict and then prevent deadly crimes before they happened. It got Gene thinking about drownings. He sometimes catches himself fantasizing about having the ability to race off to a lake and rescue the person, instead of finding their body.

Pauline Boss, the academic and therapist, wrote a short essay for the playbill of the theater production *The Ferryman* when it debuted on Broadway in New York in the fall of 2018. The play is about a family dealing with the fallout of a relative, an IRA activist, who vanished during the Troubles in Ireland in the 1970s. England and Ireland created the Independent Commission for the Location of Victims' Remains in 1999 to identify all the people who were abducted and murdered during the conflict and to locate their bodies. "For families of the missing, their narrative of loss continues indefinitely. Their story has no ending," wrote Boss.

Angela, Mick, and Ciara described feeling tightly bound to Kinbasket Lake, of living in a state of frantic stasis for the ten months between David's drowning and the recovery of his body. Their experience sounded like a kind of purgatory. They had been caught between worlds for the duration of the search. There was the world in which David was missing and they needed to find him. And then there was the world in which David had died and they needed to find a way to move forward without him. The Ralstons helped guide them through the first disorienting weeks and months after David drowned. Finding his body would have been tremendously helpful, but even the act of looking was cathartic. It relieved them from the impossible task of trying to become experts in underwater search and recovery overnight.

To add to the cruelties of what Boss calls ambiguous loss, the law, too, struggles to recognize death in the absence of a body. Courts, banks, insurance companies, and creditors need the corpse as proof. "It freezes the person who is missing, it freezes all of their assets and it freezes all of their loved ones or anybody else who's depending upon them," said Robert Jarvis, a law professor at the Shepard Broad College of Law in Florida. He has published several articles on how the law treats those who are presumed dead.

A person has not officially died until someone in a position of authority, usually a medical doctor, has acknowledged their death using the appropriate documentation. Jarvis told me about how the English legal system originally featured a presumption of life. Anyone missing was considered alive until their one hundredth birthday. That policy flipped in the seventeenth century to a presumption of death after a certain period of time, which was initially several decades. The law back then had to allow enough time for people who got lost at sea, or started a new life on another continent, to eventually find their way home or get word back to their relatives. As communication technologies advanced, and the world got smaller, that window of time for the presumption of death has shortened.

It was cut down to seven years in 1805, which is still the legal time frame in some states and Canadian provinces. Most jurisdictions in the United States, Jarvis said, have cut it down to five years and allow a judge to grant a death certificate if the "absentee," the legal term for a missing person, was exposed to a specific peril. For example, if you can prove the person had been in the direct path of a hurricane or had been in the World Trade Center on the morning of September 11, 2001, then the courts can issue a presumptive death certificate with minimal delay. Relatives still have to hire a lawyer and go to court to prove that the missing person was exposed to mortal danger.

Jarvis explained that insurance companies are highly suspi-

cious of deaths without the body as proof, but so are banks, creditors, and debtors. People in general are reluctant to presume
death. "We are always suspicious, because it is not normal. It
is not in our everyday experience to have somebody just disappear," he told me.

If there is a clear consensus about what happened in terms
of a specific peril, then Jarvis estimated the court case to get a
presumptive death certificate would take a lawyer about twenty
billable hours. And that would cost between $5,000 and $10,000.
"But it's never that way. What always happens, of course, is that
there are relatives and lovers and other people who come out of
the woodwork and they start contesting," he said. "At that point,
$100,000 would not be an unreasonable figure."

Courts are hesitant to declare someone dead because of how
difficult that is to unwind if the person ever reappears. The
people who come back are called returnees. Jarvis described
the case of Donald Miller, who had been declared dead in
Ohio in 1994, in one of his research papers. Miller materialized nineteen years later when he tried to reactivate his Social
Security number so he could get a driver's license. He admit-
ted to disappearing to avoid paying child support. "I don't know
where that leaves you, but you're still deceased as far as the law
is concerned," the judge was quoted in a newspaper as telling
Miller in court. The judge cited a law in Ohio that does not allow
a declaration of death to be reversed after three years.

Most of the families that the Ralstons have helped have
had to deal with one kind of bureaucratic dilemma or another
related to the drowning victim's state of suspended animation
in the eyes of the law. For some, the legal purgatory of an absentee creates substantial personal and financial turmoil.

In December 2006, the Ralstons went looking for the body
of a young man named Shane Pierce, who had drowned in a

boating accident on a lake in Kentucky that September. Without a body, Shane's family hadn't been able to get a death certificate, and without a death certificate, they had to continue making the payments for their son's truck and for the mortgage on his house. "It almost sunk us," Shane's father, Roger Pierce, told me. "I could have let it go by, but you lost your son. You don't want to lose his possessions."

Shane had worked as an aircraft mechanic for UPS, the shipping company, and he had a life insurance policy, but the Pierce family could not access it without a death certificate. They couldn't sell the boat that Shane was driving the day he drowned, either, because it was registered in his name. The windshield was smashed where he had apparently hit his head and been knocked unconscious before being thrown from the boat. "Man, that was tough," Pierce said. "The boat stood out here in my driveway and every time I looked at it, I'd think of Shane." At least five different search-and-rescue groups had tried to find Shane's body before the Ralstons got involved. Pierce had consulted a lawyer about trying to get a death certificate without Shane's body. The lawyer told him it would likely take a couple of years.

The Ralstons located the body within six minutes of launching their boat. "If I hadn't hooked up with Gene and Sandy, I don't know what would have happened," Pierce said. He was finally able to sell Shane's truck and boat. "My younger son lives in his house now. That made me feel better in a way. I don't know why."

~

I drove out to Kinbasket Lake on May 3, 2018, after visiting with Ciara and the Gavins in Golden. The gravel road off the main highway was muddy and riddled with potholes. It would be another month or so before the weather warmed up enough for camping, and the resort was deserted. I parked my truck and walked out onto the bridge over the Beaver River. The sky had turned gray and cloudy. A channel of green water cut a shallow, winding path under the bridge and out into an enormous basin of coarse sand and mud. It looked like someone pulled the plug on a colossal bathtub. Evergreen trees climbed in scraggly thickets up from the shoreline and over the uneven rocky shoulders of the mountains.

The railings of the bridge are made from big, square timbers. Several small painted rocks had been left on the ledge in two piles. One rock read MISS YOU, and another LOVE YOU ALWAYS. To the right of the rocks was a more permanent memorial. An inch-thick cross section of a log was engraved with David's name and the date he jumped. It was bolted to the railing and featured an illustration of a dragonfly.

The drawing reminded me of something Ciara had said earlier that afternoon: "He was picked to go and do something else." She described how her partner had been naturally good at everything he tried, from the physicality of Gaelic football to graduating with honors from university. He was tall and strong, but modest and unassuming — somehow able to blend into a crowd despite his size. "It was nearly like he'd done everything he was supposed to do here," she said. "But I don't say that every day, and I don't know why I'm saying that now, but when we're talking about him like that, he was just so good at everything."

The metamorphosis of a dragonfly is sometimes used as a metaphor for the transition from life to death. The insect hatched from an egg into an aquatic beetle, which one day crawled up the stem of a plant to the surface of the water, shed its skin, and flew away. The dragonfly, as the story goes, had no way of communicating with the beetles left behind back under the water. And the beetles could not conceive of an existence above the water. So it was as if one day the beetle just disappeared, like it somehow crawled right off the face of the Earth. It was not so much that the insect was gone but rather that it was unreachable — and it was only unreachable until the rest of the beetles made that same journey to the great beyond.

I looked over the edge of the railing and saw a patch of the muddy riverbed that had been disturbed. It wasn't a deep hole. It looked like the kind of uneven depression that's left on a beach after someone made a big sand castle. It was about a quarter of the way from the base of the bridge, a hundred feet or so, toward the bottom of the wooden steps that led back up the steep embankment. The spot where David was found was in plain view from anywhere along the ridge overlooking the lake and the river from the campground. I likely had a clear sight line to that part of the riverbed from where I sat with the Ralstons, Ciara, and the Gavin family that first evening I got to Kinbasket last summer if it hadn't been for the sixty-five feet of fast-moving, turbid water.

I called Mick on the phone about a year later. He and Angela were driving home after visiting some friends on the north coast of Ireland. We talked more about the role that the Ralstons had played in the search for David. And about the vacation that Gene and Sandy had taken in early March 2018 to stay with the Gavins in Breaffy for a couple of weeks. The trip had been Mick's idea. The Ralstons wouldn't accept any money above and beyond the cost of gas and fees for parking their motor home, so the invitation to visit them in Ireland had been a way to try to pay them back. "I think they really enjoyed the trip. You could see it meant a hell of a lot to them," he told me.

I asked Mick where David was now. "David is . . . well, I'm sure he's in heaven. He's buried in Breaffy, in our village." Mick told me they felt lucky that they were able to find him and bring him home, that they had somewhere they could go and talk to him and remember him. "That's where we're at," he said.

Most of Mick's relatives were buried in a different cemetery in a neighboring town. But Breaffy was where David played Gaelic football and where he went to school. He had a stronger connection to that community. A month before he drowned in Kinbasket Lake, Faye Lavin, a twelve-year-old girl who belonged to the same football club, had died suddenly from what the local newspaper reported as a short illness. "They're both buried side by side in the Breaffy graveyard," Mick told me.

CHAPTER FOURTEEN

Riderless Sea-Doo

On the morning of April 14, 2021, a Wednesday, three friends of Bobby Aujla, the man who'd drowned almost seven months earlier, walked down the dock next to the boat launch on Alouette Lake. They looked young, somewhere in their midthirties. They were dressed for cold weather in jeans and sweatshirts.

Gene and Sandy were getting the *Kathy G* ready, shuffling around buckets of rope and hanging the pulleys for the sonar cable on the frame for the winch and the boom. Two RCMP officers were launching another boat to take two of the friends up past the narrows where they would walk the Ralstons through what happened on the afternoon of October 1, 2020. The police boat had a metal hull, inflatable sides, and a short tower at the back with a blue siren on the top.

Two days prior, after we had seen the floating log on Monday morning, the Ralstons started searching west across the lake from Dennis Liva's boat. Later that afternoon, Gene saw something on the bottom that he thought deserved further inspection with the ROV. The object was roughly the right dimensions for a body, and there was a hint of two short legs in the sonar image. It was bent over to the side, and the shadow looked like a single, plump eyelash. We were three hundred yards west of the sunken boat, a reasonable distance for Liva and Silcock to have swum given the amount of time they were in the water.

We returned the next day, Tuesday, with the ROV, but the target turned out to be a log that split into a Y-shape at one end. Two-legged logs were the bane of Gene and Sandy's existence. They were one of the few naturally occurring objects that could trick them into deploying the submersible, which was a labor-intensive procedure. The Ralstons then used the ROV to inspect the old boat on the bottom of the lake near the narrows. The object in the middle of the boat, the one that had shown up on the sonar, was bright red and looked like a gas can.

The Ralstons heard from the Tyners last night that they had made it across the border into Canada and arrived in Merritt. Pete had already arranged for Aujla's friends to meet the Ralstons at Alouette Lake in the morning. The plan today was for two of the friends to show Gene and Sandy where they remembered Aujla going under, the point of last seen. The Ralstons would search that area until noon and then leave to make the three-hour drive east to Merritt. Gene and Sandy didn't know yet if they would come back to Alouette right away or return home to Idaho first. That would all depend on how the search for Ben Tyner went in Nicola Lake.

Aujla's friends introduced themselves to Gene and Sandy. One of them, he was wearing a toque and had a beard, showed Gene a map of the lake on his cellphone with several GPS locations. He explained that he and his friends had returned to Alouette dozens of times since the incident to try to pinpoint the spot where they had last seen Aujla. "I've thought about him, or run this through my mind so many times it's driving me crazy," he said, making a circular motion with his finger next to his head.

Gene asked if any of them were related to Aujla. He had one hiking boot on the gunnel and leaned forward with an elbow resting on his bent knee. His jeans had panels of canvas fabric over the knees. Sandy was busy with something in the pilothouse.

"We're closer than family. We're friends. You can't choose your family, right?" replied one of the men. He had a coffee in a cardboard to-go cup.

Aujla was part of a big circle of close friends. Many of them grew up together in Surrey, a city just west of Maple Ridge, and were the children of Sikh immigrants to Canada from Punjab, a state in northern India. Rick Sandhu, one of Aujla's friends who agreed to speak with me for the book about the Ralstons, looked a little younger than the two other men with him on the dock that morning. He was soft-spoken but self-assured.

"I used to love this lake," the man in the toque said. He looked out off the end of the dock at the water and mountains as he spoke. "We came here all the time, and now I hate it."

I wondered what it would take for me to hate such a beautiful place. It seemed like we were seeing the lake at its best this morning: Early in the day in early spring, before the weather improved enough to draw the crowds. The sky was an immaculate blue. The sun was high enough over the mountains that it drenched the dock in bright, warm light. The damp rain forest on the hill above the launch was fragrant, an invigorating smell of earth and wood. Alouette looked like a clean slate, like some benevolent force had swooped in overnight and polished the surface smooth of yesterday's troubles and traffic.

"Maybe if we find him, that will change," Gene told him.

The men then asked about what kind of shape Aujla's body would be in after so many months on the bottom. Gene said there was a chance that it was in relatively good condition. He told them about Morzewski, the go-to search that he and Sandy referenced when people asked about the state of a body that had been submerged for a long time.

The Ralstons got a call in the spring of 2001, only a few months after they got the sonar, to look for a young man in Hayden Lake, Idaho. They imaged a body within five minutes of lowering the towfish, but it was the wrong guy. It was later determined that it was Michael Morzewski, a thirty-six-year-old who drowned in November 1999. He was only in ninety feet of water, but Hayden Lake was part of a mountain watershed like Alouette, and the water stayed cold year-round. Gene told Aujla's friends that Morzewski was well preserved even after seventeen months. Divers performed the recovery, but a deputy sheriff who attended the autopsy told Gene that the body was in good shape. He had been found on the bottom on his back and fully clothed. His sunglasses were still on.

We left the dock at 9:00 AM. The lake gradually widened out again after the narrows, like the incremental thickening of a carrot. It then opened into two broad basins with another subtler pinch point between them. It took us fifteen minutes at top speed, about thirty-five miles an hour, to get that far down the lake.

The police boat passed us on the right and traveled farther north. Sandhu and the man with the toque were on the boat, along with two officers. The boat sat idle for a few minutes, giving the men a chance to get their bearings. The driver circled around and pulled up alongside the *Kathy G*. One of the officers grabbed a metal cleat at the back corner. Sandy was on the chair in front of the monitor. Gene was behind the wheel. He slid the driver's-side window open. Pete stood in the stern, and I was up near the bow. The boats nodded up and down in unison, as if they were coming to some kind of silent agreement. Waves lapped against the hulls.

Aujla's friends looked shaken. It obviously wasn't easy to

come out here and relive that afternoon. The man in the toque told us that he had been driving the pontoon boat. It had been a windless, overcast day. The group of eight friends had talked a lot about the calmness of the water. None of them expected it to feel so nice on Alouette in October, especially because it had been so cloudy that morning. They'd come close to calling the trip off, but Aujla was insistent. He worried it would be one of the last days of the boating season before winter.

That reminded me of Liva and Silcock, who had drummed up an excuse to skip work because it was one of the first nice days of summer back in 1974. The prison camp where the man who rescued Silcock had worked had been located on the east side of the lake, not far north of the narrows. We had passed a small bay with what looked like the remnants of a gravel road that cut into the forest from shore. I wondered if that was where the old dock for the prison camp had been, where the other two boats that had responded to the emergency radio call about Liva and Silcock had been moored.

We were trying to peel back another layer of history at the surface of Alouette Lake, trying to piece together a small stretch of time from six and a half months back instead of almost fifty years. It was possible Liva was still somewhere on the bottom within a couple miles of Aujla. And time slowed down, sometimes even stopped, at the bottom of a cold, deep lake.

The group, six in the pontoon boat and Aujla on a Sea-Doo with another friend, had started to make their way back toward the boat launch after hanging out near a waterfall on the northwest shore. The woman on the Sea-Doo with Aujla was wearing a life jacket. Boating was a relatively new hobby for the group. Aujla was not a regular swimmer, but he was comfortable and confident in the water. He usually wore a life jacket, but didn't have one on that afternoon.

No one saw or heard the Sea-Doo flip. Someone on the pontoon boat looked back and saw that it was upside down, spinning in slow circles in the water. Sandhu and the man in the toque seemed to have a good handle on where they turned the boat around to go back and pick up their friends. They pointed to a large, lichen-covered boulder on the east shoreline as a landmark. The big question then was how far back Aujla and the woman were from the pontoon boat when the Sea-Doo flipped. The friends said they were certain that it had happened somewhere before the lake widened out again, before the first big section of open water past the narrows. The area they described was roughly half a mile long. The widest section of this part of Alouette was half a mile.

The group on the pontoon boat picked up the woman first. Aujla did not appear to be in any distress when they pulled up next to him. He looked like he was treading water. He was only a few feet from the back of the boat, within arm's reach. They would have thrown him a rope or a life jacket, something, if they had any inkling that he was in trouble. And then he went down.

"He didn't scream or anything," Sandhu said. He described the incident with an incredulous look in his eyes, like he was still trying to make sense of it. He didn't understand how his friend could have drowned without warning. Several people jumped into the lake after him. All they could see was green, an abyss of dark water.

Sandhu and his friend knew that the Ralstons had only a couple of hours to search this morning, that they had to be on the road to Merritt by early that afternoon. They told Gene and Sandy that they would pick up pizza for lunch and have it waiting for them back at the boat launch.

After the police boat left, Pete, Gene, and Sandy gathered in the pilothouse.

"We could spend days here," Gene said. He had moved back to the chair in front of the monitor. The Ralstons hoped to learn something more definitive. The two men outlined a general area, but it was relatively big.

"Eight people and no one can tell us where it happened," Pete said.

The point of last seen for Aujla has been hard to pin down from the start. The original eyewitnesses accounts given to the RCMP on the day of the accident had been scattered for more than a mile across the lake. Part of the problem was the repeating landform features. The lake north of the narrows opens and then tightens back up and then opens again. One cluster of witness reports was near the first opening. A similar grouping of reports was near where the lake opened a second time, about a mile down the lake.

Gene explained that discrepancies among witnesses were not all that unusual. The Ralstons had been on several searches where they found the body a long way from where the people on scene were certain the person drowned.

Auston Strole, a twelve-year-old boy, was struck by the motorboat that was pulling him on an inflatable tube on Shasta Lake in California in early July 2017. Three witnesses on the boat provided locations for the accident in roughly the same area. Divers, an ROV operator, and another side-scan sonar team all tried to find Strole that summer. The Ralstons arrived in late September. They spent four days scanning the bottom of the lake where the witnesses who were on the boat had reported that the accident had happened. And then Gene and Sandy got new information from one of two people who had been riding Jet Skis and stopped to help soon after Strole was struck. One Jet Skier stayed with the boat, and the other left to get help. He remembered using a distinct landmark to guide himself to shore. He reported the accident happening in a spot about half a mile from the other witness reports. The Ralstons searched the new location the next day and found Strole's body in two hundred feet of water.

Eyeballing distances and judging position on water is difficult at the best of times. There are rarely any fixed reference points nearby. The human brain also works differently under stress. Gene and Sandy provide attendees to their three-day training seminar with a 131-page report that outlines the myriad ways that witness recollection can be unreliable. The authors of the report, two psychology professors, explain the well-documented phenomenon of tunnel memory. Our attention often narrows during traumatic events. We tend to zoom in on the source of the stress and can later recall that aspect of the episode in vivid detail. Intense focus on a small window of experience happens at the expense of our awareness of what went on in the periphery. We end up with little or no recollection of the big picture, but get stuck with lifelong memories of the grim minutiae. It makes sense that a life-or-death situation like a drowning would be all-consuming in the moment; that there would be little mental bandwidth left over to notice anything beyond the immediate crisis.

Back on the dock this morning, Sandhu and his friends had talked about how they had returned to this part of the lake again and again. They set up a chat group with twenty-five of Aujla's friends and family to coordinate who would search each day and when. Sandhu owned a used car dealership and always had a truck available to tow one of the boats. They had three boats in regular rotation, one of them the pontoon boat that belonged to the man in the toque and Aujla. Two of the boats had rudimentary sonar devices, but they were no match for the depth of Alouette Lake. The friends tried anyway, unsure if what they were seeing on the screen was actually a depiction of the bottom. They kept going out on the lake into November and December, dressing up in toques, parkas, and gloves. They had hired two different underwater search companies and had spent close to $40,000 so far.

"So did you get those coordinates written down?" Sandy asked.

"I did my best. We're going to pick some points and then do some scanning before we run out of time," Gene said. The plan was to search down the middle of the channel and between the boulder to the south and then up to the point before the lake widened into the first big basin of water north of the narrows.

Gene yanked the cord on the generator. I realized how quiet it had been on the boat so far that morning. We kicked into search mode with the return of the omnipresent growling of the generator and outboard motor.

"I wish they would show us a new movie. I've seen this one," Gene said, as the images of the bottom started to scroll down the monitor. We were headed south toward the narrows. It was 422 feet deep. The bottom was flat and flecked with an assortment of debris.

We passed over one object, maybe an old tree trunk from back before the valley was flooded by the dam. The shadow it cast looked like a hand reaching out of the mud. It made Gene think of Sandy. She has Raynaud's syndrome, a circulatory disease that can cause the extremities to feel numb. She'd only started to notice it the past few years, but her hands and feet were often cold. She wore fleece gloves despite the sunny weather this morning. Pete didn't like to wear hats, so he regularly spritzed his head with a spray-on sunscreen that flooded the *Kathy G* with the smell of summertime at the beach.

The Ralstons managed to scan three lines by noon. No sign

of Aujla, but the bottom was relatively smooth, a promising sign if they were able to return.

"Bummer," Gene said. "I wish we hadn't scheduled so many things."

"Fraser was added late," Pete said.

The Ralstons had more days in Maple Ridge than antici-pated. I think Gene regretted not spending more of that time on this search. Meeting Sandhu and his friends, and learning how dedicated they were to finding Aujla, had made an impres-sion on all of us. I had been locked on the screen for the past hour and a half, silently willing the body to appear as each new section of the lake floor ticked into view.

"But we can come back," Gene said.

"How long do you have between searches?" Pete asked.

"Typically a week," Gene said. That gave them time to do laun-dry, stock up on groceries, repair or replace any malfunctioning gear, and rest for a day or two before hitting the road again.

"Depending on timing, it would also be great to go to Pitt Lake," Pete said. He told us about how four men in their early twenties had disappeared, along with their boat, one night in May 1992.

Pete enjoyed being on the *Kathy G*. The Ralstons had taken him under their wing. They were teaching him how the technol-ogy worked and how to execute a search. I wasn't surprised he was laying the groundwork for more searches down the road.

"Let's just go ahead and bring her up," Gene said. The laptop on the dashboard in front of Sandy chimed when she hit the power button. Pete helped raise the towfish out of the water and onto the bow. And then we sped back down the lake to the boat launch.

The parking lot for boat trailers at Alouette was partway up the hill from the launch. The strip of concrete was hemmed in by rain forest on all sides and mostly empty that Wednesday afternoon. Pete parked the unmarked RCMP truck, which was still hitched to the *Kathy G*, off to one side.

Four of Aujla's friends set out several pizzas on the tailgate of the truck. The man with the toque had left, but another two friends had joined Sandhu and the other guy from the morning. I met Harp Dhott, who ran his own business as a property appraiser, and another stocky man with a metal bangle on his wrist. They were a boisterous group.

The friends told Gene and Sandy that they had a bad experience with Cold Water Divers, a company from Vancouver Island that specialized in salvaging boats. They felt like they had been ripped off. They said the team from Cold Water had assured them that it would be relatively straightforward to locate and recover their friend. But then they didn't provide any information on where they were looking on the lake or how the search was going. It was a tough pill to swallow for the group of friends, considering they were paying the company thousands of dollars a day and wanted to be involved as much as possible.

I reached out to Adam Coolidge, the CEO of Cold Water, but he declined to comment on their search for Aujla in the fall of 2020. Tim Cucheran, the supervisor of the RCMP's dive team, told me that he has seen that kind of relationship, the one between the family of a missing person and a commercial dive team, break down before. It can seem insensitive for a company to charge the same rate to search for a person as they do for a boat.

Cucheran was aware of instances in which a company unnecessarily extended the duration of a search to earn more money or increased their fee because they knew the family was desperate. "We've seen companies try and push for more days of searching, just tapping the families' pockets. So those do happen," he said. He didn't know whether or not that was the case with Cold Water and Aujla's friends. "I don't know what was said between them and the company," he told me.

Cold Water had recruited Mark Atherton, a world authority on sonar, to help them on the search. Atherton wrote the book *Echoes and Images: The Encyclopedia of Side-scan and Scanning Sonar Operations* and worked for thirty years for Kongsberg Mesotech, a global technology company that manufactures sonars. He was semi-retired but still provided training seminars on underwater acoustics to the FBI and other agencies. He spent three days on Cold Water's boat, looking for Aujla with a drop sonar.

Atherton told me that he tried to rent a side-scan system but couldn't find one in the area that had enough cable to reach the bottom of Alouette Lake. Side-scan, the kind of sonar the Ralstons use, was more efficient for covering large areas. A drop sonar was better at finding smaller targets, such as a body, but only when the search area was relatively contained. A scanning sonar hit the target from multiple angles because the sound pulses were emitted in a 360-degree fan around the transducer. The Ralstons' ROV was equipped with this type of sonar so that they could detect targets in the vicinity of the robot even when the visibility in the water was low.

It was hard to distinguish a body with a towed sonar if it was lying perpendicular to the direction of travel of the towfish. The sound reflected off the pads of the feet or the top of the head. On a search in California several years ago, the Ralstons imaged a body that somehow kept moving back and forth from one location to another, about twenty feet away on the bottom, depending on what direction they were heading in the *Kathy G*. It turned out Gene and Sandy had found both of the missing, twin brothers. Brian and Kevin Nannini were lying on the bottom of the lake at perfect right angles to each other. They were twenty-seven years old. Their fishing boat had sunk in high winds.

One significant limitation of the drop sonar was that you had to pick it up and move it to search the next area. Atherton said the search radius could not be more than eighty feet when trying to find something the size of a corpse. They had to raise the sonar fifteen to twenty feet off the bottom of Alouette and then move it about forty feet forward before lowering the tripod back down for the next scan. The technique provided enough overlap that they could see behind logs, rocks and other debris. The drop sonar that Atherton got from his old company, Kongsberg Mesotech, wasn't the best tool for the job considering the wide-ranging reports from the witnesses and the depth of the lake. But it was the best tool he could find at the time.

"We did as much as we could in the three days that I was available," Atherton said. "We looked where we were told to look." They scanned a long section of the bottom of the lake north of the narrows in an effort to track the path of the pontoon boat after it had turned around to go back and pick up Aujla and the woman.

The group of friends had much more positive things to say about Tim Bulman, the sonar and ROV expert they hired after Cold Water. The big difference, it seemed, boiled down to communication. Where, according to the friends, the team from Cold Water had been aloof and standoffish, Bulman involved the group of friends and made them feel like part of the search. Bulman, like Atherton, didn't have the best equipment for the conditions on Alouette Lake. His side-scan sonar only had 330 feet of cable, so he couldn't get good-quality images of the deepest parts of the lake. He did, however, invite the friends onto his boat and provided regular updates on what he was doing and how he was doing it. Bulman helped focus the search area on the section of the lake that Sandhu and his friend had pointed out to the Ralstons that morning.

Aujla's friends told Gene and Sandy about how they felt like they were on their own from the start. The RCMP and Ridge Meadows Search and Rescue responded to the initial 911 call on the afternoon of October 1, 2020. They worked late into the night. A team returned the next morning but called off the search later that day. Those initial, emergency-response resources were geared more toward rescues, and the search team found no evidence that Aujla had made it to shore. He was presumed to have drowned.

The RCMP's underwater recovery team never deployed divers or their drop sonar because the lake was so deep and the potential search area, based on the wide-ranging reports from witnesses, was immense. Plus, the dive team had been called out to another incident earlier on the same day Aujla drowned. Several people were swept into the Capilano River when a dam malfunctioned and released a deluge of water.

The group had quickly zeroed in on the Ralstons. Aujla drowned on a Thursday afternoon, and Harmin Gill, another friend in the group, emailed Gene the following Monday morning. But the Ralstons were on Duncan Lake, which is in a remote area on the east side of British Columbia. Gene and Sandy were a week into the search for Thomas Schreiber, a fifty-eight-year-old man who was presumed to have drowned in mid-September after his canoe was found washed ashore. Not only that, but Gene wrote back to Gill to explain that they would need to return to Idaho to put the long cable for the sonar on the winch before they could scan the bottom of a lake as deep as Alouette. That's when Gill and his friends decided to hire Cold Water.

The past few months had only reinforced the friends' belief that Gene and Sandy were the key to finding Aujla. The friends had seen two sonar teams come and go. They had spent count-less hours on the lake themselves, watching the surface, the shorelines, and the screens of a bewildering array of depth sounders and sonar devices. One friend even researched how to build a submarine out of a hot-water tank. They brought a priest from their local gurdwara, the Sikh term for a place of worship, out to the boat launch to do a prayer for Aujla and a blessing for a successful recovery.

Nothing had worked. Just like nothing had worked forty-seven years before for the Liva family. The group of friends had more tools at their disposal, but the result so far had been the same. The difference for Aujla and his family in 2021 was the Ralstons, except that they were leaving after only two hours of searching. Sandhu, Dhott, and the other two men didn't let on if they were frustrated or resentful. They talked over one another to share all the details of the search so far. I got the impression that the young men felt like Gene and Sandy could understand what they had been through in a way nobody else could. And they knew that patience was their only option. They couldn't secure the Ralstons' services with a deposit. And so they brought pizza and shared the story of their friend and their friendship.

"You feel desperate," Sandhu said. "You get into desperation mode and you'll do anything." He had gravitated to Sandy while we ate lunch, standing in a semicircle by the tailgate.

She nodded in response.

"He was a tough guy," Sandhu continued. He hunched his shoulders forward and flexed his arms. "So it's hard to believe something like this happened to him."

They described Aujla as the type of person whom others relied on. He had been a rock for his friends and family. He took on a lot of responsibility from a young age. His parents had a difficult marriage that ended in divorce, and Aujla helped support his mother and two younger sisters. He started a business when he was sixteen with his uncle selling fireworks. It grew into a successful company with locations across Canada. Aujla also worked as a longshoreman, a job that entailed moving cargo on and off ships. He helped put his sisters through university. One became a registered nurse. The other was a teacher.

The man with the bangle on his wrist mentioned that a prayer had been started at a gurdwara in Surrey soon after Aujla drowned; it would continue to be read until he was found and his family could have a funeral. He said that Aujla's mother sometimes visited the room in which the prayer was being read. It was comforting to know someone was always praying for her son to be found.

I asked Sandhu, Dhott, and Gill about the prayer when I spoke to each of them on the phone a few months later. I was curious how it worked. An open-ended prayer seemed like a powerful example of the kind of purgatory that families of missing people have to endure. They told me that it is customary for Sikhs to read the holy book in its entirety following a death.

The Guru Granth Sahib is 1,430 pages long and takes forty-eight hours to read from front to back. These types of uninterrupted readings of the whole scripture are called an Akhand Path. They can also be performed intermittently, as in over a period of several days or weeks. These types of prayers are done as a way to mark and bless major life milestones, such as marriage, the birth of a child, or a death.

Sikhism developed from the teachings of Guru Nanak in the late fifteenth century. He was the first in a succession of ten gurus, the last of whom decided that his successor would be the holy book itself. The Guru Granth Sahib is considered the physical embodiment of the religion's spiritual leaders. It is placed on a cushioned stand during the day; it is covered by rumalas, soft and brightly covered fabric, when it is closed and not being read. When the book is open, an attendant stands nearby and waves a chaur, a type of fan made from animal hair, to keep the book cool and comfortable. And then at night it is ceremonially laid to rest in a separate room on another cushioned stand or even a bed.

Robert Hertz, the French sociologist, proposed that our physical bodies have a life in nature and a life in culture. It is the second life that persists in the individuals and communities who remember us after we die. It was interesting to learn about the corporeality of the Guru Granth Sahib. It seemed like the holy book was an example of a body that has only a cultural life.

I looked up Aujla online after meeting his friends. I found a photo of him that looked like it had been taken at some kind of formal event. He was wearing a three-piece suit with a bow tie. He had a well-trimmed beard, broad shoulders, and large, ponderous eyes with heavy lids that made him look pensive.

A couple of news articles published about Aujla's drowning in the fall of 2020 mentioned his role in the death of a young man named Amandeep Bath. The story was hard to follow. It had taken a number of twists and turns over the course of thirteen years. Bath was killed in the fall of 2004, but Aujla was not sentenced in court until the spring of 2017.

He was twenty years old when he and a friend, Parminder Basran, got into an altercation with Bath and another man that included a car chase through a neighborhood in Surrey. The confrontation ended after Bath, a twenty-seven-year-old accounting student, was shot through the driver's-side window of his car. Aujla was arrested soon after the incident and spent five months in jail. He was released in March 2005 but then charged again in the fall of 2013 after new evidence was discovered. Aujla and Basran were sentenced four years later in April 2017. Basran pled guilty to manslaughter and got six years in prison. Aujla pled guilty to assault and was sentenced to time served. Aujla started the fight that night and chased Bath down in his truck. But it was Basran who brought and used the gun.

At the sentencing hearing in April 2017, Aujla's lawyer, Michael Klein, told the court that his client had led a constructive life since he was released from jail. He had no prior criminal record and there had been no suggestion of other criminal activity since the incident. He read a statement from Aujla, who was in court that day but didn't think he would be able to read it himself. It concluded: "To the Bath family, I want to say that I am profoundly sorry for the loss of Amandeep. His death for me was unintended and unforeseen. I know that his loss will never leave you and again for that I am truly sorry."

Klein noted that Aujla was not married and did not have children. He said that his client's life had been on hold for the past thirteen years. "He's essentially been waiting for the ultimate outcome of this matter," the lawyer said.

I'm not sure that learning more about Aujla's role in Bath's killing told me much about who he was as a person. I could see how it may have been the tragic outcome of a rash decision he made as a young man. Another aspect of Aujla's character was revealed in the fact that two dozen of his friends spent hundreds of hours and thousands of dollars trying to find his body after he drowned. The Ralstons typically dealt with the family of a missing person. Friends were often involved on searches, but usually in more ancillary ways. Gene couldn't remember another instance when a group of friends had taken it upon themselves to fund and organize such a prolonged and intensive search.

"I don't know what it was that kept us going," Sandhu told me over the phone after we had met at the lake. Every time he left Alouette, he said, starting from the day Aujla drowned, he had the same feeling: *I came here with this many friends and I'm leaving with one short.* "It just gave us that motivation to say, *No matter what, we're going to wake up. We're going to go there. We're going to search. And we're going to get this guy out of there.*"

At some point that afternoon in the parking lot on the hill above the boat launch, Sandhu and his friends discovered that the Ralstons had never tried butter chicken, one of the most popular dishes of Indian cuisine. They couldn't believe it. They kept repeating the question, *You've never tasted butter chicken?* They promised to bring some for lunch when Gene and Sandy came back to continue the search.

Aujla's friends were gregarious and polite. They had an easygoing sense of humor, but the conversation over pizza that afternoon had an undercurrent. The young men had locked onto the Ralstons as their last chance to recover their friend from the lake. Gene and Sandy must have felt the pressure to come back.

"So you get the sense of how bad these people want to find that guy," Pete said after the group had left.

"Oh, yeah. And there are probably a hundred more friends behind them that weren't here," Gene said.

Pete asked if they would come back to Maple Ridge after Nicola Lake.

"It depends on Sandy," he said. She was in the motor home getting ready for the trip. "That's the best place ever to stay with you and your family," Gene added.

They shook hands. Pete wished him luck on the next search. The Ralstons drove to a nearby campground to empty the motor home's septic tank. Then they hitched up the *Kathy G* and started the drive east to Merritt.

CHAPTER FIFTEEN

Treasure Hunters

The first time Gene saw side-scan sonar in action qualifies as one of his six-pack-of-beer stories. He and Sandy got more involved with Idaho Mountain Search and Rescue, their local volunteer search group, in the 1990s. The Ralstons were early adopters of GPS technology, which was useful for mapping the bottoms of lakes and rivers on projects for their environmental consulting business. The technology also proved helpful for training and deploying search dogs to detect human remains underwater. The Ralstons could record the location of an alert from a dog without using a buoy, which ruled out the possibility that the next dog would bark at the floating marker instead of something it smelled.

Gene heard about a search on the Wolf Creek Reservoir in Oregon in the spring of 1999. A young man had drowned after his rowboat was capsized by a gust of wind. The family hired a search team who said that they had equipment on loan from the military. The top-secret gear was supposedly 100 percent effective. Gene asked if he could join them on their boat to see what the hype was all about. The search team imaged the body of the missing man their first afternoon on the reservoir. "I didn't know what a body should look like, but it sure looked like arms and legs and a body to me," Gene said. They continued scanning the lake for another four days, upwind of where the accident happened. Eventually they made their way back to where they started the search and located the body — again. They charged the family $30,000.

Two things became clear to Gene: One, the technology was revolutionary. And two, the team using the sonar was either inept or unscrupulous — maybe some combination of both. "I will remember them until the day I die," Gene said. "That showed me right then and there that it was totally possible for someone unethical to go out and offer their services to a family, find him right away, and charge a daily fee of some sort — a couple thousand dollars a day."

I spoke with several underwater experts, people with long careers in the field, and they all have vivid memories, like Gene, of the first time they saw side-scan sonar in action. Gary Kozak was in his early twenties in 1972 and working as a commercial diver on oil rigs off the coast of Newfoundland, Canada, when he first saw the sonar at work. The image of the bottom was printed on paper. "It really opened up the possibility of not just measuring depth of water anymore, but to remove the water and see what the hell the bottom looked like," Kozak said. "And that just made my mind go wild, thinking about treasure and finding ships with valuable cargoes."

Kozak was bitten by the shipwreck bug early in life. "All of us have some Indiana Jones in us and all of us have that desire to discover and explore," he told me. Kozak grew up in Windsor, Ontario, and learned to scuba dive as a teenager. He explored the Great Lakes and learned all about the wrecks hidden some-where beneath the surface. His life, like the Ralstons', took a sharp turn after seeing how side-scan sonar could magically reveal the bottom of the ocean. He didn't waste any time orga-nizing his own treasure hunt. He found an investor, purchased a sonar, and got to work trying to find the *Dean Richmond*, a wooden freighter that sank in Lake Erie in 1893. The boat had a valuable cargo of lead, zinc, and copper. The rumors, of course, suggested that it was full to the brim with gold and silver. It took Kozak eight or nine seasons — you could only work on the lake from May to September — to find it. He ended up scanning 550 square miles of lake bottom and locating more than thirty other wrecks in the process.

Kozak has found a multitude of airplanes, ships, and submarines over the course of his career. The *San José* is probably the most famous and valuable of all the wrecks he has helped to discover. The Spanish galleon sank in 1708 off the coast of Colombia after a battle with an English squadron. It was carrying gold, silver, gems, and jewelry and was widely considered the holy grail of lost treasure ships. The president of Colombia, Juan Manuel Santos, announced the discovery in early December 2015, a couple of weeks after Kozak and his team found it using an autonomous underwater vehicle equipped with side-scan sonar. The ship was under two thousand feet of water. The estimated value of the cargo is more than a billion dollars.

"It's pure excitement to discover something that has been lost and has never been seen since the day it's been lost," Kozak said. His comment reminded me of the feeling of excitement aboard the *Kathy G* when the image of Liva's boat scrolled into view. A fifty-year-old fiberglass fishing boat doesn't have the same kind of cachet as an eighteenth-century Spanish galleon laden with gold, but the thrill of the moment seems similar — that instant when something that has been missing for a long time blinks back into existence. "Many times these are shipwrecks that have been sought by other people. And it just gives you a high satisfaction to know that you did something that others had failed at," he said.

Kozak described the way sonar technology advanced in

tandem with submarine warfare during the First and Second World Wars. The first side-scan sonars were developed by scientists and engineers working independently of each other and in secret in the 1950s for the navies of Germany, England, France, the United States, Japan, and the Soviet Union. "It was kept pretty hush-hush," he said.

Julius Hagemann, a scientist and engineer, filed a patent in the United States with the title "Facsimile Recording of Sonic Values of the Ocean Bottom" in 1958, but it remained classified until 1980. Hagemann had been an officer in the German navy and an inventor of mine warfare technologies. He and his family were relocated to the United States after the Second World War as part of Operation Paperclip, which brought more than sixteen hundred scientists, engineers, and technicians from the former Nazi Germany.

Hagemann's new job at the US Mine Defense Laboratory in Panama City, Florida, was to invent a device that could detect and locate mines on the ocean floor. Kozak sent me an article published in the magazine *Sea Technology* in November 2015 that outlined the history of Hagemann's sonar, which became known as the Shadowgraph.

The console was a floor-to-ceiling metal cabinet with a desk for the paper printout of the images of the bottom. The sonar could scan eighty feet per side and had a resolution down to three inches, perfect for small, man-made objects like mines. One of the last surviving Shadowgraph towfishes is on display at the Museum of Man in the Sea in Panama City. It has a large depressor wing fastened to the bottom near the top of the towfish as well as a haphazard array of cords, cables, and other electrical appendages. It's bigger and clunkier but still bears a resemblance to the Ralstons' stainless-steel torpedo.

Kozak explained how the concept for this new type of sonar

leaked out from the military context and into the academic community in the late 1950s. The Oceanographic Institute in England and the Scripps Institution of Oceanography in California built their own versions as a way to study the geology of the seafloor. These new systems prioritized imaging much larger areas over the capacity to find smaller objects like mines or bodies.

Marty Klein, an American engineer, developed the first side-scan sonar for commercial use in 1966 while working for a company called EG&G. Doc Edgerton, Klein's former teacher at MIT, was a part owner. Klein left EG&G in 1967 to start his own firm, Klein & Associates. Few people knew about sonar technology or understood its potential, so Edgerton and Klein tried to build a market by going out and finding famous shipwrecks. Klein used his system to locate a two-thousand-year-old Roman ship off the coast of Turkey as well as two wrecks in Lake Ontario from the War of 1812. Edgerton used the EG&G sonar to image the *Mary Rose*, which sank in a battle in 1545 near England. Both Edgerton and Klein tried to get an image of the Loch Ness monster. Side-scan sonar played a critical role in the discovery of the *Titanic* in 1985.

The key development for finding drowning victims came with the release of Klein's high-frequency sonar in the early 1980s. "It now had the resolution where you could image something like a drowning victim on the seafloor and you'd resolve it. You'd resolve his legs, his arms, his body," Kozak told me.

After the first three summers of trying to find the *Dean Richmond* in Lake Erie, Kozak ran out of funds. "I went broke, starving, married, a couple of young kids. I needed a job to actually make some real money," he said. He had yet to find his treasure ship but had become an expert with a powerful new technology. Kozak had taught himself how to use the system and how to read the shadows in the printouts to identify what he was seeing on the seafloor. Klein hired Kozak as a field engineer in 1978, and he went on to create the first training program for the sonar system. He stayed with Klein & Associates for thirty-four years and then joined EdgeTech, a company that was spun out from the oceanographic division of EG&G after Edgerton passed away in 1990.

I was curious about the two decades between when Klein released the first commercial high-frequency sonar and when Gene took part on that search on the Wolf Creek Reservoir in Oregon in 1999. I asked Kozak why it took so long for the sonar to catch on as a reliable way to find corpses in water. He told me that Klein & Associates and EG&G didn't see the police, sheriffs, or firefighters, the people responsible for drowning victim searches, as a viable market. Dive teams were few and far between back then. "Commercial manufacturers didn't invest time and money into trying to sell to them because we felt there just wasn't a lot of money available," he said. It was $30,000 for the sonar system alone, never mind the cost of the boat and winch to run it.

Kozak credits the Ralstons, even though they didn't get going until the fall of 2000, with raising the profile of side-scan sonar as an effective way to find bodies in water. "They are absolutely pioneers in exposing the technology to a wider audience in the world," he said. "It was the Ralstons, with their successful recoveries, that really brought it to the forefront that you can use this stuff to find drowning victims."

Police and fire departments in the United States eventually became lucrative customers for sonar manufacturers after the Homeland Security Act, which was drafted as a response to the terrorist attack on the World Trade Center, was signed into law in 2002. Kozak explained that a huge reservoir of grant money became available to first responders through the Department of Homeland Security for new technologies and equipment like sonar, which could be used to search ports and docks for explosives as well as drowning victims.

I asked Kozak why demand for the Ralstons' services continues to increase even as more police agencies have purchased their own sonar systems. He told me that enthusiasm, like most things in life, is the defining trait of a successful sonar operator. Even the US Navy, which has several side-scan sonar systems that they use regularly for a variety of applications, calls on a private contractor for their most serious searches, like if a military plane crashes into the ocean. Navy personnel, like police or firefighters, are competent but not always passionate. "They don't lie awake at night thinking about sonar technology," Kozak said.

Side-scan sonar makes it possible to illuminate the secrets of deep water, but it's not as simple as an on–off switch. A skilled operator has to understand the mechanics of the gear and the acoustics, the physics of sound in water, to make sense of what they're seeing on the screen. "You can take the best tool in the world and give it to somebody and they can't do shit with it. You can take the worst tool in the world and give it to a craftsman and he'll do amazing stuff with it," Kozak told me.

Gene told Sandy all about the sonar system when he got back home from the search on the Wolf Creek Reservoir. It took about a year, but they decided it was worth the investment. The plan was to buy the sonar for their business. They could use it to survey the bottoms of lakes and rivers and for detecting obstructions at the base of a dam or on the floor of a river before a new bridge was built. The Ralstons envisioned using it three or four times a year to look for drowning victims in lakes and rivers close to home. Gene and Sandy decided right from the start that they wouldn't charge anything beyond their expenses to look for a body.

It took about four months over the summer of 2000 for all the parts and pieces to arrive. They purchased a 600 kHz side-scan sonar from Marine Sonic. Crayton Fenn fabricated their heavy-duty towfish out of steel so they could search deep water. They bought nine hundred feet of electromechanical cable and a special winch drum. They already had the boat, which was named the *Sandy Jean* (Jean is Sandy's middle name) back then. They bought it in the mid-1990s for a multiyear contract with the Army Corps of Engineers to do sediment sampling on the Lower Snake and Columbia Rivers. Gene estimated that it cost $100,000 to get the boat operational with the new sonar.

The last part to arrive was the transducer, the part that generated the sound pulses and fit inside the towfish. They took it out for a maiden voyage on the Lucky Peak Reservoir, which was a half-hour drive from their house. "We'd heard that there were some old buildings and whatnot that had been flooded from the old days when it was ranchland in that area," Gene told me. "We imaged some of those. They weren't real good because we were still learning."

And then the Ralstons heard about a twenty-four-year-old man who had drowned in Bear Lake, Utah, in August 2000. Gene can't remember if he heard about the incident on the news or from someone from Idaho Mountain Search and Rescue. Brandon Larsen had been swimming from a boat with some friends and family. "He apparently was a bit of a jokester, so to speak, and they thought he was just kidding when he was splashing around," Gene said. "Then all of a sudden, he just disappeared."

Gene called the Rich County Sheriff's Search and Rescue Office in late September and told them about the sonar. The Ralstons arrived September 28 and imaged Brandon's body at a depth of 148 feet the next day. "The day of the recovery, they were there, probably twelve or fifteen of them — family members, friends — in the parking lot. Lots of hugs went around and a few tears shed," Gene said. The gratitude from the family made an indelible impression on the Ralstons. They still kept in touch with Monte Larsen, Brandon's father. His sister invited them to her wedding in the spring of 2019. They had to miss it because of a search.

Within two weeks of getting home from Bear Lake, the Ralstons got a call from Sheila Kimmell. She had heard a story on the radio about a search team from Idaho that used some kind of mysterious technology to find the body of a young man months after he drowned. Kimmell's eighteen-year-old daughter, Lisa, had been abducted, raped, tortured, and murdered over six days in the spring of 1988. Her body had been found, but they had not brought her killer to justice. Finding Lisa's car might provide clues about her murderer. Kimmell said there was a good chance it had been dumped in the Alcova Reservoir in Wyoming.

"I could hear a lot of pain in her voice," Gene told me. "It affected us a lot. I couldn't wait to get there." The Ralstons scanned all the logical places where a car could have been sent off a cliff and into the lake. "Search conditions were miserable. It was in the wintertime and snowing and blowing and colder than the dickens. We did what we could," Gene said. Lisa's car was found and dug up years later on a property in rural Wyoming that belonged to Dale Wayne Eaton. He was convicted of her murder in 2004.

The Ralstons never anticipated how far and how fast word

would spread. They went on sixteen searches in 2001. One was for the body of a young man who had jumped off the Chesapeake Bay Bridge, on the opposite side of the country in Maryland. "I don't remember how they found out about us from that far away," Gene said. "We had no idea that it would develop into such a nationwide, and continent-wide practically, situation for us." Buying the sonar, acquiring a new technology for searching underwater, had flung open a door to the suffering of perfect strangers. And for better or for worse, the Ralstons never figured out how to close it back up again.

The majority of the search requests in the early years came from the families of the missing person. "It kept us very busy. It was way beyond what we had ever expected," Gene said. The Ralstons never promoted the use of their sonar to find drowning victims. All they did was add a page about the technology to their website. The main driver, as far as Gene could figure out, was the growing number of media reports about their successful recoveries. It didn't take long for law enforcement to take notice of the married couple from Idaho and their remarkable ability to find bodies in water.

CHAPTER SIXTEEN

Black Magic

In February 2002, FBI agent Tony Tindall caught a decisive break in one of the biggest cases of his career. A suspect in a string of recent kidnappings had agreed to turn on his associates and cooperate with the investigation. Ainar Altmanis, a forty-two-year-old from Latvia, confessed that everyone abducted by the group was already dead. He then lead Tindall and dozens of other law enforcement officials to three different bridges over two reservoirs just west of Yosemite National Park in California.

The four victims went missing in late 2001 and early 2002. Their families had so far wired more than $1 million in ransom to an account in New York, which then transferred the funds to a bank in Dubai. Tindall was confident the missing victims were somewhere under those bridges that crossed the New Melones and Don Pedro Reservoirs, but as a certified scuba diver he knew it was going to be nearly impossible to recover them. The water was more than three hundred feet deep. They had come so close to solving the case but had run into what seemed like an insurmountable obstacle. "This is a trial that is very serious in the respect that it's murder, murder for profit," Tindall told me over the phone. "So there cannot be any mistakes in this case, and it has to be very tight. And without the victims, their bodies to tie in the evidence, it would be a difficult case to stand trial."

Tindall described feeling discouraged as he stood on one of the bridges and looked out over the lake. It's not like the FBI could just drain two gigantic reservoirs. Tindall thought about how people used to fire a cannon across a lake hoping that the shock wave would dislodge a body from the bottom and allow it to float to the surface. Another old technique was to pour mercury into a hollowed-out loaf of bread and set it adrift on the water in the belief that it would somehow gravitate to the spot on the surface above where the body rested on the bottom.

And that's when Keith Lunney, a lieutenant with the local Tuolumne County Sheriff's Office, told Tindall about a pair of underwater search-and-recovery specialists who happened to be using a new kind of sonar technology to look for the body of a missing man in a nearby lake. "It was kind of like black magic," Tindall said, describing his reaction to hearing about the Ralstons and their ability to see through water.

The sun was setting by the time Gene and Sandy made it back to their truck and camper after a long day on the Beardsley Reservoir in early March 2002. They had found the body of Scott Glover. It had been three and a half years since he fell off his boat while fishing. Divers performed the recovery that afternoon. The Ralstons discovered several handwritten notes taped to the doors and windshield of their truck: *Call Lieutenant Lunney as soon as you get back to town. It's urgent.*

Gene and Sandy drove to the town of Sonora later that night to meet with Lunney, who told them that their expertise was needed by some other folks, though he wasn't allowed to tell them who or for what. The next morning, the Ralstons were briefed by agents from the FBI on the series of kidnappings. Lunney told the Ralstons that they were under no obligation to help because doing so meant possible retribution by the criminal group, who were potentially connected to the Russian mafia.

Gene called his cousin, a recently retired FBI agent, for advice. He told Gene that he didn't think they would be at much risk for retaliation. The Ralstons had volunteered their sonar system on more than two dozen searches for drowning victims by the winter of 2002. This, however, would be their first search for a homicide victim. "You don't see the typical image of arms and legs out. Of course we knew that — we call it packaged, tied up, and weighted," Gene told me.

Over the next two weeks, the Ralstons successfully pinpointed all four bodies on the bottom of the New Melones Reservoir. Tindall arranged for the FBI's dive team in New York to ship an ROV to retrieve them from the bottom. The last recovery proved the hardest. People had dumped all sorts of refuse, including large appliances, off the Parrotts Ferry Bridge. It was tricky to sort through the sonar images of refrigerators and washing machines strewn across the bottom. And when Gene and Sandy managed to identify something that looked like a body, the FBI's ROV operator dismissed it as a rock after viewing it on the submersible's underwater camera.

"There was just enough stuff on her remains, which is typical of someone that's been in the water a long time, that it kind of looked like a rock from a distance. It was a gelatinous mass," Gene said. Tindall told the ROV operator to nudge it gently. "It was like bumping into a beehive. All kinds of little bugs took off."

Tindall was one of the divers who met the bodies as the ROV returned to the surface. "Every single one of those victims, I was no more than a hand's reach from them from thirty feet, to the surface, to the shore," he told me. "I just felt some connection to each one of them. I felt like someone needed to be with them. They're brought from their cold, chilly graves, all the way up to the surface, and now they're ready to tell their story."

That story included hard evidence that directly linked the victims to the perpetrators. The same type of zip ties used to bind their bodies to the weights were found at one of the suspect's homes. The FBI found receipts at the house for the weights, a kind commonly used at gyms.

Six people were sentenced for their participation in the plot. Iouri Mikhel and Jurijus Kadamovas were given the death penalty. They were considered the leaders of the group and had come up with the plan to kidnap wealthy people, extort their relatives for money, and then kill their captives anyway.

"We were able to return these victims back to the families and give the families justice. Their fathers, mothers, sisters, and brothers," Tindall said. "The crimes that were committed against these victims, their murders, how egregious the subjects were, it was just meant to be that Sandy and Gene were where they were at the right time."

Tindall, who retired from the FBI in 2018, told me that this case helped to convince the agency to expand its dive program. New FBI underwater search teams were established in Los Angeles, Washington, and Miami after the case. The FBI acquired sonar equipment based on the same setup as the Ralstons'. "It was Gene's work, and the work on that case, and the absolute positive results that he provided, that inspired the FBI to then secure the technology," Tindall said.

James Davidson left the FBI in 2015 but was one of the primary investigators on that case back in 2001 and 2002. It involved five people killed in the United States; Davidson helped with investigations that later connected the group to two more homicides overseas, one in Cyprus and another in Turkey.

Davidson interrogated Altmanis about what was motivating the group. He wanted to know why Mikhel and Kadamovas set this murder-for-profit scheme in motion in the first place. "They wanted to have their own jet plane. They wanted to have $60 million in the bank and so they were going to keep doing these kidnappings until the bodies broke the surface of the reservoir. I hadn't come across that before, that this was the beginning of a career move on the part of these two guys," Davidson said. "It's a career case. I'm most proud of it from the standpoint that we saved a lot of lives."

One morning early on during the search on the New Melones Reservoir, Davidson and Tindall walked down to the dock only to find that the Ralstons had already left. They were on the water and searching. "Gene and Sandy . . . got up early and went out on their own and located the first body on their own," Davidson told me. "That's how determined they were."

Not long after the Ralstons got home from the search with the FBI, they got a call from Dan Pontbriand, a district park ranger with Olympic National Park on the northwest coast of Washington State. Pontbriand had heard about Gene and Sandy from some of his colleagues in the National Park Service. The Ralstons had been on several successful searches in Lake Powell, which was part of the Glen Canyon National Recreation Area in southern Utah. The sprawling reservoir was more than six hundred feet deep and a popular vacation destination.

Pontbriand told Gene about Blanche and Russell Warren, a young married couple who disappeared on July 3, 1929. The park ranger was trying to find their car, a 1927 Chevrolet sedan. The couple was suspected to have veered off the Olympic Highway, which followed the south shore of the lake, and into the water. The main problem, Pontbriand told Gene, was that the bottom dropped off steeply from the spot on the shore where they thought the car had crashed. The area had presented all sorts of challenges for scuba divers. Gene told him he could be there on April 12. Their fee was $50 in gas money.

It didn't take long for Sam and Nina, Gene's parents, to notice how much time their son and daughter-in-law were spending on searches for bodies. They had started to worry. The two couples were close. They would often go on vacations together, like taking trips to fish for salmon off the coast of Vancouver Island. And Gene and Sandy would spend a night or two at his parents' place whenever they passed New Plymouth at the start or end of one of their work projects.

Sam and Nina were skeptical about the Ralstons' new venture. They understood that the work was important and helpful for the families in mourning, but it also sounded strange — finding corpses sometimes long after the person had died. Sam, in particular, was concerned that the volunteer work was interfering with his son and daughter-in-law's business. "I think Dad felt that I should be out doing environmental work and earning money and those kinds of things, or taking better care of our own property or helping them," Gene said. "It got to the point where I wouldn't go hunting with him because we were always busy doing something related to our searches. I don't think he liked that very much because I was his favorite hunting partner."

The Ralstons invited Sam and Nina to join them for their search on Lake Crescent in April 2002. They wanted to show their parents what it was that they found so exciting and meaningful about using their new sonar to find bodies.

Pontbriand ended up writing a book called *The Missing Ones* about the search for the Warrens. Blanche and Russell were in their midthirties and had two young sons when they vanished. The effort to find them spanned generations of people from the communities that surround Lake Crescent, which looks like a crooked blue smile on maps of the Pacific Northwest. Pontbriand was an avid scuba diver, and his book tracked the evolution of underwater searching technologies. The seventy-three-year history of the search on Lake Crescent highlighted the difficulty of finding anything underwater, even something as big as a car, before the invention of sonar.

Russell Warren left his sons, Frank, age fourteen, and Charles, age twelve, with a neighbor in the small logging camp where they lived near the town of Forks. He told the boys that he would be back in time to take them to a local hot springs the next day. He drove to Port Angeles to pick up his wife from the hospital. The two were last seen on the afternoon of July 3, 1929, headed west and back toward home on the Olympic Highway in their 1927 Chevrolet sedan. They had bought a new washing machine in town for $60.

Maybe it was because the couple vanished along with their car, but rumors quickly spread that the Warrens had skipped town. Jack Pike, the sheriff of Clallam County in 1929, was sympathetic to the plight of Frank and Charles. Not only were their parents missing, but the boys also had to endure all the gossip speculating that they had been abandoned.

The sheriff never suspected that Russell and Blanche left intentionally. He worked hard to find them but didn't get his first real break in the case until a month and a half after the couple went missing. Someone eventually discovered evidence of a car going off the road and into the lake at a spot about three-quarters of the way west down the ten-mile-long lake from Port Angeles.

Pike burned through most of his annual budget on the search for the Warrens that summer. He organized several dragging operations, including one by a commercial diving company from Seattle that used a barge and a ferryboat. The sheriff also recruited a local diver to look for the car and the Warrens in the lake.

"A dive operation in 1929, in fresh or salt water, would have gone something like this," wrote Pontbriand. A diver dressed in a suit of heavy, waterproof canvas that was fitted with a thick rubber collar. The giant brass helmet had three or four viewing ports. The diver risked rolling over forward if they tried to look down at their feet. An air hose was mounted to a valve on the helmet and supplied by a hand pump on the surface. The diver wore heavy lead shoes to compensate for the flotation of the suit. All told a dive suit back then weighed about a hundred pounds. The divers couldn't swim. They had to walk on the bottom, so it couldn't be too steep or muddy or crowded with debris.

Pike was out of luck and out of money by September 1929. He was confident he had located the spot on the road where the Warrens had crashed into the lake. He had found a small number of items in the water, including a sun visor that was confirmed to be from the same model sedan as the missing one, but not the car itself or the Warrens. Bertha Matheson, Blanche's mother, took Frank and Charles to her family's farm in Montana.

And that's where the story would have ended if Bob Caso, a longshoreman from Port Angeles, had not taken up the new sport of scuba diving in 1953. Jacques Cousteau, the famous underwater explorer, and Émile Gagnan, an engineer, developed the first commercially successful scuba system, which they called the Aqua Lung, in the early 1940s. The streamlined equipment allowed divers to swim freely without ropes or hoses connected to a boat at the surface. The gear made underwater exploration accessible to the general public, although it was still considered on the extreme end of recreational activities in the early 1950s.

Gary Kozak, the treasure hunter, told me that the exhilaration of scuba diving, the sensation of moving and breathing in an otherworldly environment, can only hold your attention for so long. Every diver eventually has to find something to do while they're below the surface. For some, that's photography. Others take an interest in aquatic life or explore caves. Kozak turned to shipwrecks, and Caso had been drawn to a similar path. He visited the library in Port Angeles to research lost ships that he and his dive buddies could try to find. But then one of the librarians introduced him to the story of the Warrens and how they had likely crashed their car into Lake Crescent.

Pontbriand described how the unsolved case got under Caso's skin. He started collecting all the material he could find about the couple. He tracked down Jack Pike, who had retired as the sheriff by then, and visited him at his home in Port Angeles. He talked to the nurse who cared for Blanche when she was in the hospital. Caso used his research to plan several dives in Lake Crescent over the years, but he and his friends never saw any signs of the Chevy sedan.

Pontbriand began his book with a story about meeting Caso at his office at the Storm King Ranger Station, which was next to the Olympic Highway and had a clear view of the north end of Lake Crescent. It was April 2001, and Caso, who was in his late seventies, arrived with several rolled-up maps under one arm and a thick file folder labeled THE MISSING ONES. The two men, both experienced divers, sat down next to the cabin's stone fireplace and discussed the events from the summer of 1929.

Something passed that afternoon, like a baton in a relay race, between the park ranger and the retired longshoreman. The librarian in Port Angeles had handed the story of the Warrens off to Caso in 1953, and now he had given it to Pontbriand. It was remarkable how the mystery neatly stepped from one generation and into the next. The question of what happened to the Warrens offered Pontbriand, like Caso before him, a reason to spend more time beneath the surface of Lake Crescent, which is six hundred feet deep in some places.

The mystery also held the promise of finding something that had been lost. And I think that type of discovery — finding a ship, an artifact, or even a corpse — is a uniquely satisfying accomplishment. Something clicks back into place, some misshapen contour of reality gets bent back into form. Finding missing things serves as a reminder, the kind of reminder that we need to hear over and over again to believe, that the universe plays by a predictable set of rules and we therefore have a measure of agency and control over our lives.

Pontbriand read all the old newspaper articles in the file later that night after meeting Caso. He learned how all the communities around Lake Crescent had closely followed the search for the Warrens during the summer of 1929. A hundred people turned up on the shoreline to watch the dive operation organized by Pike to search for the car. Pontbriand wondered about Frank and Charles, how their lives had turned out. He looked them up in the phone book that night and found a listing for each brother in Port Angeles. He dialed the numbers. "Thus began the journey that would change the lives of many people, including myself," he wrote.

Pontbriand organized several dives over the summer and fall of 2001. He found a trail of evidence, which included a lid to an antique washing machine, on the bottom of the lake next to a bend in the road. The artifacts led the divers to the edge of an underwater cliff that was only about forty or fifty feet from the rocky shoreline. The pristine, blue-green water of Lake Crescent turned pitch black beyond the lip of the dropoff. The car seemed close at hand, but Pontbriand and his team of divers were at the limit of their abilities. None of them were certified as technical divers.

Almost all scuba divers, about 98 percent, don't go below 130 feet because it's too dangerous and requires extensive training and additional equipment. The atmosphere at sea level is 21 percent oxygen and 78 percent nitrogen. The other 1 percent is made up of inert gases like helium. These gases are dissolved and absorbed by the body's tissues when under pressure. The deeper a diver goes and the longer they spend at depth, the more nitrogen and oxygen build up in the body. The oxygen is consumed and used up in normal cellular metabolism, but the nitrogen doesn't have anywhere to go and becomes increasingly concentrated. High levels of nitrogen affect the central nervous system and cause light-headedness, tunnel vision, impaired judgment, and anxiety. Jacques Cousteau called this sensation the "rapture of the deep." Gene calls it "the woolly buggers."

Mike Clement, a friend of the Ralstons who is certified as a technical diver, told me that the effects of nitrogen narcosis vary from one person to the next. Some level of confusion starts to creep in for most divers at around ninety feet. The disorientation can be exacerbated by a number of factors, like if the visibility is low or there is a strong current or dense vegetation. "Narcosis is really, really serious approaching two hundred feet," Clement said. "You have to take a note down there if you're changing a shackle on an anchor or something. You have to take a slate down with you to remind yourself what the heck it is you're doing there."

Technical divers adjust the mixture of gases in their tanks to minimize the amount of nitrogen that accumulates in their body. They have to make a series of decompression stops as they return to the surface. A slow, staggered ascent ensures that any dissolved nitrogen off-gases safely from the lungs. The bends, or decompression sickness, happens when a diver comes up too fast and the nitrogen in their bloodstream starts

to fizz. Bubbles collect in the joints and organs, causing excruciating pain.

Pontbriand went on two dives in early 2002 to a depth of
150 feet. He and his diving partner used an oxygen-enriched
mixture of air and spent only four minutes at that depth. They
discovered that the bottom at the base of the cliff was at about
160 feet. It was made up of the same shale rock and continued
to slope down at a forty-five-degree angle. Beyond the abyss
was more abyss. They didn't see the car. The ranger figured it
was time to call in additional resources.

Gene and Sandy set up their search grid in the deep water off
the south shore of Lake Crescent at 9:00 AM on Saturday, April 13,
2002. Sam and Nina, who were in their early eighties, decided to
watch from shore instead of aboard the *Kathy G.* Meldrim Point,
the bend in the road where it was suspected that the Warrens
had crashed into the lake, had a small beach of gravel-sized
rocks that jutted into the lake right next to the highway.

At about 2:00 PM, Gene motioned to Pontbriand to join him
on the *Kathy G.* The park ranger was on another boat with Bob
Caso and two deep-water technical divers. Gene showed the
ranger something strange that he had picked up in one of the
sonar images. He was, as usual, cautious in his assessment.
"Gene could not even begin to guess what it was other than to
say that it appeared to be man-made," Pontbriand wrote. The
object was long and angular. It had a circular shape at one
end and cast a large shadow. Gene estimated that it was under
about two hundred feet of water. It was hard to gauge the depth
exactly because of the steep pitch of the bottom.

The Ralstons dropped their marker, two plastic milk crates
stacked on top of each other, next to the target so the divers
could follow the rope down to the bottom. Pontbriand had a
terrible time waiting for them to return to the surface. It was

one year to the day since Caso had first told him the story about the Warrens. "I wanted to jump in the lake," he wrote. "I needed to know!"

The divers surfaced about fifty feet from the ranger's boat. "Did you find the washing machine?" Pontbriand shouted across the water. "No, we found the car!" one of them responded. The divers had looked inside the vehicle but didn't see any evidence of human remains. It would take another two years of intermittent searches, but another diver working with Pontbriand found a femur bone and skull not far from the wreck. DNA analysis confirmed it was from Russell Warren.

The park ranger included a photo of the car in his book. It was lying on its side and was half buried in the rocky slope. The front wheel was covered in rocks, but the back wheel, the one that appeared so clearly on the sonar image, was free of debris. It took five hours for the Ralstons to help solve a case that had haunted a community for more than seventy years.

Pontbriand called Rollie Warren later that same day to tell him that they had found his grandparents' car. He had been in touch with Charles Warren's son, who lived close by on Whidbey Island, since the summer of 2001. Rollie arrived at Lake Crescent with his wife and daughter the next morning.

Sam and Nina met the grandchild and great-grandchild of Blanche and Russell. They learned more about Charles and Frank and how difficult life for the two brothers had been. Neither of them had talked much about their parents and what had happened. The brothers found it too painful to revisit the memories and unanswered questions from the summer of 1929. They both died young. Charles, the younger of the two Warren boys, was forty-six when he disappeared on June 14, 1964. He never returned from a fishing trip off the coast of Northern California. Some evidence points to the likelihood that his boat was struck by a freighter in the fog and then sank. Frank died at fifty-seven from health complications related to an alcohol-use disorder.

Gene told me that he and Sandy noticed a change in his parents after they got home from Lake Crescent. Where Sam and Nina had before expressed skepticism and disapproval about their work finding drowning victims, they now asked lots of questions. They were curious about the details of each new search. The elder Ralstons were more understanding when Gene and Sandy were unable to visit for months at a time. "I think that trip really made them understand the importance of what we do," Gene said.

Sam and Nina started to cut out and collect newspaper articles about Gene and Sandy and their searches in lakes and rivers across Canada and the United States. They invited a reporter to come to their house in New Plymouth so they could talk about the value of what Gene and Sandy were doing. "He says it makes him feel good to help somebody," Sam told the journalist from the *Argus Observer* about his son.

The Ralstons went on eleven more searches in 2002. They spent the first three months of 2003 working with police to look for Laci Peterson, a pregnant woman who had been murdered by her husband. Her body was discovered in April, washed ashore in San Francisco Bay. Gene and Sandy went on fourteen more searches that year and found seven bodies.

They reached a turning point in 2004. They decided to stop promoting their business because it was getting in the way of the searches for drowning victims. "I would have to tell a family that we couldn't come for two or three weeks, and that bothered me," Gene said.

The surprising level of demand had pulled the Ralstons deeper into the world of underwater recovery than they ever anticipated. It was their disillusionment with environmental consulting, however, that pushed them to embrace the volunteer work full-time. Gene and Sandy had grown frustrated and weary of federal and state regulators. "We discovered that even though we would write a lengthy report, a very detailed report about something, most of them didn't even read it," Gene told me. "It was crushing that they wouldn't even read it."

He described giving presentations on how a company could mitigate the environmental effects of a proposed industrial project, like a new hydropower station on a river, only to realize that the people in charge of the approval process were asleep in the back of the room. It seemed like their reports, which were often the result of weeks of work in the field, were just a box that companies had to check and not a real factor when it came to deciding whether a project should go ahead.

The consulting work provided a substantial paycheck but felt hollow. Underwater recovery flipped that equation on its head. It cost them money to look for bodies, but the sense of satisfaction and purpose was profound.

The Ralstons were in their late fifties when they decided to scale back their business. They realized they had enough savings to support their modest lifestyle into retirement. They didn't aspire to travel the world or buy a new car every other year. "We were happy with what we had," Gene said. "We felt that it was more important to do the drowning victim searches rather than to go out and make a bunch more money."

Gene liked to return to the same point whenever we talked about the reasons underwater searching took over their personal and professional lives. He rationalized the decision by explaining that he has always been the type of person to help someone change a flat tire on the side of the road. "I'm usually the first one to stop to help fix it even when I have an appointment for a meeting that I'm an hour drive away from. I stop and help them. And of course I'm late for the meeting. It's something that I do."

And if you look past all the technology and grisliness associated with body recovery, maybe it was as simple as stopping to check on a family who was stranded on the side of the road. The Ralstons found a unique way to help people get moving again. And they had the presence of mind to recognize that it was in those moments, the ones in which they dropped what they were doing to fix a stranger's flat tire, that they found the most meaning.

CHAPTER SEVENTEEN

Riderless Horse

It was early afternoon on Thursday, April 15, 2021, by the time the *Kathy G* was on the water. The truck had to back up far enough into the lake that the boat could float up off the trailer and drift backward out of the wooden supports. The water level on Nicola Lake was extremely low, even for that time of year. Gene had scouted out two other boat launches so far that morning. He had driven up and down both sides of the fourteen-mile-long lake before reluctantly agreeing to try the launch at Monck Provincial Park, which was part of a small campground on the north side of the lake.

Richard Tyner, who was sixty-nine years old, balanced on the narrow metal beam of the trailer where it connected to the truck hitch so he could help push the boat off its supports and into the lake. He looked like he was dressed for the golf course in a windbreaker jacket and yellow baseball hat. The trailer wheels cut deep furrows in the gravel that extended for several feet beyond the concrete slabs of the launch before reaching the water. Gene was worried the truck would have a hard time pulling the boat back out on such soft ground. There was no dock at the campground, so we climbed into the bow of the boat from shore.

"So this is the best body-hunting boat in the world, huh?" Jack Tyner said to me as we found a place to sit at the back of the *Kathy G.* Sandy was at the wheel, and Gene was beside her at his station in front of the monitor. We left Richard, Jen, two FBI agents, and two RCMP officers, the lead investigators on the murder case, behind at the boat launch. Sandy kept the boat close to shore and headed west down the lake. The water was fifty-seven feet deep. The bottom looked clean and smooth on the monitor.

Jack's question caught me off guard. It was an astute way to describe the Ralstons' boat, one that hadn't occurred to me. Jack had a narrow face with a scruffy beard and a subtle under-bite. He was thirty years old — two weeks away from thirty-one, the same age as his older brother when he vanished. Jack had a habit of standing close to people when he talked, leaning forward on the balls of his feet and towering over the person. It was hard not to move back in response. He was wiry and tall, all the more so because of his weathered cowboy hat. He reminded me of the Man with No Name, the character that Clint Eastwood played in Gene's favorite movie, *The Good, the Bad and the Ugly.*

"You want me to clean that windshield off for you, Sandy?" Jack asked. He noticed a squeegee on board and dipped it into the lake and started washing the glass before she could respond. He was alert for ways he could pitch in.

"Did that help or hurt?" he asked. His voice had a slight nasal quality.

"That's beautiful, thank you," Gene said.

The lake was flat. The day was hot. Sandy was wearing big, dark sunglasses. She steered the boat to follow the contours of the base of a broad, low mountain. So far the slope of the shoreline was relatively gradual. The hillside was covered in sagebrush, dry grass, sparse trees, and rocky outcroppings. It looked like rough country, the kind of dusty, cracked landscape where vegetation struggles to survive. The Ralstons were on the lookout for steeper terrain.

The Nicola Valley was in the rain shadow of the Coast Mountains. It was much drier than Maple Ridge, almost desert-like. The lake was part of the Nicola River. The concrete dam on the southwest end was built in the 1920s to provide water for irrigation and power generation. The headquarters for the Nicola Ranch, the place where Ben worked, was half a mile west of the dam; Merritt, a city of eight thousand people, was another seven miles down the two-lane highway.

"There's a bear," Jack said, about half an hour into the search. He nodded in the direction of shore. It took me a moment but I picked out the shape of a large brown animal mostly concealed by the wide trunk of an evergreen tree.

"That's a pretty good-sized bear," he said.

I asked if he thought it was a grizzly.

"You ever seen a grizzly?" he replied.

I launched into a story about an encounter I had on a camping trip with a grizzly, but stopped short when I realized that Jack was asking because he thought the difference between a grizzly and a black bear was obvious. And that it was clearly a black bear behind the tree. He said there's no mistaking a grizzly. They have a broad head and short, round ears.

"I've killed four bears," Jack said. And then after a brief pause, he added: "All in self-defense."

He told me about working as a hunting guide in the Yukon. The bears up north, unlike those in places like BC or Wyoming, had never seen people before. They were curious and always came to check you out, which could get dangerous.

Jack divided his time between working as a cowboy and as a hunting guide. The Tyners' ranch, the one he'd started with his brother and father ten years before, was relatively small. They had 150 cattle on a lease for a thousand acres. Jack freelanced for other ranches in the area near Laramie. He also trained and sold horses. It sounded like you needed to be entrepreneurial to be a cowboy these days. You had to hustle. It didn't take me long, talking to Jack at the back of the *Kathy G* that afternoon, to get the sense that he was exactly the kind of brother you would want to come looking for you if you ever got into trouble.

The search on Nicola Lake was the first time that the Tyners had been back to Merritt and the ranch since Ben went missing during the winter of 2019. A crew of loggers had found a riderless horse, outfitted with a saddle and reins, early on Monday morning, January 28. The mare was wandering up and down a back road on Swakum Mountain, which overlooked Merritt from the north. It was eventually identified as Gunny, a horse that belonged to Ben Tyner, the new manager of the Nicola Ranch. Someone Ben worked with remembered him talking earlier in the week about going to look for stray cattle, but Ben had never said where or when he was going. No one had seen him since Saturday night. He had not shown up for work on Monday morning.

There were several ranches in the valley, and so it was not all that uncommon for someone to find a horse without a rider. "We scrape at least one cowboy off these mountains every winter," Lynne Broekhuizen, the manager of Nicola Valley Search and Rescue, told me. A riderless horse usually meant one of two things. One, the horse got away from the rider. Or two, the rider had fallen off and been injured.

Nicola Valley SAR and the RCMP started looking for Ben on Monday afternoon with what's called a hasty search. The theory was that the missing person was either lost or injured and needed help quickly. You wanted to reach them fast, so you started with the areas of highest probability. Searchers hiked into the bush in every direction from the point of last seen, which in this case was the spot on the mountain where the horse was found.

The Coquihalla Highway was the main road people took to travel across the interior of British Columbia. It was a four-lane divided highway that ran north–south between the ranch and the mountain. Cowboys had to ride through one of a handful of underpasses built under the busy, high-speed road. It had snowed not long before Ben went missing, so it should have been relatively easy to pick out his tracks and find the path that he had taken from the ranch. Not only that, but the local SAR team had several experienced trackers, people trained to follow subtle disturbances in the snow and vegetation. "We couldn't find a trace of how that horse got up there," Broekhuizen said. That was the first indication that Ben's disappearance was not as straightforward as it initially appeared.

Gunny provided another clue. She was known as a gentle and reliable horse. It was unlikely that she had bucked Ben off and then bolted away. The bridle was missing one rein, but otherwise the horse and rigging were in good condition. There likely would have been fresh spur marks on Gunny's side if Ben had encountered some kind of trouble in the bush, like an attack from an animal.

Planes with heat sensors flew over the mountain Monday night. SAR volunteers started a grid search the following morning. "Take a specific area and just very carefully comb it, looking for information, looking for any clues," Broekhuizen said. They didn't uncover any evidence of how Ben got to Swakum Mountain. The theory started to evolve. Someone must have driven the cowboy and his horse to the mountain, but nobody came forward to say they had given Ben a ride.

With no new information to narrow down the missing man's whereabouts, the search area and the search effort kept expanding. It turned into the largest Broekhuizen had ever seen. Nineteen other volunteer SAR groups from across the province arrived to help as the week progressed. More than two hundred SAR members took shifts looking for Ben. Broekhuizen estimated that another hundred people from the area, including ranchers on horseback and members of the Lower Nicola Indian Band, one of four First Nations groups in the valley, volunteered to help.

People searched on foot, snowshoes, snowmobiles, and ATVs; they scanned the valley from above in helicopters, from planes, and with drones. They scoured the mountain over a nine-mile radius north from Merritt. They walked through forests, creek bottoms, grasslands, rock bluffs, and knee-deep snow at the higher elevations. The weather was mild at the outset of the search but got much colder later in the week.

Jack jumped right into the middle of it all. The Tyners arrived in Merritt on Tuesday afternoon, the day after Gunny was found, and Jack went out on horseback the next morning. He found the missing rein along the same road where the loggers had come across Gunny. The rein was the only tangible evidence related to Ben ever found on the mountain.

The RCMP called off the search on Sunday, February 3, a week after Ben was reported missing. The temperature had plummeted to minus thirteen degrees, and the roads were so icy that searchers had to ride in a helicopter up the mountain to start their shifts. Broekhuizen told me that SAR would have gladly kept looking, even in the severe cold, but they never found any sign that Ben was on the mountain. All the evidence pointed to the fact that someone drove the horse up to that road to make it look like Ben was lost on the mountain. Gunny was a decoy, a way to keep the police from finding out what had really happened.

The Tyners drove home on February 13. They took Ben's truck, trailer, three horses, and two dogs back to their ranch near Laramie. A month later, on March 19, the RCMP released a statement that Ben's disappearance was being investigated as suspicious and that it may involve criminality.

Broekhuizen told me there were three main outcomes on searches for missing people. The first kind you felt really good about — the kind where you succeeded and brought someone who was lost or injured back home. "Those are the happy searches," she said. The second type was where you found the person, but they were deceased. It was tragic but you still provided the family with an answer to all the open-ended questions. "Then there are the searches that we all wonder about forever because we never found a trace. And those are the tough ones," she said.

~

Sandy followed the north shoreline of the lake around a corner and into a small bay. A series of cliffs lined the water on one side. A cluster of cabins was built above a rocky beach on the opposite end.

"Is this where the road comes close?" Gene asked.

Jack had driven up and down the lake that morning with one of the FBI agents, looking for places where someone could have dumped a body into the lake. He told Gene that there was a rough, two-track road branching off the highway at the top of the hill. He said a four-wheel-drive truck could get you pretty close to those cliffs.

The rock walls were furrowed by a constellation of cracks and crevices. The bottom ten feet were marked by distinct horizontal bands of black, white, and gray — a sign of how low the water level was this spring. Someone had wedged a couple of wood planks into a wide crack at the top of the tallest cliff. It looked like a fifty- or sixty-foot plunge into the lake from the slipshod platform.

Sandy kept the boat close to shore. The bottom near the cliffs looked like a field of craggy boulders, which made it difficult to get a clear reading on the sonar. The rocks registered as bright-yellow swatches with little to no definition on the monitor. The fissures and gaps between the rocks looked large enough to hide, and maybe even trap, a body. Gene was excited about the potential of the location.

The Tyners and the RCMP were reluctant to talk to me about the open investigation, but it seemed like the working theory for this search was that whoever killed Ben either didn't have access to a boat or didn't have time to launch one and take his body out to the middle of the lake. Search and rescue had flown drones over the lake as part of the big, initial push to find Ben back in the winter of 2019. Broekhuizen told me the lake was mostly open water at the end of January. The extreme cold snap in early February quickly froze the surface over.

"It's hard to imagine he could be sixty feet from us and we don't even know," Jack said at some point that afternoon. He was sitting on the gunnel, which was wide enough to serve as a bench if you kept most of your weight forward on your feet. The surface of the water reflected a tremulous version of the clear blue sky. I'd had that same thought on searches. We might have been within thirty-three feet of the missing airplane a few days before on the Fraser River. It was incredible how water, something so commonplace and seemingly innocuous, could present such an insurmountable barrier. I'd felt tempted at times to grab a pair of goggles and leap overboard, exasperated by the lumbering pace of the *Kathy G.*

Someone had told me about a local superstition that Nicola Lake hid her bodies. I'd learned of similar myths about other lakes on my travels with the Ralstons. An old farmer once told Gene and Sandy that Slocan Lake, which was more than a thousand feet deep, never gave up its dead until they arrived in the spring of 2014 and recovered the bodies of three young men. The Ralstons told me a legend about a lake in Nevada where malevolent spirits lead people to drown by mimicking the sound of a crying baby on the water at night. And then there were the monsters and leviathans, like the Ogopogo, an aquatic dragon that inhabits Okanagan Lake.

It was understandable that a community would develop uneasy feelings about a lake over generations as more people slipped below the surface never to be seen again. And it was a plain and ordinary fact that deep, cold lakes did not give up their dead for most of history. Powerful natural forces — the crushing weight of water, the peculiar property whereby water at thirty-nine degrees, a temperature that inhibits bacterial growth, sinks and sits at the bottom — all conspired to hide and trap corpses. Each successful recovery that the Ralstons performed took another step toward unwinding the time-worn intuition that someone lost in water was lost forever.

"I'm going to say we put eyeballs on it," Gene said, after Sandy had made several passes back and forth along the steep shoreline. He wanted to come back tomorrow with the ROV and search the area at the foot of the cliffs with the robot's video camera. He tried to gauge the visibility of the water by extending a metal pole with a hook on the end into the lake. The water was green with an orange, metallic tinge. Gene estimated he would be able to see for about ten feet underwater with the ROV.

The sturdy pickup truck that the Tyners had borrowed from the ranch had no problem dragging the boat out of the water. Jack and his parents went to Merritt to find something to eat. I followed the Ralstons as they towed the boat back to the ranch, where they had parked the motor home.

Going to the ranch felt a bit like going back in time. It operated out of several old houses and buildings that were once part of the townsite of Nicola, which was founded in the valley bottom in 1886. The ranch had the feel of a reincarnated ghost town. The courthouse, a general store, and maybe half a dozen or so historic homes with gabled roofs and wide front porches were used by the staff and clustered around a short stretch of the highway. There used to be a gift shop and lodging for visitors, a way for tourists to get a taste of the Old West, but I think that side of the business had been shut down for several years. The Liu family had bought the property in 1989 and ran it as part of a larger company called the Coquihalla Development Corporation.

Someone had burned down the Murray Church, the most distinctive of the original buildings, in early 2019, only three weeks before Ben disappeared. It was built in 1876 and had been one of the oldest structures in the region. The community raised money to rebuild a replica of the quaint one-room church, and it looked like construction was almost done when we were there in the spring of 2021. The new church occupied the same footprint as the old one. It was surrounded on three sides by disorganized rows of weathered gravestones leaning out of the yellow grass at odd angles.

A local news program had talked to Ben about the fire. He had lived in one of the heritage homes across the highway from the church. You could watch a short clip of the interview online.

"I know a lot of people have told me before what this church meant to them," Ben said to the reporter, who was off camera. He was in front of the burned ruins. The only thing left standing was a skinny brick chimney. "It was definitely heartbreaking to a lot of them. Like I said, it was just a tragic and senseless act."

Ben was wearing a black-and-red woolen cap with a short brim. He had dark eyes and a thick, long beard. He had softer, rounder features than Jack. I didn't see an obvious likeness between the Tyner brothers. Ben was plainspoken and to the point in the interview. He had a deep voice and a patient way of talking. Richard, Jack, and Ben all spoke with a similar drawl, like they enjoyed stretching out and rolling over certain sylla-bles and words. Ben had overseen a team of eight cowboys who looked after fifteen hundred cattle and two thousand yearlings, cows between the age of one and two years old, on a property that extended for three hundred thousand acres. Thirty-one seemed young for that kind of responsibility.

I got the sense from Ben's family that he was someone who had a clear vision from a young age of what he wanted out of life. His dream had been to own and run his own ranch, one large enough to support himself and maybe a family. The manager position at Nicola had been a big step on his way to realizing that dream.

The Ralstons turned right onto a gravel road across the high-way from the church. Their motor home was parked at the end of a field and in front of a cavernous green barn. Sandy went inside to get dinner ready. Someone had left a hose coiled and hanging off one end of a hitching post. Gene hooked it up to the water supply for the motor home.

"I think the ranch goes as far as you can see," he said. We looked west down the valley. The landscape rose gradually toward the horizon. Flat fields of grass folded into gentle hills and then up into low, blunt mountains covered by forest. A series of fences crisscrossed the fields into grids. I could make out the dark shapes of cattle and a few horses grazing in the late-afternoon sun.

"That's a calf placenta," Gene said, after I just missed stepping in what I thought was a pile of cow excrement. "This is manure. It's more like sawdust." He pointed to a dried-out pancake of dung with the toe of his hiking boot.

Gene looked right at home on the ranch. It was a similar kind of landscape to where he grew up on the dairy farm next to the Snake River. His collared shirt was partially untucked and his hat rested high on his head. It looked like he might have spent the afternoon on horseback or tinkering on the guts of some rickety piece of farm machinery.

I asked him how he thought the first day had gone. He had seemed energized after finding those cliffs, but he and Sandy were always hard to read when on the boat. They were careful of what they say in front of a family or the police. Gene told me that it didn't look promising. The lake eventually reached 180 feet deep, but that was way out in the middle. The bottom descended more gradually from shore than he had expected. And a body in less than fifty feet of water, even if it was weighted down, would have surfaced over the past two years. Gene wanted to check the crevices between the rocks under the cliffs with the ROV, but he didn't sound optimistic.

"I think we're going to be going back to Maple Ridge pretty soon," he said. Then he told me that in some cases just being asked to go on a search was enough of a reason to go on a search. You could sometimes help just by trying.

"You can't even imagine, in fact you don't need to imagine the pain and the grief they must feel. You know," he said. "It's one thing if someone drowns and you lose them, that's hard enough. But these people, their son was killed and they can't find the body. The guy who did it, some jerk, has also got away with it. It must be doubly, triply hard."

CHAPTER EIGHTEEN

Scratch the Surface

Jen brought donuts to the boat launch the next morning. It was one the few small ways she tried to celebrate Richard's seventieth birthday despite the circumstances. That same Friday, April 16, Gene turned seventy-six.

Jen was a language arts teacher at a middle school in Cheyenne for most of her career. More recently, she has worked with special needs kids on a one-on-one basis. She looked younger than her husband. Her short brown hair didn't show any signs of gray. She had a small and slender frame but shared a clear resemblance to Ben. They had the same sharply defined, close-set eyes.

It was another calm, cloudless morning. Smoke from a nearby fire, a controlled burn a few miles west of the ranch, blanketed the valley in a thin, dreamlike haze. Richard joined the Ralstons on the *Kathy G*. Sandy outfitted him with a yellow life jacket with metal clasps. Jen, Jack, and one of the FBI agents drove back down the highway to scope out the cliffs from above. The other agent had left the day before. I think his main goal had been to help the Tyners cross the border into Canada. The agent who remained at the lake was stationed out of Vancouver and would stay with the family until they drove back to Wyoming.

The ROV had a rubber-ducky aesthetic. The top was made of a thick plank of hard foam that was bright yellow. The lights, camera, thrusters, and wires were all tucked underneath and mounted to a rectangular steel frame. The scanning sonar, which provided a picture of what's on the bottom around the robot, stuck out of the foam board like a stubby periscope. Gene used the video feed to steer the ROV from inside the pilothouse. Sandy was up near the bow feeding the neon-green umbilical cable into the water. The cord was coated in some kind of spongy material and spun on a drum inside a black hardcase.

It was tough going under the cliffs. Gene tried to fly the ROV in parallel lines next to the shore, but the boulders on the bottom made it difficult to keep the robot going straight. The poor visibility of the water cut the camera's field of vision short, so he didn't get much warning before almost colliding with the rocks. He found a beer bottle. And then an old tire. And then the ROV got hung up. The cable looped around something on the bottom. There was enough slack in the line that Gene could pull the robot, which weighed forty pounds, back into the boat. He disconnected the cable and was able to shake the cord loose from whatever had snagged it. He worried that if it got stuck again, they might not get so lucky.

We were back at the boat launch by 12:30 PM and in need of a new plan. Lynne Broekhuizen, the manager for Nicola Valley SAR, met us there along with Jack and Jen. She brought homemade sandwiches, egg salad and smoked salmon, for lunch. Jen offered everyone a mini cupcake. The group sat in the sun, which had warmed the concrete slabs of the launch, and talked about what to do next.

Broekhuizen's first search as the leader of the local SAR group had been for Brendan Wilson and Austin Kingsborough back in 2013. She joined the volunteer search group in 2010, soon after she and her husband had retired and moved to an acreage north of Merritt. She had worked as an environmental consultant and, like the Ralstons, specialized in aquatic ecosystems. She suggested looking in that same bay where Gene and Sandy had found the bodies of the two teenagers. It was on the other side of the lake and about four miles northeast of Monck Provincial Park. The Ralstons had imaged the bodies in seventy-five feet of water, but Broekhuizen thought there was a deeper section in that bay, a depression in the bottom, where a corpse could possibly get trapped for years. And it was right beside a two-lane highway.

"We can certainly take a look," Gene said. He stood at the edge of the water and looked out over the lake. He seemed skeptical but didn't have any ideas of his own left to try.

Brandi Hansen, one of the SAR volunteers who'd helped with the initial search for Ben back in 2019, arrived at the launch as we were preparing to leave. She had driven three hours to meet the Tyners and Ralstons in person. The search for Ben on Nicola Lake was originally her idea. She'd reached out to Gene in early January with a message on Facebook. She described what had happened to Ben and the massive search. "We relentlessly scoured the mountains and land in an effort to find him. To the best of my knowledge the areas that were not searched were bodies of water of the surrounding lakes close to the Nicola Ranch where he worked," she wrote. Gene responded to her within minutes. He was on the phone with Richard the next day.

Hansen looked very put together, but also ready for a day outside on the boat. She was wearing cowboy boots and a black baseball hat. Her blond hair was tied in a single braid. She was outgoing and attractive. She was a dual American and Canadian citizen and had served for several years in the military. Gene told me that she had been on the Air Force One presidential security detail for Barack Obama and was a championship marksman. She currently worked as a flight instructor.

The young cowboy's unresolved disappearance had stayed with Hansen. "It's been heartbreaking over the past couple years watching the sadness and pain that his family has had to go through," she wrote to Gene in that first social media message. She was a member of a Facebook group called Missing: Ben Tyner, where the six thousand or so members shared information about the Nicola Valley and theories about the case. They also posted inspirational material, like prayers, aphorisms, and memes that included images of cowboys on horseback, to show their support for the Tyners.

Jen posted to the group every once in a while. She reminded people about the ongoing investigation and that Richard was in contact with the RCMP and FBI. She shared memories and photos of Ben, usually on his birthday, which was August 25, or on holidays like Christmas and Thanksgiving. One of the images she posted was a childhood photo of Ben with Richard, who was wearing his flying uniform and holding his young son to his chest. Ben, a toddler, grinned while he tried to keep his father's pilot's hat from slipping off his head.

Hansen had been keeping tabs on the Ralstons in the media since she first heard about them in August 2012 after they had found the body of Ralph Der in Carp Lake in northern BC. She was living in the nearby city of Prince George at the time and was a member of the local SAR group. She worked hard with her team to find the missing fifty-nine-year-old, who had drowned while on a fishing trip with friends. Hansen knew the RCMP dive team had also done an extensive search of the lake so she was incredulous when she heard that a couple from Idaho had shown up and found the body within minutes of launching their boat. That same trip to Carp Lake was memorable for the Ralstons because, as Gene told the story, he almost died.

Gene was sixty-seven in the summer of 2012. He had noticed, and been trying to ignore, that he felt unusually winded after doing run-of-the-mill activities like walking one of the trails near home. He eventually went to see his doctor, which led to several tests, which discovered a partial blockage of a coronary artery, the one with the nickname widow-maker. He had a stent, a steel-mesh tube, inserted into the artery to prop it open. The procedure was done on the morning of August 8, and Gene left the hospital that afternoon. The doctor warned him not to lift anything heavier than ten pounds for the next ten days.

The Ralstons loaded up the motor home and left for Prince George three days later. They stayed the night with Sam and Nina in New Plymouth and then split the thousand-mile drive over two days. They arrived at the Der household on a Monday afternoon. The first thing they did was examine the chart plotter, a device that integrated GPS navigation with maps of lakes and coastlines. The Ralstons matched the time of the accident with two little circles — they looked like a pair of swimming goggles — made by the boat's track line on a map of Carp Lake. The goggles showed where Der's friends had turned the boat around to try to pick him up. He had jumped into the lake to grab his hat and cool off. The Ralstons began their search the next day by scanning right down the middle of those two circles. And bingo, there was Der on the bottom.

Downloading track lines from a chart plotter, or another GPS-enabled device on the boat, was low-hanging fruit in terms of investigating a drowning. It was the first question the Ralstons asked about any potential search, and it was surprising how often they were the only ones to inquire if that type of information was available. Photos taken with smartphones also included location data and could help narrow down the point of last seen.

One of the most dramatic examples of the value of track lines was on the search for Daniel McGuckin in Lake Powell, Utah. The forty-one-year-old jumped off a houseboat near a place called Iceberg Canyon on September 22, 2018. Teams from the National Park Service, Kane County Sheriff's Office, and Utah State Parks all tried to find McGuckin.

His family eventually connected with the Ralstons, who asked if the boat had any GPS devices. The Ralstons arrived on the afternoon of Monday, June 24, 2019. They followed the track line that they had downloaded off the houseboat's chart plotter. McGuckin had been missing nine months. The Ralstons found him in five minutes. They imaged his body in 321 feet of water. "Pretty much exactly where the track line shows the houseboat slowed and turned to port," Gene wrote to me in an email at 3:43 AM the day after they had imaged McGuckin. He was awake long before his alarm in anticipation of doing the recovery later that morning.

The Ralstons drove back to Prince George after working with the RCMP to recover Der's body in August 2012. They parked the motor home in front of his family's house for the night and had a big breakfast with everyone in the morning. That's when Gene started to feel woozy. One of Ralph's nieces was a nurse and convinced him to go to the hospital. He credits her with saving his life.

Gene passed out in the emergency room and ended up in intensive care. The medication he had been prescribed after his surgery had diluted his blood so much that it had been leaking through his stomach lining. It took four days in the ICU for his body to replenish all the blood and fluids he had lost. The

Ralstons spent another two nights with the Der family after Gene was discharged from the hospital. Sandy drove home.

~

I stepped onto a small stool on the beach and then swung my leg into the bow of the *Kathy G*. Hansen and Jack climbed aboard. Gene took us north down the lake. I had not seen any other boats on the water so far this trip. Maybe no one else was willing to risk launching one when the water level was so low. A variety of docks and rafts were beached high up on the rocky shore and in front of the houses that were built in small clutches around the lake.

And then, within minutes of leaving the launch, I saw a woman in a turquoise T-shirt running down a set of stone steps and onto the beach on the north side of the lake. She waved at the *Kathy G* as she ran. Gene banked left. The boat tilted sideways in the water as he made the sharp turn toward shore. He told us that the woman was Connie Wilson, the mother of Brendan Wilson, one of the two teenagers that the Ralstons had found in Nicola Lake eight years before.

Gene slowed the boat as we approached shore. Connie had one hand on her hip. The other was up covering her mouth, like she was having a hard time processing what she was seeing. I wondered if this was the first time she had seen the *Kathy G* since the spring of 2013. She and her husband, Barry Wilson, had sold their cabin in the Nicola Bay RV Park and built a new one on this side of the lake. The three-story home was part of a row of palatial cabins on a grass hill overlooking the water. Gene nosed the bow up onto the beach. He had texted Connie before we left the launch to let her know they would be passing by on the lake.

"We're looking for the brother of this young man," Gene said. Jack sat on the gunnel next to the pilothouse.

"I'm sorry for your loss," Connie said.

"Thank you," Jack replied.

"We've been there," she said.

Barry joined his wife on the beach. They told the Ralstons that they had been in their new place for about six weeks. They have seven grandkids and were looking forward to hosting everybody up at the lake.

Gene explained that this search involved a homicide. He asked the Wilsons if there were any places near a road where someone could have disposed of a body into the lake. He said they already tried looking under Cowboy Scuttlebutt — the local name for the cliff-jumping spot with the wood platform. Barry suggested checking the shoreline farther east and on the north side of the lake, where the road cut into the side of a near-vertical hill that dropped directly down into the water.

The steep hillside the Wilsons described was a five-minute drive east down the lake at top speed. The depth sounder didn't register anywhere on the bottom near shore deeper than fifty feet. The more places the Ralstons checked, the more they confirmed their assessment that the depth of Nicola Lake didn't support the theory that someone could have disposed of the body without the use of a boat. The lake just didn't get deep enough fast enough. The Ralstons headed to the bay by the RV park next.

I helped Gene lower the towfish. They started scanning the bottom, heading south toward the RV park. A semitruck carrying dozens of crushed cars drove by on the two-lane highway, which closely followed the contours of the bay. The road was maybe twenty feet from the water and separated by an abrupt slope.

Gene pointed out the dock where the RCMP had transferred the bodies of the two teenagers to the coroner. It was next to a concrete boat launch that connected with a gravel road. It looked like the road that Jim and Anna Ward had described, the one where the community had stood and cheered as the white van left the dock and drove away.

The Ralstons called off the search after about an hour. They scanned most of the bay but had not seen any depressions in the bottom. The deepest section we saw that afternoon was eighty feet. Broekhuizen, Richard, and Jen had been watching the *Kathy G* putter back and forth from the rocky beach next to the road. Gene took us to shore to meet them. Richard sat on the bow with his feet on the beach to hold the boat in place. Jack climbed out and sat next to Jen on the rocks.

"We didn't find any big holes," Gene said. "If he was in the water, sixty to eighty feet, he would have come up in two years."

The group brainstormed other possibilities, other lakes in the area and other theories about what fate might have befallen Ben. The suggestions seemed halfhearted, though. Nicola Lake was by far the largest and deepest in the region. And the closest to the ranch.

"We knew it was a long shot, but we appreciate what you guys have done," Richard said.

"We knew it was a long shot, too," Gene said. He explained that they needed to get back to Alouette Lake, but the next day was Saturday and the lake was going to be too busy to search. Pete had warned them that the weekends on Alouette would be a zoo of boat traffic once the weather warmed up. He had texted Gene yesterday with an update on the search for Dennis Liva. Pete had tracked down Herb Silcock, the man Liva had gone fishing with in 1974. He still lived in Maple Ridge.

"So we have two more days," Gene said.

"Well, you're probably ready for a day's rest anyway," Richard said.

Another semitruck passed. It was carrying a load of milled lumber. We felt the gust of wind that the immense vehicle generated as it whooshed by just a few feet up the hill.

"All right, you ready?" Richard asked Gene. "We'll get the old guy in the boat again." He turned his hat around backward so it wouldn't blow off when the *Kathy G* got up to speed. Jack drove back to the ranch with Jen. We sped across Nicola Lake one last time.

$$\sim$$

I met the Tyners and the Ralstons in front of their hotel in Merritt early in the evening the next day. Richard had paid for Gene and Sandy to spend the night there instead of in the motor home at the ranch. I was startled by how good the Ralstons looked. They must have caught up on some much-needed rest. I was used to seeing them on the boat or at the end of a long day on the boat. Gene's hair was neatly combed to the side instead of poking out haphazardly from under a hat. He was wearing a crisp collared shirt and a fresh pair of jeans. Sandy's white hair was lustrous, and her dark sunglasses contrasted with her pink cardigan, which had snap buttons. They had gone shopping earlier that day, restocking supplies in the motor home.

We walked to a pizza restaurant down the block and sat at a picnic table on the patio, which was enclosed by tall panels of frosted glass. The Tyners had met with several high-ranking members of the RCMP that afternoon to discuss the investigation. Jack seemed encouraged by what he had learned, but his parents were less sure. Richard looked worn out by the last couple of days. The Tyners planned to drive home to Wyoming the next day.

At some point over dinner, Sandy nudged me with her elbow. She was beside me on the bench and passed me her cellphone so I could see a photo she had just shown to Richard and Jen. It took me a moment to realize that I was looking at a picture of an old picture of her and Gene. They looked so young I almost didn't recognize them. I had been talking to Jack, who was across the table from me, so I wasn't sure what prompted Sandy to show the Tyners the photo.

It had been taken during that trip to Mexico back in college when they first started dating, so fifty-one years back. They were in the back seat of a car. A friend had taken the photo from the front seat. Gene was next to the window, his head tilted back on the headrest. He had his arm around Sandy. She rested her head on his chest. They were fast asleep, which gave the scene a feeling of intimacy and vulnerability.

I was struck by something about Sandy's expression. Maybe it was her large, closed eyes or the way her head and upper body rested so comfortably against Gene. She looked content. I asked her a few weeks later if I could get a copy of the photo. She said no. It was personal.

I asked Sandy once if she ever looked back in surprise at the path that her life has taken with Gene. "I didn't have any preconceived notions about how things were going to go or anything," she said. She explained that becoming experts at finding corpses happened the way that most things happen in life, a series of gradual steps that felt reasonable at the time. It was only when you looked at it all at once, or from the outside, that it seemed remarkable or unusual.

I had attributed her nonchalance about their unconventional life to her general unflappableness. I suspected she was wary of how I was trying to a make a fuss about them and their work. The photo of them in the car, and the fact that she kept it with her on her phone, made me think I had misinterpreted her perspective. It wasn't that Sandy thought finding bodies was a perfectly ordinary way to spend your time; rather, it wasn't a defining aspect of how she saw herself and Gene. It was just something they had been doing, like how they used to race jet boats.

The photo reminded me that the Ralstons first met on a road trip. They got to know each other, and got an inkling of what it was like to be a couple, as they explored the Mexican countryside and slept in tents by the side of the road. That nudge from Sandy at dinner felt like a nudge to look at their life beyond search and recovery. It was a nudge to see how they had discovered a feeling of home, a feeling of sanctuary in each other, and how they were able to take that feeling with them wherever they went and whatever they did.

Someone arrived at the restaurant who knew the Tyners, and Jack offered to move to another table so they could sit with his parents and the Ralstons. I joined Jack at the other table. He told me about tie-down roping, a rodeo event in which a cowboy chased down a calf on horseback while swinging a lasso over his head. The goal was to catch the calf by looping the rope around its neck. You then flipped the animal on its back and tied off its legs. The best ropers secured a calf in less than seven seconds. Some cowboys made upward of a million dollars a year in prize money as they toured from one rodeo to the next. Jack had been competing at a high level, qualifying for some of the marquee events across the United States, before Ben disappeared.

Jack had a habit of cracking his neck every few hours. It was an aggressive movement. He would put one hand on his chin and the other on the back of his head and then jerk his head to the side suddenly. He would keep at it until there was an audible crack. And then do it again, but in the other direction. Tie-down roping sounded dangerous. You had to leap off a galloping horse after you had lassoed the calf. I wondered if

Jack's homespun chiropractic treatments were related to an old rodeo injury.

He had stopped training because his parents needed more help at home. "A ranch always needs work — always," he told me. You're responsible for the welfare of all those animals. Richard had experienced a heart attack this past September. He had got a call from his cardio therapist when we were having lunch on the boat launch the day before. He told them he would visit the clinic when he got back home. "He won't go," Jen had said. Richard had been spending most of his time researching and advocating about Ben's case.

There was another reason, a deeper reason, that Jack had not picked back up where he'd left off in terms of competing in rodeos. He felt stuck. "I can't do me anymore," he said. He would wake up feeling good and start to think about practicing. But then he would think of Ben. And everything that had happened. That took the wind out of any motivation he had to train.

He still followed all the big rodeos and who had been winning the tie-down events. "I know I can beat those guys," he said. He had his eye on a few local competitions coming up this summer as a possible way to get back into the sport. Jack said he found it helpful to meet Connie and Barry Wilson. It was a brief encounter, but he got the impression that they were doing okay, that they had mostly come out the other side of something similar to what he and his parents were going through. The Wilsons had built that nice cabin and now had lots of family who visited.

Talking to Jack that night, I got the sense that he had been the cooler, more popular brother. He was a brash and talented athlete. Ben had been bigger, taller and broader, but more reserved and thoughtful. He seemed more like the kind of person to have a small but close circle of friends. "He was proud of me," Jack said.

At some point that evening, he showed me a social media post on his phone that he had written back in the winter of 2019. It was dated February 11, two days before he and his parents returned to Wyoming in Ben's truck and with his dogs and horses. Friends and family back home had been anxiously waiting for an update on the search. Jack was at a loss of what to say, and so he wrote a story about one of the last times he and Ben had gone riding together, which was only a few days before his brother left for his new job at the Nicola Ranch in Canada.

Jack described spending the day with Ben doing odd jobs on the ranch. "The wind was quiet, it wasn't too cold, and it was a good day to be on horseback doing what we loved. Although our family operation is small I know we both took pride in it, because it is something we both dreamed of since we were young," he wrote. After lunch, Jack got bucked off his horse. Ben teased him for getting two-jumped, which I guessed meant that he was knocked off relatively quickly. The post concluded:

> I know there isn't much of a point to that story but the sound of his laughter and his voice that day is something I will never forget and I will always treasure. My brother loved life to the fullest. He loved being a cowboy and always looked forward to the next adventure. The things he valued most are the things many of us forget. Honesty. Integrity. Loyalty. My brother taught me so much about life and I never even knew he was doing it.

CHAPTER NINETEEN

Unfriended on Facebook

It feels like anything can happen at the outset of a search, like the body will appear at any moment. Everyone on board the *Kathy G* is vigilant, watching the monitor, studying it, trying to puzzle it out like it's a qualifying exam for becoming an astronaut. That anticipation, that focus, inevitably falters. Joints get stiff. Muscles need stretching. And all that optimism ebbs away, like a sand castle eroded by high tide. Minutes turn to hours turn to days, all at the same maddening metronome of 1.2 miles per hour.

Zombie-like is how Gene describes the altered state of consciousness induced by long days, or weeks, on the water. "You can be sitting there staring at the screen and not see a thing. You just go blank and your eyes are wide open. You're not asleep, your eyes are wide open, you're sitting there. You know, just life passes you by," he told me.

The Ralstons' capacity to endure withering monotony is one of the secrets of their success. They stay at their posts, Gene at the monitor and Sandy at the wheel, long after the rotating cast of visiting crew members lose interest and find a place to sit out on the deck. Some circuit in Gene's brain, some benthic tangle of neurons, remains awake to the subtle cue that something on the screen doesn't belong, doesn't quite match the contours of anything else he has seen on the bottom of that particular lake or river. And Sandy keeps the boat arrow-straight on the search line, which looks like it could be infinite on the tiny screen of her antique laptop because both the start and end points are hidden from view.

It occurred to me on one of those long afternoons I spent aboard the *Kathy G*, as more of the endless canvas of lake bottom inched down the computer monitor, that Gene and Sandy were likely the first and only people to ever see those submarine landscapes. And exploring a new frontier, regardless of how ordinary, is an extremely rare experience in the twenty-first century.

At the end of every search season, usually sometime in November, Gene archives all of the sonar images he and Sandy have recorded that year. They generate six to ten gigabytes worth of overhead pictures of lake and river bottom every year. Most of the archive is stored on hundreds of CDs. Gene prefers the old-school format because he once lost two full seasons of images when a hard drive failed. A few years ago, someone from the US Geological Survey emailed Gene to ask about getting a copy of their archive. He wanted to create some kind of database for images of the bottom of lakes and rivers in the United States. Gene replied to the email but then never heard back. And so all those CDs, all those pictures of never-seen-before-or-since underwater worlds, continue to collect dust in the basement of their house in rural Idaho.

The first day back to search for Bobby Aujla on Alouette Lake on April 19, 2021, was discouraging. The Ralstons picked up where they'd left off five days earlier. They used the same landmarks, the ones pointed out by Sandhu and his friends: the lichen-covered rock on the east shoreline to the south and the spot on the lake before it broadened into the first basin past the narrows to the north.

Some of the bottom within the search area looked smooth, but much of the west side of that part of the lake was strewn with rocks and boulders. Gene thought they were likely the remnants of a landslide off the mountain. Those sections of lake floor looked like a bulbous head of cauliflower on the monitor. Another part of the bottom featured a steep rock formation, like a submarine mountain peak. Gene had to raise and then lower the towfish hundreds of feet as Sandy piloted the boat forward. All that vertical movement of the sonar interfered with the quality of the images.

"No wonder the other guys couldn't find him," Gene said about an hour into the search. He zoomed in on a suspicious-looking object later that morning. We were close to the point where the lake widened and were headed south toward the narrows. Gene measured it at just over five feet long.

"That a stick, Sandy?" he asked.

"Strange looking," she said, which was shorthand for saying it deserved another scan. It was down more than four hundred feet.

Gene agreed it was worth a second look. Sandy started her turn and we heard a thud up at the bow.

"I did not tell you to turn!" Gene said, raising his voice.

"You did!" Sandy barked right back.

"Put it in neutral," Gene said.

He went up front and started yanking on the cable for the sonar. It had been knocked loose from the pulley at the bow because he had not raised the towfish before Sandy started the turn.

I had seen that same type of terse exchange play out in a variety of ways aboard the *Kathy G*. It usually happened during moments of high consequence, like when they were trying to image something a fourth or fifth time but it was in a difficult spot or the wind made it hard for Sandy to keep the boat on track. Gene would start pointing, his index finger jabbing into the air with increasing intensity, for Sandy to correct course. She could tolerate his insistency up to a point before she snapped and told him to back off. The bickering escalated and then deflated in a matter of seconds. Everyone else on board would find something to study, whether it was their feet or the surface of the lake. Those brief quarrels were as far as I saw the Ralstons get in terms of a fight. They flared up and then burned out without a trace. It seemed like Gene and Sandy could let them go in the moment without holding a grudge. For the record, at least in that instance, I had also heard Gene ask Sandy to make the turn.

And then, as the day wore on, Pete questioned if we were even in the right area on the lake. He wondered what stage in the group of friends' sequence of recalling the accident was the most trustworthy. Was it the location they had told the RCMP on the day of the accident, only hours after Aujla had drowned? Or was the consensus that the group arrived at later, the one that took months to congeal, more accurate?

"I regret not taking them all the way down to that second point," Pete said. He was referring to the other, larger basin of the lake that was another mile north from where the Ralstons had been searching. Pete had started to grow a beard. He was more tanned, and therefore more freckled, since we had seen him last.

"I'm wondering if it's not farther up that way, toward the narrows," Gene said. His hunch was that the friends might have misjudged the other end of their search perimeter, the one demarcated by the boulder.

"Or we just can't see him because of the rocks," Sandy said.

"Or we just don't know what we're doing," Gene said.

"Sounds like you guys need more practice," I said. Sandy smiled at my joke but kept her eyes fixed ahead on the lake.

Gene selected half a dozen objects on the bottom that day for another pass with the sonar. None of them looked promising after the second scan. We were back at the boat launch by 5:00 PM. It had been an eight-hour day on the lake. I had seen the Ralstons split a sandwich and a small plastic bottle of cold coffee.

The next morning, Gene saluted me as I pulled into Pete's driveway. He had just stepped out of the motor home. He straightened his back, stood at attention, and lifted a flat hand to the brim of his hat to complete the humorous gesture. It was 8:00 AM, but he had likely been up for three hours already. He caught up on responses to search requests first thing in the morning and checked in on social media.

~

The Ralstons stay in touch with many of their friends, a diverse group who are spread across Canada and the United States, on Facebook. The site has also been the downfall of some relationships, including those with the relatives of people he and Sandy have recovered. The Ralstons told me about this volatile element of their online activity during my first meeting with them back in 2017 at the library in Idaho. I had asked them about reaching out to the parents of Kathy Garrigan, the young woman whom they had named their boat after.

"Unfortunately, or fortunately, whatever, probably unfortunately, the family, most of the family, is extremely liberal, and, of course, we're fairly conservative so we have some different political views," Gene said. He added that they were not on speaking terms anymore, although Marian, Kathy's mother, still sent him the occasional private message.

"But you can't make everybody happy," Gene said.

"Or you can just keep your mouth shut," Sandy said.

"No, can't do that." Gene's tone made it sound like he considered his forthrightness on social media somewhat heroic.

I waited a long time, probably too long, to read his Facebook page. I worried about what I would find. And it was easy to ignore. The content he posted was private. I eventually got around to sending him a friend request in early 2022.

Much of what I read on Gene's page was not surprising. There were cheesy jokes and cartoon memes with puns. He included photos of their property, images of wildlife, and views of the dramatic sunsets from their back porch. Many of the people whom he and Sandy have helped on searches over the years posted heartfelt messages on the anniversary of the day their relative drowned or their body had been found.

There was a deluge of political content. The Ralstons, like many Idahoans, were fans of Donald Trump. I saw a few memes about heterosexual pride with obtuse slogans like, "It's natural, it's worked thousands of years and you can make babies." Gene also posted material that ridiculed people who are transgender.

Gene in person, or Gene on the phone, is different from Gene on social media. He is more thoughtful and nuanced. He has told me that he supports gay marriage. He and Sandy have lifelong friends who are gay. The Ralstons don't discriminate in their friendships or in terms of who they help as search-and-recovery specialists. The degree of need is the only criterion they use to judge when and whether to go on a search.

I asked Gene during one of our semi-regular afternoon phone calls how he reconciled his sense of himself as compassionate with the way that he made fun of marginalized groups of people on social media. "There are several sides to compassion," he said. "We are very compassionate on some things. Does not mean you have to be compassionate on everything."

Criminals don't deserve any sympathy in Gene's view. He is an advocate for the death penalty. The Ralstons are very law-and-order-ly. Many of their friends are police officers. Personal responsibility trumps everything. You make your bed, you sleep in it. Guns don't kill people, people kill people.

Gene emailed me a link to a meme after we had a debate about personal responsibility versus systemic racism. I appreciated that he never shied away from discussing controversial topics. The meme featured a photo of two luxury buses with the words BLACK LIVES MATTER printed in giant letters along the sides. The text above the photo explained that Black Lives Matter had raised more than a billion dollars but had not helped any African Americans in a practical way. "They haven't had 1 neighborhood cleanup, sent 1 poor black child to college . . ." The list went on. "Where is the money going other than to buy huge charter buses to transport members to riots!" the meme concluded.

I emailed back arguing that Black Lives Matter was a social movement and not a single entity. It included hundreds of organizations, many of which were helping people in pragmatic ways. I pointed out that the meme didn't source any of the information. It was not signed by anyone or affiliated with any kind of group or media agency. It was free-floating. It had no footing in the real world. I later googled the meme, and it turned out the buses belonged to the Toronto Raptors, an NBA basketball team. They had printed BLACK LIVES MATTER on the buses in solidary with the movement.

I think memes like the one Gene emailed me and many of the conspiracy theories about the vaccines for COVID-19 share the same rhetorical strategy. They offer people an escape hatch from difficult and challenging aspects of reality. They simplify the world. All you ever need to do is follow the money. The meme about the buses took the issue of racism right off the table. It gave people unwilling to accept the existence of systemic racism in policing a way to criticize the Black Lives Matter movement by fabricating a story about greed. Conspiracy theories about the vaccines offered no end of creative moral justifications for people unwilling to make a minor personal sacrifice to prevent the spread of a deadly virus.

Gene never responded to my email about the meme. I don't think he is all that judicious or careful about what he puts on social media. He posts half a dozen links most mornings. He is in conversation with a private audience of his friends. People who get offended usually opt out. Every once in a while someone they have helped on a search tries to debate him on a charged topic like gun rights or abortion. I understand the impulse. They're trying to resolve the gap between the sensitive and conscientious person who found the body of their lost loved one and the strident social conservative they meet later online.

Angels on earth is one of the most common ways people describe Gene and Sandy. I appreciate why someone they have helped would see them in that light, but I think the description flattens them out. It circumvents the chance to understand who they are and why they do what they do in three dimensions.

The banner at the top of Gene's Facebook page reads, ALWAYS HELP SOMEONE. YOU MIGHT BE THE ONLY ONE WHO DOES. The white letters are set against a blurred photo of lush foliage. In most contexts that sentiment feels like a cliché, the kind of tired phrase that inspires eye rolls. But those words carry real weight for the Ralstons. Those words inform their actions. Gene and Sandy have lived those words for the past twenty-some years.

I felt uneasy about questioning the integrity of the Ralstons' compassion from my desk chair. They have done an undisputable amount of good in the world. Their sense of compassion is messy and contradictory, but ultimately it's practical. It's a value that they act on.

Mick Gavin said something to me that I'll never forget. We were wrapping up our conversation at the cabin they were staying at in Golden. It was early May 2018, a couple of days after his son's body had been found and exhumed from the riverbed. Angela and Ciara had already gotten up and left the living room when Mick brought up how Ciara had asked me to leave Kinbasket Lake back in the summer of 2017. The family had decided against having a writer along for the search. He said that back then he couldn't understand why I was there at the lake if I wasn't there to help them find David. I liked Mick. I respected him. His words hung in the air between us. I got the impression that it was something he still felt. I was at a loss for how to respond. I knew the Ralstons' story had value and that highlighting the experience of families like his could perhaps lead to change in terms of additional public resources for underwater search and recovery. But that answer felt hollow in the moment. It was so abstract when measured against the concreteness of his loss.

CHAPTER TWENTY

Back from the Deep

Pete, Sandy, and Gene had a long talk in the pilothouse before leaving the dock. It was the morning of Tuesday, April 20, two weeks since the Ralstons had left Idaho. They planned to start the drive home the next day. They would stop in Seattle to see Crayton Fenn and pick up a refurbished winch for Cory Reeves, the undersheriff in Montana who was putting together a sonar system. Today was the last chance to find Bobby Aujla. They had already scanned the area outlined by Sandhu and his friends and so decided to create a grid farther north into the first wide section of the lake past the narrows.

Gene spotted something on the surface that he thought looked like a body as we sped down the lake. He slowed the *Kathy G* down and brought us alongside what turned out to be a gnarled hunk of driftwood. The spring melt had picked up speed while we were in Merritt. The water level had risen, lifting all sorts of debris off the shores and carrying it out onto the lake.

I helped with the towfish, guiding it away from the bow as Gene lowered it into the water with the winch. We started out in the middle of the wide section of the lake and headed south back toward the narrows and the boat launch. The towfish made an orange, diagonal slash on the depth sounder as it descended 450 feet.

"Okay, I'm going to choose a line at random," Gene said.

The sun poured in through the window beside him. He had a hard time seeing the monitor even after dropping the mesh blinds. He grabbed a black tarp from the hatch beside the motor, and we helped him secure it over the outside of the window with metal alligator clips.

"Is this a body bag?" Pete asked. It had a zipper down the middle. "Ours are usually white or gray," he added.

The bottom of the lake was as flat as fresh asphalt and flecked with small objects that looked like the shards of broken toothpicks, great conditions for searching. Gene told me once that underwater searchers, especially those who used sonar, were vulnerable to something called the streetlight effect. It was tempting to gravitate to the places on the lake with the smoothest sections of bottom because that was where the technology worked the best. It was a type of cognitive bias that also affected researchers and scientists. It was more appealing to do the experiments that produced definitive and easy-to-measure results, even if they didn't advance understanding in the field. The concept got its name from the analogy of someone looking for their keys at night under a streetlight even though they knew they had lost them somewhere else.

And then, about twenty minutes into that first search line of their last day on Alouette Lake, Gene said matter-of-factly: "I think we have a body." He zoomed in on something close to the edge of the sonar image. He was scanning with a 131-foot range out the portside of the towfish. The left side of the monitor displayed a narrow strip of black, which represented the area directly below the steel torpedo.

"Wow. Wow. Wow." Pete repeated the word softly.

"I'm not saying it is, but that's the best thing we've seen yet," Gene said.

The object on the screen was not much bigger than a thumb-tack. I had seen a similar form scroll into view two years before when the Ralstons imaged Alexander Bravo Marroquin on the bottom of a lake in Washington State. The head, torso, and legs were clearly visible. We were near the spot where the east shoreline expanded into the first basin. The Ralstons had stopped just shy of scanning this far north yesterday. It looked like we were within the area described by Rick Sandhu and his friends, but the boundary they had used at this end was trickier to judge because it was more general — the widening of the lake — versus the one to the south, a big rock on shore.

Gene recorded the location in the navigation program and then raised the towfish a couple hundred feet so Sandy could turn the boat around to scan it from the other direction.

"Did your heart skip a beat, or are you trying to stay calm?" Gene asked.

"It skipped a beat," Pete said.

The atmosphere on board was hushed as we approached the target from the south. Gene murmured course corrections to Sandy. A graphic on the monitor showed that the boat was passing over the object, but the towfish was still several hundred feet behind us. The more cable that was needed to reach the bottom, the farther back the towfish got pulled behind the boat. We watched the bottom inch down the monitor. Tick. Tick. Tick. Tick.

"We're not going to have a lot of wiggle room," Gene said. The deeper the lake, the more challenging the recovery. The ROV had 500 feet of umbilical cable. The depth sounder read 428 feet. The deepest recovery the Ralstons had ever done was in 375 feet of water.

"Boom!" Gene clapped his hands. "Make the call."

The image of the body was brighter and better defined on the second pass. A sizable log lay flat on the otherwise empty lake floor about ten to fifteen feet west of the corpse.

"You sure?" Sandy asked.

"That's a body," Gene said.

"We got a Gene guarantee. I'll take that to the bank," Pete said.

It was 10:24 AM. There was still time to drive back to the motor home, pick up the ROV, and return to perform the recovery. Everyone started moving at once. We had been shaken out of a trance by the apparition of the pixelated figure on the monitor. Pete called the dive team on a satellite phone. I helped Gene raise the towfish. Sandy shut down the computers in the pilothouse. And then we raced back to the boat launch. Gene had to swerve from side to side to dodge all the sticks and logs drifting on the surface of the lake. Sandy stayed with the *Kathy G* at the dock. She cut an intriguing figure in her black sunglasses, black fleece jacket, and white hair billowing in the breeze.

I followed Pete and Gene up the hill through the rain forest to the parking lot. The trail was only a few hundred yards, but it was steep. Gene stopped at the top, leaned against a tree, and tried to catch his breath. It was the only time I had seen him winded. Pete and I had been moving fast. I think we were both full of adrenaline.

It took an hour to drive to Pete's place, load the gear, and return to the boat launch. The ROV was stored in four hard cases: one each for the computer, the robot, and the umbilical cable, then a smaller yellow case for the grabber jaws and scanning sonar. Gene untangled various buckets and containers of rope on the dock. He needed every last inch he could find to deploy the anchor in that part of the lake.

We were back to the spot north of the narrows by 12:45 PM. Pete had confirmed that Tim Cucheran and the RCMP dive team were on their way with their own boat. The wind was blowing from the south. It felt like it was getting stronger. It took two tries, but the Ralstons managed to set the marker on the bottom within thirty feet of the body. The two stacked milk crates, which contained an anchor and registered as a bright square on the sonar image, were attached to a white buoy that floated on the surface. Pete helped Gene raise the towfish so they could drop the anchor. The chains clattered and banged against the metal deck. The *Kathy G* had to stay in a fixed position on the surface for Gene to navigate the ROV on the bottom.

He drove several hundred yards upwind from the white buoy. The anchor had an articulating design. It unfolded and then snagged into the floor of the lake as it was towed backward. The last few times Gene tried to get the anchor to hold firm in the soupy bottom of Alouette Lake, it ended up dragging. The boat had so far been blown off position on the lake even in light winds.

Gene entered the talking-to-himself phase of the search. He coached himself through each successive step, like the next knot he had to tie or which way the wind was shifting. "So much stuff," he said under his breath as he prepared the pilothouse to fly the ROV. He moved one of the chairs onto the deck so he could raise a sheet of metal that was bolted on hinges to the inside wall. This became the table for the ROV computer, which was built right into the black hardcase. He secured the lid of the case, which contained the screen for the video feed, to the window frame of the pilothouse with a bungee cord. He then plugged the monitor that was usually used for the side-scan sonar into the ROV computer so it could display the images generated by the robot's scanning sonar. Gene has refined this system over years. He took pleasure in the way everything fit together in such a small space.

The RCMP boat, which looked like the same one with the inflatable sides that had brought Sandhu and his friends to this spot on the lake six days ago, arrived at 2:00 PM. Cucheran had four other RCMP officers with him. He and one other officer were wearing dry suits folded down to the waist. They pulled up alongside the *Kathy G*. Cucheran told Pete to call the coroner on the satellite phone as soon as he saw the body with the ROV's camera. The coroner would then meet Cucheran and his team back at the boat launch. Gene tied off a rope on one of the metal cleats next to the outboard motor and handed the other end to one of the officers. We were already dragging the anchor and getting pushed down the lake. Gene asked Cucheran to put his boat in reverse and hold the *Kathy G* in position upwind of the white buoy.

He then picked up the ROV and turned it toward the officers. "Smile, you're getting your picture taken," he said. Gene leaned back and pitched the robot out over the side of the boat. He took up his post in the pilothouse. Pete stood in the doorway. I was outside on the deck, looking over his shoulder at the screens. Sandy was upfront feeding the neon-green cable into the water. She wore a pair of gloves with rubberized palms to protect her hands. We watched the video feed as Gene caught the rope for the marker in the robot's grabber jaws and then started the descent. The controller for the ROV was big and clunky. It had a black joystick and a four-by-four grid of sixteen buttons; it was connected to the computer with a coiled cord, the kind used for an old landline telephone. Gene was on the edge of his seat, more leaning against it than sitting on it. He held the controller tight against his stomach and moved the joystick with the thumb and forefinger of his right hand.

He called out the depth every hundred feet over a loudspeaker. The screen faded from turquoise to dark blue to black.

The depth sounder read 424 feet when the ROV reached the bottom. The lights from the robot illuminated the marker in the gloom. The bottom crate was almost entirely buried in the silt, which was so fine that it looked more like a wispy, gossamer material than sand or mud. The camera only panned up and down so Gene had to fly the robot around to see what was in the vicinity. The thrusters kicked up thick plumes of sediment that obscured the video feed whenever he got too close to the bottom.

"Ah, dammit. I think we're stuck," Gene said, after only a few minutes of trying to get his bearings on the bottom. He heaved a dramatic sigh, his shoulders and head collapsing forward for a moment. I realized that this was far from a done deal. I had assumed the hard part was over, that locating the body on the bottom was the biggest obstacle. The feeling on board was tense. The five police officers waited and watched from their boat a few feet behind us. When the ROV got hung up in Nicola Lake, Gene had enough slack in the line to bring it aboard and disconnect it. Now it was more than four hundred feet below us.

Gene had about twenty feet of leeway left in the cord. He darted the ROV around until he located the green cable in the water and followed it back down to the bottom. He crashed into the muck and the screen exploded in a cloud of silt. "We'll have to sit here all night waiting for it to clear so we can see," he said. The fibrous material eventually settled enough that Gene could decipher that the cord was looped around the end of a chunk of wood lodged into the soft bottom. He caught the cord in the grabber jaws, closed the interlocking pincers, and then reversed. It worked. He was free again. He asked Sandy to pull some of the slack back into the boat. And then Gene started to fly the robot along the log, the one that had appeared beside the body in the sonar image.

"Straight ahead. There he is," Gene said. It was hard for me to make out what was on the screens from outside the pilothouse.

"Yep," Pete said. "We got him."

"Not yet," Gene cautioned.

"Well, you found him," Pete replied.

And then, as the robot got closer, I saw the body. He was on his back. He was covered in a thin, white substance flecked with a few small patches of something green and fuzzy. John Wallace, the aquatic entomologist, called this organic shroud a biofilm. It was a mixture of algae, fungi, and bacteria. Gene had seen it before. He said it could usually be washed off. The body appeared fully intact. The biofilm covered and smoothed over any subtle details. It looked like someone had draped a sheet over Aujla's body as it lay on the feathery bottom.

Gene brought the robot up beside Aujla's shoulder. I caught a glimpse of the horizon line, if you could call it that on the bottom of a lake, where the barren, submarine landscape met an unfathomable expanse of ink-black water. I was looking south toward the narrows and then, beyond that, the boat launch. It was an intriguing vantage point. I knew that if I walked forward into that dark world for another mile or two I might stumble across the remains of Dennis Liva or James Carmichael.

The brim of Gene's hat had been knocked high on his forehead. His hair bristled out at odd angles around his ears. His eyes were narrowed. He had a strained look on his face like he was trying to remember something. The stressful situation had put Gene into a flow state. He was completely absorbed in the task. I could see Sandy through the windshield. She held the cord of the ROV gently in her hands and gazed off at the shoreline. It took about twenty minutes of Gene trying various maneuvers and then waiting for all the silt that was stirred up to drift back down, but he managed to get a firm grasp on the right wrist.

"I think we got him," Gene said. It had been an hour and a half since he dropped the ROV into the lake.

Pete got the satellite phone from the hatch at the back of the boat to call the coroner. I went upfront to spool the cord back into the case as Sandy started to pull the ROV, and the body, back to the surface. She asked me to take over after about fifty feet. "I don't know if he's caught on something or just really heavy," she said. Aujla had been a muscular guy.

I took the spongy cord from her, leaned out over the gunnel, and started to pull. I went slowly, like Sandy had demonstrated. The line felt heavy. And precarious. I worried about screwing up. I was scared that I might somehow compromise that tenuous hold on the body four hundred or so feet below the surface.

Thomas Lynch, the poet and undertaker, wrote about the ways that the presence of a body could change the feeling and atmosphere in a room. "The ontological stakes are always raised, the existential ante upped, and the press of our impermanence, our mortality, flexes its terrible gravity in every aspect of our being," he wrote. I think I understood what he meant. He was trying to articulate the instinctual dread inspired by close proximity with a corpse. He was trying to chart some of the intractable ways in which the experience of life felt incompatible with the finality of death.

The context of a search for someone who drowned was radically different from that of the antechambers of a funeral home. The intimate interaction with corpses, however, seemed similar. I was connected to a body in that moment. It was on the other end of that long, neon-green cord. That nearness, that up-closeness, didn't inspire any insights or fears about my own mortality. My single preoccupation was Aujla's family and friends. Their sense of desperation was fresh in my mind. I was helping to bring a body back from the deep, and at the same time helping to return someone to their family. I felt the burden, but also the great privilege, of that responsibility as I pulled on the cord, one carefully placed hand over the next.

Pete tapped me on the shoulder and took over on the ROV after he had called his boss, who was then going to contact the coroner. I spelled Sandy off from coiling the cord back into the case. It was exhausting work to spin the drum, which got harder to turn with each new coil that was reeled in. Gene monitored the progress of the recovery on the video feed in the pilothouse.

Cucheran and his diving partner put on their oxygen tanks and masks in the police boat. They had untied the *Kathy G*, and we drifted north on the lake. Pete stopped pulling the line once the body was within twenty feet of the surface. The police divers placed Aujla in a white body bag under the water. The bubbles from their respirators made a whooshing sound as they broke to the surface. I sat on the gunnel opposite from Pete to help balance the weight on board and keep the boat level.

The dive team secured the body onto the side of their boat and started making their way south back to the boat launch. Gene and Sandy had to pack up the ROV, raise the anchor, and then raise the marker before we could follow them.

"Hang on, because we won't be able to see the logs with the waves and the sun," Sandy warned Pete and me. The boat rattled and shook as Gene traveled at speed in the rough water.

Aujla's friends had heard that the Ralstons were back in Maple Ridge to keep searching on Alouette Lake. A group of them arrived at the boat launch at around 5:00 PM to discover several police vehicles and the coroner's van preparing for the dive team to return with the body. They realized that the Ralstons must have been successful. They met with them a couple of hours later at the parking lot up the hill from the launch. Gene and Sandy talked quietly with the group of young men next to the *Kathy G* on the trailer. Their mission to bring their friend home had finally concluded.

"You do what no one else can do," one of them said.

"We are just so glad we could find him," Sandy said to Sandhu.

I talked to Sandhu over the phone a few months later. He told me that he got a premonition when he first met Gene and Sandy on the dock that morning before he was escorted by the RCMP out onto the lake. Sandhu believed some people had an inexplicable ability to go beyond what others could do, whether that was with a particular skill or an art form. "Sometimes, it's luck. And, sometimes, it's just a gift that somebody has. And you don't question it. You don't argue it. You appreciate it. And you go with it. And I feel like with the Ralstons, that's exactly how I felt," Sandhu said.

We drove home in the dark on the night after the Ralstons had recovered Bobby Aujla. The cab of the truck was filled with the rich, spicy aroma of Indian food. Sandhu and his friends had come to the lake that afternoon to give the Ralstons dinner, which included several take-out containers of butter chicken.

~

The Ridge Meadows RCMP presented Gene and Sandy with a certificate of appreciation at Pete's house the next morning. "Our members have witnessed your investigative minds, exceptional knowledge, and the physical prowess it takes to do this work," the document read. It was signed by Inspector Wendy Mehat, the officer in charge of the detachment. She was one of five officers in uniform, which gave the meeting on the driveway the feeling of a formal ceremony. Nate Olson and Pete were dressed casually.

The Ralstons were packed up and ready to go by 11:30 AM. Gene had taken the towfish apart and stowed it away. He swung the boom around to face the pilothouse and secured it to the frame for the winch with a bungee cord. Mike Clement said you need to master a thousand skills to be good at body recovery. You also need a thousand bungee cords.

Pete hugged Sandy and shook Gene's hand.

"You've been a prince," Gene said. He told Pete how impressed he was by his dedication and compassion.

"Well, there are only a few things that stand out in my career and this is one of them," Pete said. He was already working it out with his detachment to bring them back to continue where they left off on the search for Dennis Liva.

Many of the law enforcement officials I spoke with told me something similar, that finding and recovering a corpse was uniquely satisfying work. It had something to do with how the job involved a high degree of complexity, was both a physical and logistical challenge, and at the same time provided an important kind of humanitarian value. Tony Tindall, the FBI agent who was with the Ralstons when they found the homicide victims in the lake in California, was so inspired by the experience that he joined the FBI's underwater search-and-evidence-recovery team in Los Angeles. He said his work as a diver was often dangerous, but tremendously fulfilling. "The end goal of getting that person back to the family and finishing that question, and now putting an answer to that question," Tindall said.

Pete and I watched the Ralstons drive off, towing the *Kathy G* behind their motor home. Gene made a wide, slow turn, taking up both lanes of the highway. He missed the ditch and didn't crush any of the plants that lined the driveway.

~~

"It was sad, and it felt like we all relived it again," Raman Aujla told me about getting the call that her older brother had been recovered. "It felt like the day we found out about the initial accident."

The funeral took place a couple weeks later. The family and some of Aujla's close friends visited his favorite stores and bought clothes, shoes, and a belt for him. His mom picked out fabric for a turban. It was the color she had hoped he would wear when he got married. They planned to have a closed casket, but the funeral director assured Raman that they would make her brother look as good as possible and dress him in the clothes they had purchased.

Raman and Aujla were close, more like best friends than siblings. Her brother had always looked out for his sisters and mother. Raman and Jasmin, the youngest in the family, each moved out of the family home in Surrey after they got married. Aujla continued to live there with his mom. He helped pay the bills. He was always renovating, upgrading something every couple of years. Raman told me that her brother was the hardest-working person she had ever met. He loved to garden. He grew vegetables and fruit in the backyard and had flower beds out front. "He had that tough-guy exterior, not very approachable," she said. "When you actually spoke to him, you quickly learned he was very sweet."

Aujla was missing for close to seven months. "It was torture for our family, almost every day," Raman said. It was discouraging when the other search teams couldn't find him. The family didn't understand why it was so hard if they knew he was in the lake. The failed attempts added to their feelings of uncertainty and confusion about his disappearance. After a few months passed, Raman convinced herself that her brother was not in the lake, that he had decided to leave and start a new life somewhere else. "My mind just started to play these tricks on me. I think it was a protective factor," she said.

People suggested they organize a funeral without the body, but Aujla's mother never considered it. It was important to her that the family hold a religious ceremony in a particular way. Raman said her mother had nightmares while her son was missing. He appeared to her in dreams and told her that he was trapped at the bottom of a lake and couldn't get to the place where he needed to go.

Raman had a professional photo of her brother taken on her wedding day in 2017. They had it enlarged to life size and displayed it next to his casket. She and Jasmin gave a speech. Raman described something that happened to her mother during the funeral. "She kind of zoned out while the prayers were going on," she said. Her mother had a vision. Her son walked out of the photo and up to her. He told her that he had been in the water for seven months, but now he was finally free to go where he needed to be. He told her that he would wait for her when he got there, but that now she needed to let him go.

"Since then my mom has been so much stronger," Raman said. She still grieved and missed her son, but she was in a better place. Raman and her family felt tremendous gratitude that the Ralstons gave them that chance to finally put their beloved brother and son to rest.

Aujla was cremated. His family scattered his ashes in the ocean.

CHAPTER TWENTY-ONE

Searching for Answers

A few days after the Ralstons left Maple Ridge, the RCMP dive team tried to investigate the object with the bunny-shaped shadow on the bottom of the Fraser River. Gene had given them the GPS coordinates. The current was too fast to safely deploy the divers. The team probed the river with drop cameras, but the water was so murky they couldn't see much of anything. They left without confirming whether the plane, and perhaps the pilots, was on the bottom in the middle of the river just down-stream from the power lines. That's how many searches end for the Ralstons. It's one thing to image something on the bottom; it's a different and more complex thing to get down there and retrieve it.

Gene got an email from Pete at the end of April 2021. He found out that Dennis Liva married, and his wife was five months' pregnant when he drowned. His daughter, Denise, was named after him and raised by her grandparents in Maple Ridge. The Ralstons agreed to return to Alouette Lake in early June to continue the search for Liva.

They went on two other searches in May. They spent a week on Duncan Lake, which was in a sparsely populated and moun-tainous region of southeastern British Columbia. It was their third trip to try to find Thomas Schreiber, the fifty-eight-year-old who'd vanished while fishing from his canoe in September.

The Ralstons searched the lake for two weeks in the fall of 2020 and then, after Gene got home and reviewed the sonar images, drove right back in early December with the ROV in their pickup truck. They borrowed a boat to launch the robot. The body-like object on the bottom of Duncan Lake, the one that had looked so convincing that the Ralstons had driven seven hundred miles to see it with the ROV's video camera, was an old tree trunk that had been cut close to the base. Spindly, leglike roots curled out into the soft mud.

Gene and Sandy had become close with the Schreiber family. They parked their motor home in front of the missing man's parents' house, which was down a tree-canopied gravel road from the boat launch. Annalise and Wieland Schreiber were in their early eighties. Thomas had a younger brother named Jorg and a variety of friends from the hodgepodge of communities built on the beaches and forested slopes that overlook the giant lakes in the area. He had met the same group of friends for years at a local sawmill every afternoon for a beer.

Someone was always available to help out on the *Kathy G.* Annalise made everyone breakfast, which included fresh eggs from their chickens, and then dinner at the end of each search day. Wieland has Alzheimer's disease. Thomas was a big reason why his parents were able to manage at home in such a remote place. Losing their son meant facing hard decisions about where and how they were going to live. "We're two hands short and those two hands it almost seems like you're ten people short trying to get the job done looking after the folks," Jorg told me. The Ralstons searched for close to a month on three separate trips. They never found Thomas.

The Schreibers were only a few years older than the Ralstons. Meeting Annalise and Wieland made Gene and Sandy think about their own future. "We don't really have anyone that's going to take care of our myriad stuff once we're not capable of doing that, and you never know when that day is going to come," Gene told me. He posted a question on Facebook a few years ago asking what people would do if someone gave them $100,000. He got a range of answers. Someone said they would buy a car, another would travel to Europe. Many of the responses were about donating the money to a search-and-rescue group. Gene said it was a flippant experiment, an off-the-cuff idea, but he brought that social media post up more than once when we talked about their longer-term plans.

He told me about a neighbor in Kuna who went to an estate sale and bought a cabinet that was full of woodworking tools and drill bits. He paid $10 for something that was likely worth $1,000. An entire life's worth of possessions was thoughtlessly put up for sale at the event. "So that's my worst fear, that somebody would do something like that," Gene said. He has spent his life fixing, maintaining, and caring for everything that they own, including photos, family heirlooms, and the archive of sonar images of lake and river bottoms. Respect for the inherent value of things was instilled in Gene from childhood. Nina Ralston saved the cotton sacks that sugar used to be sold in to patch jeans or to sew entirely new shirts. "Tools are one thing, but it's the historical pictures and mementos, and those kind of things. All my dad's handwritten notes from when he went on motor home trips visiting family and things like that, that we need to sort out what to do with," Gene said.

Sam Ralston died in the fall of 2009. Nina passed away during the summer of 2011. Sandy's father, Fred Odell, had died at the age of sixty-eight, only a few years after Gene and Sandy were married. Her mother, Jewel, passed away in 2000.

Gene's parents had asked him to be the executor of their estate, which ended up further straining his relationships with his sister and brother. It took the Ralstons seven years to go through his parents' belongings. They sold Sam and Nina's house in December 2018.

The senior Ralstons lived in New Plymouth, a fifty-mile drive northwest from Kuna. Gene and Sandy called his parents' place the beach house because it was west from where they lived and so technically closer to the coast. They would often get there with a plan to spend a few days sorting through things only to get a new search request and then have to return home and mobilize the boat and motor home.

Gene and Sandy took the same methodical, detail-oriented approach to Sam and Nina's stuff as they do on searches. They sorted diaries into one container, trinkets in another. They emptied every box and read through all the documents. Their meticulousness yielded treasures that otherwise would have been lost. Gene found a Purple Heart, a medal awarded to soldiers who died or were wounded in battle, in an old case for eyeglasses. The name Adolph Blotter was inscribed on the back. Gene's aunt, his mother's sister, was Mable Blotter. She and her husband had died years ago, so he reached out to his cousin who had some of Mable's possessions, including letters that mentioned an Adolph. He served in the US Army in the First World War. The letters indicated that he had relatives from Logan, Utah. Gene turned to the internet and was able to track down some of Adolph's family. He and Sandy met them at a gas station in Tremonton, Utah, in June 2019 on their way to Lake Powell to search for the body of Daniel McGuckin. Gene gave them the old medal. "They were just incredibly excited to get it," he said.

The Ralstons have been on the lookout for a successor for the *Kathy G* and all their search-and-recovery gear for several years. They would likely bequeath the entire setup to the right person, someone who didn't see the sonar as dollar signs. Someone who could drop what they were doing at a moment's notice and leave home for indefinite stretches of time.

Gene broached the idea with Brandi Hansen, the search-and-rescue technician and flight instructor, one evening by the motor home at the Nicola Ranch in April 2021. I think Gene saw Hansen as a kindred spirit. She was smart and industrious. The way that she followed Ben Tyner's case long after she volunteered on the initial search effort had made an impression on the Ralstons. They invited her to join them in Maple Ridge on the search for Bobby Aujla in Alouette Lake. Hansen was flattered but had to decline.

"I just think what they do is incredible. It's remarkable. It's an anomaly. It's unusual," she told me on the phone in the fall of 2021. She called Gene and Sandy do-gooders. "I mean I don't know anyone in the world that does that, like the entire world. I've been all over the world. I lived in Mexico City for five years as an investigator. I've been all over Japan. I've never encountered anybody like the Ralstons," she said. I had asked Hansen a few times what she meant by working as an investigator. It came up during the search for Ben in Nicola Lake. Her answers were always vague. My guess was that it had been for the military, but perhaps in a covert or classified capacity.

"I'm afraid that one day when Gene and Sandy are too old to be doing this that there is not going to be anybody to replace them," Hansen said. But she was a single parent of two kids and had a full-time job. "I mean, if I won the lottery, sign me up. I would love to do it," she said.

The Ralstons have found other ways to pass on their knowledge even if they have yet to find an heir for the *Kathy G.* They often teach by example. Dozens of law enforcement agencies have purchased a sonar system after Gene and Sandy arrived at a lake in their jurisdiction and performed a successful recovery. These agencies sometimes then send an officer to join the Ralstons on other searches to learn how to use the equipment. Or they will organize a training seminar and invite more agencies from nearby counties to attend. Gene and Sandy have taught these short, usually three-day, courses all over the United States.

The first day is in a classroom. Gene explains how the sonar generates a picture, what it takes to get a good-quality image and how to see a corpse for the shadows it casts on the bottom. Sandy interrupts him if he gets too far into the weeds of a particular story. They show videos of past recoveries. They talk about re-float intervals for corpses and how to talk to a witness to get accurate information about the point of last seen.

The rest of the instruction happens on the water. Some type of target, like a weighted dummy, is set up on the bottom in advance. Gene and Sandy split up and move from boat to boat to provide hands-on instruction. The previous experience of attendees varies immensely. The most common participant is from a marine patrol unit for a county sheriff's office. Some of these officers do several underwater searches a year. Others have yet to turn on their sonar system. The class size is limited to thirty so there is a manageable number of boats on the water.

Gene and Sandy have focused more on these training sessions lately. The schedule is more predictable, and the work is not as physical. Teaching people all their secrets is theoretically an effective way to reduce their workload. One challenge, however, is that the officers they train are often rotated out of their positions within a year or two.

I asked Gary Kozak, the treasure hunter, if the technology is getting to a point where it could replace experts like the Ralstons. Most of the side-scan sonars that companies like Marine Sonic sell nowadays are designed for autonomous underwater vehicles, known as AUVs. These systems are preprogrammed to search a particular area. They navigate the seafloor independently and then surface when they have completed the grid. The images generated by a sonar on an AUV are not affected by rough weather at the surface. They can search day and night.

Advances in artificial intelligence make automatic interpretation, such as picking out targets like a mine or body, increasingly plausible. Kozak called this type of program computer-aided detection. He said it was something that militaries around the world have been working on for decades. Kozak went head-to-head with one of these systems on an experiment for the Australian navy. "They ran automatic target detections and then they ran me," he said. "I had probably 90 percent detectability of meaningful targets and they had like 30 percent." Sonar imagery is variable from moment to moment and objects look different depending on what angle the sound pulses are traveling. Experience and intuition are key factors for success.

Crayton Fenn, the Ralstons' friend who built their towfish, agreed with Kozak about the limitations of automation. "I learn something new every other time I go out there. And I mean I have got tens of thousands of hours on sonar, hundreds of thousands of hours. I mean I don't even know how many hours," he said. Regardless of how advanced these systems become, Fenn said they will always need people to launch the gear and troubleshoot glitches. And that brings you back to the same issues that law enforcement officials face today, which is mainly the expense of the equipment and the fact that they may go months or years without having a drowning in their county. It's rare for the police to use a sonar system enough to become proficient. The Ralstons got so much experience because they were willing to travel to wherever the drowning happened. Fenn didn't think AUVs could fill the void left behind when the Ralstons retire.

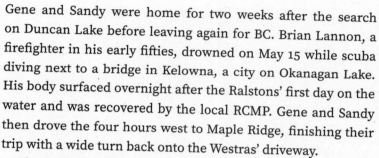

Gene and Sandy were home for two weeks after the search on Duncan Lake before leaving again for BC. Brian Lannon, a firefighter in his early fifties, drowned on May 15 while scuba diving next to a bridge in Kelowna, a city on Okanagan Lake. His body surfaced overnight after the Ralstons' first day on the water and was recovered by the local RCMP. Gene and Sandy then drove the four hours west to Maple Ridge, finishing their trip with a wide turn back onto the Westras' driveway.

The Ralstons spent the first two days back on Alouette, June 3 and 4, searching the area just south of the narrows and west of where they found Liva's boat on the bottom. Gene marked dozens of objects to scan a second time. Nothing looked promising enough to evaluate with the ROV. Pete advised against searching on the weekend because of how busy the lake got now that it was the summer season. Gene used the time to review images on the laptop in the motor home.

I met Denise Powell, Liva's daughter, on a Saturday afternoon in early June at her house in Maple Ridge, only a few hours after I talked to Herb Silcock, the man her father had been fishing with the day he drowned. They lived less than a mile apart.

Silcock and I sat on lawn chairs on the patio behind his house. It was an overcast and blustery day. His son had set up a portable gas fireplace. Silcock turned seventy-nine on June 6, the day after we met. He had been married fifty-two years and worked at that same mill on 207th Street, the one he and Liva shut down on a whim that Friday afternoon, until he retired in 2010. The mill had closed for good in 2019. The Haney Hotel, the spot where he and Liva got the idea to go fishing, was still open. Silcock thought it might be a strip club now. I passed the two-story building every morning on the way from my hotel to Pete's place.

Silcock had enjoyed his job. He described how each new log coming down the line to his saw presented a unique puzzle for him to solve, in terms of where and how best to make his cuts. All those years of manual labor had been hard on his body. "The disks in my back have all disintegrated," he said. Standing and walking was painful. He was bald with a scratchy beard of white hair that almost matched the pallor of his skin. He had large, pendulous ears that framed his head like a set of parentheses.

We talked about the afternoon of June 14, 1974. He had vivid memories of that day. He described how fast Liva reacted after falling in the lake, how shocked he had seemed by the cold water. Silcock was still amazed at how the boat had just fallen away beneath his feet, like somebody kicked out a support beam that had been holding it aloft. "The wave came over the back of the boat and it was gone — like, bam," he said.

He remembered lying on his back in the water, trying to swim and thinking it would be a miracle if he survived. The doctors put him in a hot tub when he got to the hospital. He had swallowed a lot of water. His chest and lungs hurt like he had broken ribs. He asked for time off work, but his foreman told him to show up Monday morning. The best therapy was to get right back to work, his boss had said. Silcock was in a daze for weeks after Liva drowned. "I felt my strength was coming back, but I was in a disassociated mood." He wondered what might have happened if they had never walked off the job that day. It had been such a spur-of-the-moment idea, a case of spring fever. Silcock didn't know Liva well, but had liked him. He enjoyed working along-side the quiet and capable young man.

Silcock tried swimming in a pool in the backyard of a friend's house a few years after the accident. He dunked his head under and then immediately got out. He never went swimming again. Something about the sensation of being suspended in water had become intolerable.

We moved to a couch inside so I could use my laptop to show him some photos of the boat on the bottom of the lake and a map of the area the Ralstons had searched. The images were stills clipped from the ROV's video recording. They were blurry, but you could clearly see the bow of the boat, which was covered in a thin layer of grime. It was resting on the bottom at an angle. I asked Silcock about the red, square object in the boat. "I wonder if that would be a tackle box, maybe. I can't remember what would be red." After a pause he added, "Darn. Wish I could."

I showed him the map with the blue track lines that displayed where the Ralstons had searched. A square cursor marked the location of the boat. "Interesting. It looks pretty well equidistant to each shore," Silcock said, like he had expected it to be closer to the side they had swum toward. He had told me there had never been any doubt about which direction to swim. They both instinctively went west. Silcock didn't have any suggestions for where else the Ralstons could look for Liva's remains.

The Powell family lived in a tidy row house that backed on to a lush ravine with a creek that drained into another creek that then connected with the Fraser River about ten miles downstream from the power lines. Denise, her husband, Jay, and their fifteen-year-old daughter had been observing a family of owls lately, particularly the babies, from the large windows in their adjoined living room and kitchen. "They're really neat, little fluff balls," Denise said. She had big, warm eyes and long brown hair. Her feet, unlike Jay's, didn't reach the floor when she sat on the couch in their living room. The couple were a study in contrasts. He was tall and languid. She was short and animated. Jay moved in slow motion. Denise was set on fast forward. They had been married nineteen years and also had a son who no longer lived at home.

It had been a strange few weeks for the family. It all started with a phone call. Denise worked from home as a data researcher in the construction industry. Corporal Westra called on a weekday afternoon. It took her several minutes to grasp what the RCMP officer was talking about. She told him that her father wasn't missing. They didn't know exactly where he was, but they knew he was in the lake. Pete told her about the Ralstons and their ability to find bodies, even ones that have been gone for decades.

Denise talked to her grandmother, who was ninety years old. "She's very feisty," she said about the woman who raised her. She discussed the search with her aunt and uncle, Liva's brother and sister. Her relatives preferred to leave him in peace. "That is, to them, his resting place," she said. Denise had more conversations with Pete. He answered her questions about why the RCMP had to search even after all this time and what the Ralstons might find if they were successful. "He can tell you awful stuff and make it okay. He's a very kind man," she said.

Exhausted all possible options was the phrase Denise's family used to describe the original effort to find Liva after he drowned. Denise had heard stories about the search, how hard they had tried and how frustrating it had been. They had so few tools. The water was so deep. It got so dark that the divers couldn't even see to the bottom, let alone search it. And so, eventually, the family tried to let go.

"They know he's not there, right? His body might be there, but he's not there," Denise said. "That brings comfort, to think that he's not actually in turmoil at the bottom of the lake. His body might be there, but he's at peace."

Denise told me about her large and tightly knit extended family. Her father's parents divorced and then remarried when he was young. Liva grew up with two sets of parents and many siblings and step-siblings. His mother and father first met in Maple Ridge, but they had both escaped from Estonia when they were young. The country was repeatedly invaded and occupied, first by the Stalinist Soviet Union and then Nazi Germany. "The luxury of emotion was not something my grandparents grew up with," she said. "They know, more so than a lot of people I think, that you have to keep going. You just don't have the option of coming undone."

Denise described how she internalized the example her family set of not talking about her father, including what had happened on the lake that day in 1974. She absorbed from a young age how painful his death and disappearance had been for everyone. She tried to suppress her curiosity about her father as a way to care for her family, especially her grandmother.

The same handful of stories were told about him as she grew up. He had a motorcycle and a Volkswagen Bug. He loved French toast. He had an ear for music and could play any song on the piano after hearing it once. He was soft-spoken but mischievous. He was a swimmer and a bowler. One of the few possessions she had of her father was a trophy from a bowling tournament. Denise's son reminded her grandmother of her father. They have some of the same facial expressions and mannerisms.

"It's just so strange when you have this parent, this person, that you are so connected to but not connected to at all, because you never knew them," Denise said. "It's so strange to grieve a person you've never met, and apparently you just keep grieving. It just keeps happening when these things come up."

There were layers to the absence of her father. His body was missing, but he was missing from her life in other ways because the memory of what had happened was too traumatic for her relatives to revisit. Pauline Boss, the academic and therapist, defined ambiguous loss as having a person in your life who was no longer around in a physical sense, but remained present in powerful emotional and psychological ways.

When she was around twenty, Denise decided to read the police report about her father's drowning. She was living with her grandparents and waited until they had left town on vacation. She visited the Ridge Meadows RCMP detachment in Maple Ridge to access the report. "I just felt like I needed some answers," she said. The story she had grown up with was that her father had been testing fishing boats for the government on Alouette Lake when he drowned. Several things in the report upset Denise. She didn't understand why the prison guard or his wife didn't jump into the lake to save her father. She reached out to Silcock soon after reading it to learn more about what had happened. She didn't get much from their conversation. Looking back now, Denise thought Silcock's guardedness might have been related to feelings of guilt — not because he was responsible for what had happened, but because he had survived.

The Powells had two dogs. Nala looked a bit like a fox. Tucker had long, shaggy white hair and harassed Denise for attention. He sat in her lap even though he was too big to fit. He got edgy if she didn't pet him intentionally with both hands. Denise seemed to appreciate the constant distraction of her dog's neediness. She used to run her own daycare business. I could see how she would have thrived in that atmosphere of organized chaos.

Denise told me that at some point over the past few weeks, although she couldn't say exactly when or why, she'd realized that she wanted her father's remains to be found. And she wanted to be there on the lake in the event that it happened. She had talked with Pete again recently. Denise and Jay were going to bring a boat to Alouette Lake tomorrow to meet the Ralstons. Gene had found something during his review of the sonar images that he wanted to investigate with the ROV. Pete explained to Denise that the Ralstons were working to rule out the object. It was a precautionary step. He was careful to moderate her expectations.

Denise described how she had tried to explain to her grandmother the rationale for joining the Ralstons on the search for her father. "I've never been to where he was. I've never seen it. I've never been that far down the lake," Denise said, summarizing their conversation. "You guys all got to go there. You went out there. You searched. You had your time to do that. You had your vigil."

CHAPTER TWENTY-TWO

The Past Is Present

I heard an Indigenous woman singing on the radio, which was tuned to CBC News, as I drove to Pete's place on the morning of Monday, June 7, 2021. The song was part of a ceremony that had taken place at the Kamloops Residential School, which was an hour drive north from Merritt. It had been ten days since the chief of the Tk'emlúps te Secwepemc First Nation, Rosanne Casimir, announced the discovery of the remains of more than two hundred children in unmarked graves on the grounds of the school. The news shocked the country and the world. People set up shrines of stuffed animals and pairs of kids' shoes at government buildings and other public places across Canada. Flags were at half mast.

It had been an odd experience to hear on the radio that people had used ground-penetrating radar, which involved firing high-frequency radio waves into the earth and then using the reflections to generate images of what was underground, to detect the remains of buried children as we drove to a lake to use sonar to look for a man who had been missing for forty-seven years.

It was no secret that thousands of children had died at residential schools. The physical and sexual abuse, neglect, and cruelty had been assiduously documented in the *Truth and Reconciliation Report* that was published in 2015. An entire volume of that report was dedicated to missing children and unmarked burials. The Canadian government created the residential school system, a network of 139 schools run by Christian churches, in the late nineteenth century as a way to assimilate Indigenous people. Children were forcibly taken from their homes, separated from siblings, and punished for speaking their language. The last school closed in 1996. The kids who attended died at increased rates of diseases like tuberculosis and scarlet fever because of malnutrition and unsanitary living conditions. Others disappeared without warning or explanation. The government refused to pay to transport the body of a child back home. Families were sometimes never notified that their child had died.

The previous Thursday morning, as we drove to Alouette, Pete talked about how the discovery of these clandestine graves was a good thing. More people would learn about the injustice of what had happened. "It brings it into the present," he said. Canadians had by and large brushed aside the testimony of survivors of residential schools who spoke about friends and relatives who never made it home. No one could ignore the physical remains of children, especially of those who had been mistreated in life and then callously disregarded in death. The discovery of the bodies, and the searches it inspired at other schools across the country, brought a disgraceful chapter of Canadian history back into the present.

I heard another story that week by Tanya Talaga, an Anishinaabe journalist and author for *The Decibel*, a podcast by the *Globe and Mail*. Members of the Skwah First Nation carried a wooden canoe on their shoulders out into the middle of the field by the residential school in Kamloops. They invited the children to climb into the boat so they could finally be free of their captors. The ceremony was accompanied by drumming.

"They were there with their canoe to take their spirits home," Talaga said.

~

It was overcast and humid at the boat launch that morning. Low-lying clouds obscured the tops of the mountains and got snagged like clumps of gauze among the trees. Sandy was wearing the most impressive fisherman hat yet. It was the color of straw and had a magisterial brim that started as a short peak above her forehead but extended into a wide fan that covered her neck and upper back.

The object Gene wanted to investigate was directly between the sunken boat and the west shoreline, so along the path that Silcock and Liva had swum. It took a few tries to get the marker close enough to the target on the bottom that Gene felt satisfied he could find it with the ROV.

Denise arrived at about 9:30 AM. It was raining in a fine mist. Her cousin, Aaron Liva, was driving the classic-looking ski boat. It had a blue tarp for shelter. Jay was in the back seat.

"Right here? Really?" Denise asked Pete after her cousin brought them alongside the *Kathy G*. She wiped her eyes with the sleeve of her sweatshirt, which was a bright, seafoam-green color. Her hair was pulled back in a ponytail. Denise was shocked that her father had been so close to shore. "I thought it was farther out in the middle of the lake," she said. The boat had sunk east of us, but I think Denise meant the area in general. She had pictured the accident happening in a much more remote part of the lake. It looked like we were within three or four lengths of a swimming pool from the nearest point on land.

Pete walked Denise through what the Ralstons were doing, how the two blue buoys on the surface were connected to a marker that would help Gene find the target on the bottom. It took an hour or so, but he eventually nosed the ROV up to the object. It was a log. He heaved one of his theatrical sighs and then continued to probe around on the bottom. The light from the robot caught the outline of some kind of fabric not far from the log. It was mostly buried in the muck. Gene snagged it in the jaws. Pete pulled the cord, and I coiled it back into the case on the deck, just as we had done for the corpse a month ago. This time, however, we had raised a tattered beach towel covered in mildew.

Aaron brought the ski boat back over. Pete explained that the suspicious-looking object had been a log with roots that looked like legs on the sonar. He told Denise that the Ralstons would drop the marker beside the sunken boat next. Gene had noticed several objects in the vicinity of the boat when he reviewed the images over the weekend that he wanted to see on camera. "If you can't tie a knot, tie a lot," Gene said to himself as he went through the laborious routine of raising the anchor.

He clapped his hands after he got the marker within a foot or two of the back of the boat. The blue cylindrical buoys now showed the position of Liva's boat on the bottom. One buoy lay flat on its side. The other was vertical, only the top third was visible above the surface. Denise had a visual cue, a floating cenotaph, of the spot where her father's boat had come to rest after sinking 285 feet.

The robot approached the old boat from the side. The larger chunks of suspended sediment looked like leaves in a breeze. We saw the motor. It was missing a cover. "That's an antique," Gene said. The rusted and exposed engine looked like a messy, multilayered sandwich. The robot moved farther into the boat. We got a side view of the red object. The word CHRYSLER was legible in white, capital letters even though we were reading it upside down and backward. The cover must have slid off the

motor as it sank. Then Gene snagged a fishing rod in the grabber jaws. Pete pulled it to the surface.

The ski boat was drifting behind us on the east side of the
buoys. Aaron gave the Ralstons a wide berth while they worked.
Pete motioned for them to come over. He asked Denise if she
wanted the rod. The reel was rusty, and it had come up along
with a short strap of metal that looked like it had been part of
the boat.

"Yes," she said, nodding. "They never found the rods or
anything."

A few minutes later, Aaron brought the ski boat up next to
the two buoys. Denise tossed a white rose onto the lake. The
rain had stopped. The clouds had thinned, allowing more
sunlight to hit the surface of the water. The color of the lake
had changed from dark blue to jewel green. It was a windless
day, but the space between the buoys and the flower gradually
widened. The rose drifted toward the east shoreline.

Denise, Jay, and Aaron left not long after Pete gave her the
fishing rod. She thanked the Ralstons before they drove back to
the boat launch.

"We appreciate it so much," she said.

"We sure tried. It's been so long," Gene replied through the
open window of the pilothouse.

He managed to recover the other fishing rod. Then the
Ralstons made one last-ditch effort to find the body of Dennis
Liva. Gene flew the ROV along the bottom and toward the west
shore from the sunken boat, retracing the route that Silcock
and Liva had swum in 1974. The ROV's lights didn't reach more
than a few feet into the planetary darkness. Sandy was up front
feeding the cable into the water. Every object on the bottom was
full of possibility from a distance. I saw a shoe, and not just
any shoe, but Silcock's steel-toed loafer, right up until we were

inches away and it suddenly transformed into a lumpy stick. The last thing the ROV encountered looked like a homemade diving board, something that had once been nailed to the back of a raft. The RCMP file for Liva would remain open until he turned 110 years old, which would not be until 2064.

We sped back to the boat launch on Alouette Lake one last time with an old towel in a plastic bag and an antique fishing rod on the shelf under the gunnel. I think the Ralstons had wanted to return for that last day less because of the objects Gene had identified over the weekend and more to give Denise a chance see where they had found the boat and to see them make an effort to find her father. It was a special kind of application for their equipment and expertise. I had heard them talk about similar types of searches, instances when the *Kathy G* helped perform a ritual instead of a recovery.

They found Sid Neville's two fishing rods on the bottom of François Lake and gave them to Marley, his widow. They anchored a wooden cross on the bottom of Kalum Lake to create a submarine monument on the spot where they had imaged the body of Jody Frocklage. Gene told me about ferrying people to funeral services on the water. Every search became its own kind of vigil for the missing person.

I called Denise a few weeks later to ask her about her experience on the lake that day. "It was very emotional. It was very peaceful. It was very healing," she said. The two buoys on the surface had reminded her of a roadside memorial that people used to mark the spot of a fatal car accident.

She talked about trying to inhabit her father's perspective, trying to imagine what he had been thinking and feeling that day. It was a way to feel connected to someone she had never met. That was why the fishing rod was so special. It was tangible. It was something her father had held that she could now hold. Denise was going to refurbish the rod and hang it on her living room wall in the basement. "I have very few things of my dad's," she said.

Pete gave her a video of the ROV exploring the boat and recovering the fishing rods. She watched it for the first time with Jay and her children. The four of them huddled around a laptop on the island in the kitchen. She put a copy on her iPad and had watched it over and over again. "Everybody knew what boat he was in, everybody knew what motor it was, everybody knew everything except me. So for me, I'm finally in the loop," she said.

I asked Denise if she was glad she got that call from Pete, the one that had set the tumult of the last couple months in motion. "Yes," she said without hesitation, but then added that her grandmother and Liva's brother and sister felt differently. News of the search had stirred up difficult memories for them. But the Ralstons had given Denise a reason to ask her cousin to take a day off work so they could go out in his boat to see where on the lake her father had drowned four months before she was born. "And to know that he's still there in some capacity, it was quite possibly the closest I ever have been to him physically," she said.

I spoke to Denise again on the phone a few months later. I told her about my theory that Liva, being a good swimmer, might have chosen to stick by Silcock in the water instead of going ahead to shore. And that her father had been the one to call out to the prison guard and his wife for help. The boat would have likely passed them right by if he hadn't got the woman's attention. The guard had thought the two men were out for a swim on a sunny afternoon. In other words, it seemed plausible that Liva had saved Silcock's life. Denise told me that she grew up with the feeling that her father was goodness personified.

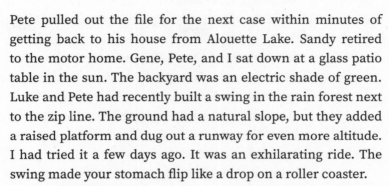

Pete pulled out the file for the next case within minutes of getting back to his house from Alouette Lake. Sandy retired to the motor home. Gene, Pete, and I sat down at a glass patio table in the sun. The backyard was an electric shade of green. Luke and Pete had recently built a swing in the rain forest next to the zip line. The ground had a natural slope, but they added a raised platform and dug out a runway for even more altitude. I had tried it a few days ago. It was an exhilarating ride. The swing made your stomach flip like a drop on a roller coaster.

Pete unfolded a map of Pitt Lake. "So the boat launch is right here." He pointed to a spot at the south end. Gene had his elbows on the table. He leaned forward as Pete identified the reference points for the next search. His hat read JACKSON COUNTY SEARCH & RESCUE. Pete's T-shirt had a faded image of an RCMP badge printed on the chest.

I had read a few old newspaper articles about the accident. Four young men, all in their early twenties and two of them brothers, vanished in early May 1992. Their boat was found overturned and close to the opposite side of the lake from their campsite. The motor was missing. The point of last seen was actually a point of last heard. Another group of campers heard the four friends get into their boat in the middle of the night. Then there was a loud bang out on the lake somewhere.

Pete relayed the details of the case to Gene. He had learned a lot about what kind of information they needed. He talked about the direction of the wind that night and the size of the waves. He described the search-and-rescue response, where the evidence was found and what time they found it. Gene asked questions to clarify certain points and told stories about past searches with similar circumstances. Jay and Denise had remarked on the teamwork between Pete and the Ralstons, how his investigation complemented their skills, when I was at their house on Saturday. "The bond that he probably has with the two of them is such that they work really well together," Jay said.

The back-and-forth started to yield a picture of what might have happened and an area on the lake where they would start the search tomorrow morning. It was hard to say if it was Pete's idea or Gene's. It was something they arrived at together, supporting each other to take small logical steps until they found themselves with a working theory.

The conversation drifted after they had a plan in place. Gene mentioned that Sandy was feeling tired. "She's got the hardest job of all, and her arthritis and scoliosis and neck pain," he said. She had been awake at 2:00 AM with soreness in her shoulder. Gene massaged her neck and shoulders until she fell back asleep.

"When you're seventy-seven years old . . ." Gene paused, realizing he'd gotten his age wrong. He'd turned seventy-six on the search with the Tyners. "Whatever, she is way much younger than I am."

"Is there much of a difference between you?" Pete asked.

"Yeah, at least three years," Gene said.

He described how he only started to feel old five or six years ago, but when it happened it happened all at once. He got old in a heartbeat. "Can't do the stuff that I used to do. And probably shouldn't do the stuff I used to do," he said. Gene has been having trouble with back pain. It was tricky because it didn't happen in the moment. He could lift the ROV, which was forty pounds, and sometimes even the case with the umbilical cord, which was a hundred pounds, without feeling much discomfort. The pain in his back arrived later, sometimes days later.

Gene associated aging with fatigue. "The older I get, the more tired I get," he told me once. It was hard for him to tell if the weariness was a symptom of age or fallout from grief. He missed his parents. "A lot of what we did, they were a big part of," Gene told me. He missed telling them stories about their searches and showing them photos of the places they'd been. "I've noticed that's been bothering me a bit, that I don't have them to share things with of what we do."

Sandy talked about aging more in the context of specific ailments. Her arthritis was frustrating. She could no longer sign her name legibly on a check. A few years before, when the Ralstons were going on more searches and still driving across the continent, Sandy's wrist swelled up and started to hurt. She developed a ganglion cyst from the repetitive movements required to steer the boat. She had a procedure to remove it, and her wrist has worked fine ever since. "It has really helped not to have to travel so much," she said. She was feeling healthier and stronger now that they had slowed down.

Gene told Pete that he got a lift, a boost, at the outset of a new search like the one they were discussing on Pitt Lake. "I tend to get a little up when we get a request to go on a search that we can do, that we think we can have a chance at success, or it's a mystery like this, and we can help somebody out." He'd gotten an email recently from John Zeman, who was eighty-two years old. Zeman wished he could have joined them on these searches but felt it was too risky because of the pandemic. "It's killing him not to be here, because he really wants to keep doing it," Gene said.

I think Sandy felt more at home at their house in Kuna than her husband. Gene got restless. If the *Kathy G* was his domain, then their place in Idaho was hers. She had her plants to take care of and the wild pets that roamed their property to keep tabs on. Sandy has found ways to make life at home feel meaningful. Gene worried about not having enough to do. I think the winters could grind him down in ways that no search, no matter how long or grueling, ever could. He was at his best when his skills and knowledge were being tested, when he was in the thick of battle and juggling the manifold tasks required to bring a body back from the deep. All those jobs, however, were physically taxing, especially when they didn't have an extra set of hands to help out on the boat.

Pete told Gene that he understood now, after the past two months, why he and Sandy had been dedicated to search and recovery for so long. "It's tedious and it's hard work but then you get on the phone and you talk to the family and that's kind of a whole new level of energy again — just the impact it makes." He told Gene that he felt lucky he was the person from his detachment who got to work with them.

It had become clear to me, as it had to Pete, why the Ralstons devote themselves to this type of work. It's equal parts challenging and rewarding. Gene and Sandy found a way to help people who have nowhere else to turn. The job brings them to some of the most beautiful places in North America. They make new friends with each new search.

It's fascinating to look at a life in reverse. The trajectory can seem inevitable, like fate. The Ralstons met in college on a road trip across Mexico. They spent their wedding night in a makeshift camper on the back of a pickup truck. Gene and Sandy were predisposed to a life on the road. Their education and work experience furnished them with the requisite knowledge and skills for underwater work. They built and raced jet boats. They were involved in an accident on a river, and their friend drowned. The Ralstons experienced the gnawing uncertainty of expecting a missing person to return at any moment. They bought a revolutionary technology for searching underwater.

"There must be something special about our relationship," Gene likes to say about his life with Sandy. Colleagues and friends had warned them not to start the environmental consulting firm together back in the late nineteen seventies. They'd told the Ralstons that they were putting their marriage in jeopardy. But it had all worked out. Gene and Sandy have been living and working together for close to fifty years. They have dozens of friends all over Canada and the United States, but they're alone in some respects. Their lifestyle in Kuna is reclusive. They're a family, a self-sustaining unit. It's hard to know where one Ralston ends and the other begins. It's that dynamic, their closeness, that allows them to spend so much time on searches for drowning victims. They bring their world wherever they go.

The story of why the Ralstons are so good at what they do, why they succeed after others fail, is ultimately a love story. It's their partnership, the fact that they tow the *Kathy G* behind their home, that enabled them to master the thousand skills required for body recovery.

What makes Gene and Sandy unique is also what makes them irreplaceable. Other nonprofit search groups — like the Canadian Canine Search Corps; police divers, like the RCMP's underwater recovery team; and even advances in technology, like AUVs and computer-aided detection programs — will all help to fill at least part of the gap left behind when the Ralstons retire. I doubt another couple will ever follow in their footsteps, will ever choose to invest their life and livelihood in such difficult and macabre work.

Comparing the Ralstons to the ferryman of mythology was a way to highlight the timelessness of their work. Finding the dead, honors the dead. And honoring the dead is fundamental to being human. The instinct often finds expression in religious beliefs and practices, but it's rooted in something deeper, in the way we connect and bond with the people we love. A corpse often retains a social existence, a feeling of personhood, because death is too abrupt for us to comprehend. The body becomes, as Mary Roach described, a receptacle for emotions that have no other place to go. The dead are "creatures who need to be eased out of this world and settled safely into the next and into memory," Thomas Laqueur, the historian, wrote.

The Ralstons work in the service of grief. They guide people through purgatory, like in the myth. They help families cross a barrier they cannot cross on their own. The myth, however, misses the essential ingredient of their success. The ferryman, throughout time and across cultures, has been a solitary figure. A weary old man rowing a boat, alone with his responsibility to transport a ceaseless tide of lost souls. No one to rub his shoulders when they get stiff. No one to patiently entertain his cheesy puns.

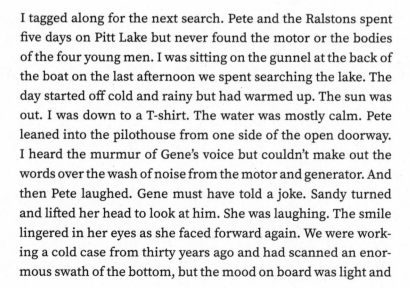

I tagged along for the next search. Pete and the Ralstons spent five days on Pitt Lake but never found the motor or the bodies of the four young men. I was sitting on the gunnel at the back of the boat on the last afternoon we spent searching the lake. The day started off cold and rainy but had warmed up. The sun was out. I was down to a T-shirt. The water was mostly calm. Pete leaned into the pilothouse from one side of the open doorway. I heard the murmur of Gene's voice but couldn't make out the words over the wash of noise from the motor and generator. And then Pete laughed. Gene must have told a joke. Sandy turned and lifted her head to look at him. She was laughing. The smile lingered in her eyes as she faced forward again. We were work-ing a cold case from thirty years ago and had scanned an enor-mous swath of the bottom, but the mood on board was light and playful. The Ralstons enjoyed spending time with Pete. He was curious about what they were doing and helpful with the equipment on board. The team returned to the task at hand. Pete and Gene studied the scrolling images on the monitor. Sandy kept the boat on the grid. The engines rumbled. Waves sloshed against the hull. This was what Zeman, the veteran deckhand of the *Kathy G*, called their happy place.

ACKNOWLEDGMENTS

Thank you, Gene and Sandy Ralston. You invited me onto your boat and into your lives to tell an incredibly intimate and remarkable story. I tried my utmost to approach your life story with diligence, respect, and compassion. I'm grateful for how generous you were with your time and knowledge.

Telling this story meant revisiting the worst moments in some peoples' lives. This book was made possible by the participation of people who lost someone whom the Ralstons tried to find. Thank you to all those who shared their experiences about a search. I understand that working with me was largely an expression of gratitude for the Ralstons, but I don't expect that made it any easier to talk about such profound loss. Thank you for working with me. I know it wasn't easy to discuss those experiences during our interviews, and I realize it might be even harder to read about them in a book years later. This book would not exist without your help.

Thank you to Corporal Peter Westra, or Pete, and his family for their warm and welcoming hospitality during my reporting trips to Maple Ridge. And thanks to the Ridge Meadows RCMP detachment for the access to accompany your officers and the Ralstons on the searches on the Fraser River and Alouette Lake in the spring and summer of 2021.

Thank you MaKenzie Ditto and Virginia McDorman for talking to me about your accident on the Little River in Alabama. I know those are difficult memories, but your experiences helped elucidate aspects of the physiology of drowning and also served as a powerful reminder to exercise caution on the water, even when in familiar surroundings.

I appreciated the time, information, and insight provided by all the experts and researchers I spoke with and whose work I sourced. I'm particularly indebted to Thomas Laqueur's book *The Work of the Dead: A Cultural History of Mortal Remains*. I drew on only a small portion of his comprehensive study of this topic, but the material helped me to write about some of the deeper reasons that motivate the Ralstons, and others like them, to devote themselves to search and recovery.

Thank you Christina Frangou, a friend and talented writer and journalist, for your careful consideration of important sections of the manuscript as it was being finalized. I would also like to thank author Marcello Di Cintio for his counsel on elements of the publishing industry. Your advice and perspective was always well-timed and appreciated.

This book first found footing as an article that was published in the *Guardian* in early 2020. Thank you David Wolf, the editor of the publication's long reads section, for taking a chance on this story. I appreciated the incisive editorial guidance from you and Alex Blasdel about how to do justice to the dramatic nature of the Ralstons' story. Thank you Jessica Mileo and Maria Whelan of Inkwell Management for seeing the potential of a book in the article and for your help and enthusiasm to get this project off the ground. I'm grateful to Chip Fleischer and the entire team at Steerforth Press for their work in bringing this book to completion.

Thank you to my partner, Leanne Hosack. We missed many weekend adventures together so I could work on this project. Your wide-ranging support, in the form of thoughtful feedback or delicious snacks, made all the difference in terms of getting across the finish line. I would also like to thank my parents, Nora and Norval Horner, for their varied and sustained encouragement over the years. And thank you to Pat Horner, a brother and friend and writer who listened to me ramble about this project for years and provided steady encouragement to see it through. And, finally, thanks to Dean Mutrie for introducing me to the idea of writing about Gene and Sandy Ralston and for checking in now and again with words of support.